Culture and Economics in Contemporary Cosmopolitan Fiction

Elif Toprak Sakız

Culture and Economics in Contemporary Cosmopolitan Fiction

palgrave
macmillan

Elif Toprak Sakız [iD]
Dokuz Eylül University
Izmir, Türkiye

ISBN 978-3-031-44997-0   ISBN 978-3-031-44995-6 (eBook)
https://doi.org/10.1007/978-3-031-44995-6

© The Editor(s) (if applicable) and The Author(s), under exclusive license to Springer Nature Switzerland AG 2024

This work is subject to copyright. All rights are solely and exclusively licensed by the Publisher, whether the whole or part of the material is concerned, specifically the rights of translation, reprinting, reuse of illustrations, recitation, broadcasting, reproduction on microfilms or in any other physical way, and transmission or information storage and retrieval, electronic adaptation, computer software, or by similar or dissimilar methodology now known or hereafter developed.
The use of general descriptive names, registered names, trademarks, service marks, etc. in this publication does not imply, even in the absence of a specific statement, that such names are exempt from the relevant protective laws and regulations and therefore free for general use.
The publisher, the authors, and the editors are safe to assume that the advice and information in this book are believed to be true and accurate at the date of publication. Neither the publisher nor the authors or the editors give a warranty, expressed or implied, with respect to the material contained herein or for any errors or omissions that may have been made. The publisher remains neutral with regard to jurisdictional claims in published maps and institutional affiliations.

Cover illustration: SEAN GLADWELL/Getty Images

This Palgrave Macmillan imprint is published by the registered company Springer Nature Switzerland AG
The registered company address is: Gewerbestrasse 11, 6330 Cham, Switzerland

Paper in this product is recyclable.

Acknowledgments

I would like to express my sincere gratitude to those who have been instrumental in bringing this project to fruition. First and foremost, I am deeply indebted to my Ph.D. supervisor, Assoc. Prof. Dr. Nil Korkut Naykı for her unwavering support both throughout and following my doctoral research upon which this monograph is based. Her invaluable feedback, enthusiasm, and dedication to academic depth have enhanced the quality of this book. I would also like to extend my heartfelt appreciation to the members of my examining committee, Prof. Dr. Nursel İçöz, Prof. Dr. Aytül Özüm, Assoc. Prof. Dr. Elif Öztabak Avcı, and Assoc. Prof. Dr. Mustafa Kırca, for their guidance, expertise, and constructive criticism.

I would also like to take the opportunity to thank all my professors at METU for their stimulating classes and intellectual support. My special thanks go to people at Dokuz Eylul University, in the departments of Comparative Literature, Foreign Languages, and the Faculty of Tourism, for making it possible for me to conduct this research and creating a warm working atmosphere meanwhile.

A special mention goes to my editors at Palgrave, who believe in this project, and to my two blind reviewers, whose insightful comments and commitment to thoroughness have greatly contributed to the refinement and quality of this monograph.

Last but not least, my heartfelt gratitude goes to my family. My mother and my father have provided infinite love and persistent support not only during this period but also throughout my life. I would like to express my special thanks to my sister, Esma Toprak Çelen, for her supportive and loving heart throughout this journey. I wish to thank my husband, A. Çağlar Sakız, from the bottom of my heart for his generous love and encouragement as well as being by my side in each and every step of this process. My greatest thank goes to son, Poyraz, whose unconditional love and energy of life have always strengthened and inspirited me. To all those who have contributed in one way or another to the creation of this monograph, I extend my heartfelt thanks.

Contents

1 **Introduction: Cosmopolitanism's New Orientations**   1
    The New Cosmopolitan Fiction   7
    What Is Cosmopolitanism?: Diverse Points of Departure   12
    From Universalism to Particularism in Cosmopolitanism   20
    Particularist/Vernacular Cosmopolitanism: Emphasis on the Parochial/Local   24
    References   32

2 **New Intersections in Fiction: Cosmopolitanism, Culture, and Economics**   37
    Narrative Glocality: Interaction Between the Global and the Local   38
    Allegiances as a Matter of Choice   42
    Everyday Difference   45
    Cosmopolitanism's Veiled Ideologies: Relationship with Neoliberal Capitalism   50
    The "Cosmoflâneur": Existence in City Spaces   53
    Narrative Immediacy and Political Hyper-awareness   61
    References   64

3 Narrative Glocality and the *Cosmoflâneur* in Ian
  McEwan's *Saturday* 69
  Narrative Glocality and Vernacular Cosmopolitanism 72
  The Cosmoflâneur as a Globally Conscious City-Wanderer 85
  Perowne's Transformation and the Vernacular Feelings 98
  References 103

4 Vernacular Cosmopolitanism, Cosmopolitan Culture,
  and Economics in Zadie Smith's *NW* 107
  Cultural Communication in Vernacular Cosmopolitanism 111
  Narrative Glocality: Cosmopolitan Spaces in NW 119
  Cosmopolitan Outlook of Identity 129
  Toward Political Hyper-awareness: Economic Dimensions
  of Vernacular Cosmopolitanism 136
  References 144

5 Cosmopolitan Identity and Narration in Salman
  Rushdie's *The Golden House*: The Move Toward
  Vernacular Cosmopolitanism 147
  Cosmopolitan Identity and Choice 153
  Cosmopolitan Narration: Compositeness, Narrative
  Immediacy, and Political Hyper-Awareness 162
  Considerations About the Economic Dimensions
  of Cosmopolitanism 173
  The Vernacular Ending 176
  References 183

6 Posthuman Cosmopolitanism and Post-COVID-19
  Sensitivities in Kazuo Ishiguro's *Klara and The Sun* 185
  Posthuman Cosmopolitanism: Do Androids Dream of Being
  Cosmopolitan? 189
  The Cosmoflâneur as a Carrier of Posthuman
  Cosmopolitanism 198
  Post-COVID-19 Sensitivities: Engagement with Health
  and the Ecological World 206
  The Vernacular Ending and Healing 213
  References 216

7 Conclusion: The Genre of The Contemporary	219
References	227
Index	229

CHAPTER 1

Introduction: Cosmopolitanism's New Orientations

Literature has always been attentive to crises of all types. Crisis of epistemology, crisis of ontology, crisis of values, crisis of self, and crisis of language, to name only a few, have always been the focus of literary production. Crisis has been primary in both modernist and postmodernist literature, yet post-postmodernism has redefined it by expanding its scope and range. Twenty-first-century literature is involved in crisis on a global level since globality has had a sweeping impact on the scope of crisis as on everything else. As for its range, even more challenging forms of crises can be added to the list: crisis of global culture, crisis of money, crisis of (post)human, crisis of environment, and crisis of health without denying the fact that they may have existed to a certain extent long before our contemporary age. It can be argued, however, that twenty-first-century fiction feels an urgency to scrutinize all these issues and seeks new ways—both thematic and formal—to look at these realities. At the core of this book crudely lies the idea that contemporary cosmopolitan fiction was born as a response to these crises. The term cosmopolitan in this book encompasses two main aspects in its definition: the first involves culture in its reference to a culture of the world as a whole, yet equally to a local and particular one; the second, perhaps less typically, relates to global economics which is inherent in the term's connotations of the workings of neoliberal capitalism.

© The Author(s), under exclusive license to Springer Nature
Switzerland AG 2024
E. Toprak Sakız, *Culture and Economics in Contemporary Cosmopolitan Fiction*, https://doi.org/10.1007/978-3-031-44995-6_1

My aim here is primarily to define twenty-first-century cosmopolitan fiction with a view to two intersecting areas within it: culture and economics. My argument in general is that contemporary cosmopolitanism in fiction is primarily defined by these two areas. To be more specific, cosmopolitan culture is characterized by the notions of everyday difference and individualistic choices without prioritizing communal affiliations such as ethnicity, race, and nation. Likewise, global economics and the mechanisms of neo-capitalism also inform the subject matter in contemporary fiction. All these standpoints are manifest in the particular themes, attitudes, and narrative devices employed in Ian McEwan's *Saturday* (2005), Zadie Smith's *NW* (2012), Salman Rushdie's *The Golden House* (2017), and Kazuo Ishiguro's *Klara and the Sun* (2021), which will be elaborated in the following chapters. With a view to contemporary theories of cosmopolitanism in the field of Anglophone literature, I will also suggest a number of definitions for analyzing these novels which can well-deservedly be categorized as cosmopolitan.

Critical engagement with the world and its prevailing problems, be they cultural, economic, or ecological, has emerged as a dominant aspect of social, cultural, and literary studies with the turn of the century. As the world is considered a whole in the face of common global issues, a critical term to define this recent condition of the world has gained validity: cosmopolitanism. The first three decades of the twenty-first century have witnessed a renewal of interest in the concept of cosmopolitanism that keeps receiving attention increasingly every day. With the emergence of this new type of cosmopolitan world, which is unparalleled owing to the technological capacity to connect everyone and everything across its borders, new debates around the concept of cosmopolitanism and its meaning have been inaugurated. The need to trace these changes in the realm of literature has become the departure point for this book. The scope of culture has expanded, and conventional forms of cultural communication have undergone unprecedented changes. Likewise, individuals and governments have faced certain economic challenges, especially in the aftermath of 2008 global economic crisis. These challenges have exacerbated with two important global events of the second decade of the twenty-first century: Brexit and the COVID-19 pandemic (2020). New meanings and forms of cosmopolitanism have been emerging to address these changes. Drawing upon broader theories of cosmopolitanism from a range of diverse disciplines, this book tries to explore the repercussions of twenty-first-century cosmopolitanism on postmillennial British fiction. The argument here is that twenty-first-century novels reflect the transformations in the conception of cosmopolitanism with its new implications in contemporary culture and economics.

Culture and economics intersect in the book's title not coincidentally; as the most important defining elements of cosmopolitanism, these two areas are also central to twenty-first-century cosmopolitan fiction. Probing into theories of economics is beyond the scope of this book, which instead centralizes a certain understanding of contemporary economics as a way of analyzing novels. Transcending a well-defined Marxist class system based on means of production, contemporary economics is now informed by global connectedness, and cosmopolitan mobility of not only capital, but also people, information, resources, and cultural products. However liberatory it may seem in terms of borderless cultural and economic activities, this mobility gives rise to growing global inequalities and socioeconomic imbalances whose impact upon local communities might be devastating. Type of local cosmopolitanism advocated in this book is concerned with the less obvious consequences of such mobilities by drawing attention to economic disparities and problems in the face of increasing global connectedness. An idea of economics is then no longer limited to power mechanisms premised on production or capital since it undergoes a redefinition with a view to multi-layered factors including global wars, pandemics, posthuman developments, and environmental crisis. In "New Climate, New Class Struggles", Nikolaj Schultz (2020) underscores the strong connection between socioeconomic and ecological problems ("the social question" and "natural question"), which lead to the emergence of new class struggles[1]. What determines a new class system in Schultz and Bruno Latour's (2019) conception of "geo-social classes" is not possessing means of production or surplus value obtained from exploitation of labor, but struggling with others in the processes of "engendering" through an advantageous positioning within territories and soils for reproduction[2]. Thus, these new ways of engaging with economics as a culmination of global mobilities which contribute to further economic discrepancies in the world have become central to cosmopolitan fiction.

The COVID-19 pandemic has also revigorated thoughts on cosmopolitan economics. The global pandemic is far from being parochial in its range and impact. The emergence of the novel coronavirus in a specific part of the world has in fact impacted on very distant territories across the world. Then, the phenomenon calls for cosmopolitanism to cope with its adverse effects on the global society with a sort of global solidarity. It may seem to work on a surface level, with the aids including medicine, test kits, masks, and vaccines roaming across the world. Yet, such global mobilities fail to address the whole matter. Economic factors render its effects disproportionate across diverse communities. Slavoj Žižek, in *PANDEMIC! 2: Chronicles of a Time Lost* (2020), argues that the COVID-19 pandemic has made us rethink about global solidarity, which has been replaced by different concerns and attitudes toward the issue:

> The ongoing pandemic hasn't just brought out social and economic conflicts that were raging beneath the surface all along; it hasn't just confronted us with immense political problems. More and more, it has become a genuine conflict of global visions about society. (p. 3)

Global solidarity gives way to global conflicts, with each country eventually turning to its internal social and economic problems. For Žižek, "we are not all in the same boat" in that the pandemic reveals and explodes class differences (p. 2). Some classes, including those that David Harvey calls the "new working class", and that Latour and Schultz call "geo-social class", Žižek argues, become more visible after the pandemic (p. 20). These less privileged classes are at the one end of the wide range of spectrum, and at the other end, the super-rich finds extreme ways of escaping the coronavirus outbreak.

Žižek (2020) contends that "[t]he contours of corona-capitalism are gradually emerging, and with them new forms of class struggle" (p. 29). It is both down to the exploitation of ecosystems and the collapse of the health system that class has come to the forefront in the global agenda perhaps in an unprecedented way. Harvey's category of "new working class" corresponds to a vulnerable group of people who need to choose between getting infected by the virus because they are obliged to be physically present at workplaces, and becoming unemployed if they fail to do so. Health personnel, agricultural workers, delivery staff, and staff in provision and services sectors like sale assistants are among the members of the "new working class" (Žižek 2020, p. 21). These classes also become visible in contemporary cosmopolitan fiction. Cosmopolitan novels like *Klara and the Sun* (2021) make this interrogation into the ecology and health crisis its central theme. Klara and other AFs designed as a caretaker and companion to children are self-sacrificing workers of the "new working class" whose sole aim is to serve their human owners. Yet, Klara seeks ways of taking an active role in the construction of a posthuman cosmopolitanism. As humanoid robots become an integral part of our contemporary life, cosmopolitanism comes to have broader connotations of inclusion, interconnectedness, and implications of an openness toward not only local and global fellow humans but also the nonhuman other in every sense of the word—be it androids or other living existences in the ecological system.

Posthuman cosmopolitanism embraces the nonhuman as well as the human in defining who / what a cosmopolitan subject is. As we share the same world with each and every nonhuman being—be it other species, notably animals, or humanoid robots, and considering their contribution to a cosmopolitan coexistence, they deserve to be accepted as an integral part of this "one-world" community. With the increasing concerns with ecological problems as well as the integration of robots into our everyday lives, a cosmopolitanism without the posthuman element would be incomplete. Human and nonhuman interaction as well as hierarchy, the mistreatment of species other than human, posthuman and robotic ethics as well as the commodification of robots and artificial intelligence are the common themes of posthuman cosmopolitanism. Kendall et al.'s account of a very material form of everyday cosmopolitanism entails both human and posthuman subjects: "[T]he emergence of cosmopolitanism within everyday spheres, there should be identifiable 'carriers' who play a role in diffusing or sowing the seeds of cosmopolitanism", which "is accomplished by humans and non-human alike" (2009, p. 101). In this sense, the role of the nonhuman as "carriers" of cosmopolitanism cannot be denied. Another rationale behind this convergence between posthumanism and cosmopolitanism is the idea of ethics installed within the principles of each. Braidotti's idea of posthuman ethics has connotations of and many commonalities with posthuman cosmopolitanism: "Posthuman ethics expresses a grounded form of accountability, based on a sense of collectivity and relationality, which results in a renewed claim to community and belonging by singular subjects" (2016, p. 26). Very much like cosmopolitanism, posthuman ethics is profoundly predicated on a sense of community whose internal connections are made through accountability and responsibility not only toward others but also toward the planet itself.

Brexit and its economic implications give rise to even more debates on the cosmopolitan thought that has developed thus far and required a revision of its basic premises thereafter. The responses to Brexit are varied and lack a unique anchoring point—be it cultural or socioeconomic—from which Remain and Leave camps originate their reactions. For some, the EU membership provides the British with greater mobility and dialogue with the European culture while for others its economic ramifications are grimmer. In his introduction to *Brexit and Literature: Critical and Cultural Responses* (2018), Robert Eaglestone hails those writers and literary scholars who explicitly or implicitly support the Remain campaign "cosmopolitan" as they "feel attached to intellectual work and culture from the wider world" (p. 6). Cultural consequences of Brexit, as Eaglestone emphasizes, may last for centuries. From an economic point of view, Shaw (2019) concedes that economic threats underlie the decision of Leave voters, those "who feared that refugees would struggle to assimilate in a new culture, place a significant strain on host economies and public services and increase competition for jobs thus reducing national wages" (p. 41). Within this camp, immigrants are seen as intruders into the ordinary British life with their potential rivalry within professional and public domains, and through this approach, they disputably distance themselves from the cosmopolitan idea of hospitality. By distinguishing the universalist cosmopolitanism envisioned in the unison with Europe as an economic advantage of globalization from the vote of the non-elite population that suffers from poverty, unemployment, and less beneficiary aspects of globalization, Calhoun (2017b) maintains that Brexit "was a vote against cosmopolitan elites who brought Britain into the European Union (EU), who benefited from the EU, and who were widely believed to look down on those who felt they did not" (p. 57). Then the question concerns cosmopolitanism at its root: Does Britain's decision to abandon its EU membership mark an inclination toward parochialism, a total denial of cosmopolitanism, or a local form of cosmopolitanism? Lacking a straightforward answer, this question remains in the forefront of Brexit debates spanning several disciplines. The "deformed cosmopolitanism" of the EU, as Ulrich Beck and Edgar Grande (2007) call it, is manifest in the "egoism of the member states, economic self-interest and the asymmetries in influence on political decisions" (cited in Shaw 2018, pp. 16–7). In this sense, aligning Brexit with anti-cosmopolitanism would be a reductionist approach. Although the relation between Brexit and cosmopolitanism is complex in nature, it is important to note that its economic interpretations surpass discourses of cosmopolitanism with abstract and idealist meanings.

On the literary front, Kristian Shaw coins the term BrexLit to refer to "fictions that either directly respond or imaginatively allude to Britain's exit from the EU, or engage with the subsequent socio-cultural, economic, racial or cosmopolitical consequences of Britain's withdrawal" (2018, p. 18). Shaw's *Brexlit: British Literature and the European Project* (2021) comes as a significant contribution to literature on post-Brexit fiction in its attempt to explore the literary responses to Brexit and its implications for cosmopolitanism. Ali Smith's *Autumn* (2016), for many commentators, is the first serious post-Brexit novel. Anthony Cartwright's *The Cut* (2017) and Mohsin Hamid's *Exit West* (2017) are among the other novels of BrexLit due to their attempt to negotiate the disparate concerns of both Brexit camps. BrexLit fiction may or may not be cosmopolitan depending on their broader or narrower focus. The first wave of post-Brexit fiction, as Shaw observes, is "updated forms of state-of-the-nation novels that retain a narrow focus on British society and its isolation from the continent" (2018, p. 28). This parochial focus is not adopted by some cosmopolitan novels that have emerged after Brexit as "they espouse an outward-looking cosmopolitan engagement as a form of resistance to an increasingly nationalistic and inward-looking cultural landscape" (Shaw 2018, p. 28). Then, even if Brexit politics seems anti-cosmopolitan to some extent, post-Brexit fiction may well be cosmopolitan with a sustaining emphasis on world engagement, empathy, and hospitality.

The New Cosmopolitan Fiction

These new directions on the cultural and economic front have also been taken up on the literary front. With the turn of the century, fiction has tended to become more cosmopolitan and more interested in the world's political, economic, and ecological conditions. Especially, as an upshot of 2008 global economic crisis, cosmopolitan fiction has become more overt and hyper-sensitive in its engagement with contemporary politics, especially with regard to neo-capitalism and global economics. Following this crisis moment, Brexit and the global pandemic, both with an economic dimension as well as ramification, have also reinforced this propensity in fiction. The departure from multiculturalism and universalism, and orientation toward particularism in postmillennial novels can be explicated with a view to twenty-first-century cosmopolitanism—vernacular cosmopolitanism in specific terminology—in literature. In this vein of thought, differences in race, ethnicity, and culture are accepted as ordinary and everyday aspects of cosmopolitan living while class divides and economic inequalities gain renewed significance in the definition of this new interconnected community. As such, cosmopolitanism's implications in neo-capitalism and in class have come to be the core of twenty-first-century novels with a hyper-aware approach to cosmopolitics revolving around global, financial, cultural, and environmental crises.

In fact, the title "cosmopolitan novel" emerges in the literary context in an unparalleled way, signaling the birth of a new type of fiction. This does not mean a denial of the fact that cosmopolitanism as an idea has ancient roots and it appeared in literary texts as a theme in the past; however, the term "cosmopolitan novel" has emerged as a new conception of this idea in contemporary literary studies. This is partly because of the simultaneous inauguration of critical debates on post-postmodernism, and also in account of the need to respond to the ever-increasing interconnectedness across the world. Craig Calhoun (2017a) gives three reasons for the boosting popularity of cosmopolitanism since the late 1990s: the fall of the Soviet communism, the need for transnational cooperation against global risks including infectious diseases and nuclear weapons, and globalization's call forth cosmopolitanism (p. 190). It is also the intensification of global diversity that draws more attention to cosmopolitan theory as Bill Ashcroft (2020) avers: "[C]osmopolitanism is being reinvented as the latest Grand-Theory-of-Global-Cultural-Diversity" (p. 77). More recent developments in the global agenda, involving climate- and health-related breakdowns, have further renewed the attention to cosmopolitanism since they are beyond the narrower scope of nations and smaller communities.

The concept of cosmopolitanism is enshrined in another trending term of the twenty-first century: post-postmodernism. Post-postmodernism is a new tendency that has emerged after postmodernism which is defined by a lack of foundations, roots, and certainties. Post-postmodernism, on the other hand, emphasizes the intensifying need to address both cultural and economic conditions brought about by globalization in more direct ways. It is this attitude of directness that merges cosmopolitanism with post-postmodernist ideology in certain respects. In fact, like the former, post-postmodernism remains a slippery term, which, nevertheless, can be delineated in terms of a time span from the late 1990s onwards. Jeffrey T. Nealon's *Post-Postmodernism or, the Cultural Logic of Just-in-Time Capitalism* (2012), playing with the title of Fredric Jameson's *Postmodernism, or, the Cultural Logic of Late Capitalism* (1992), emphasizes the timeless prevalence of, and the impossibility of going beyond, capitalism within contemporary discourses, and defines post-postmodernism in alignment with this capitalist reign. The post-postmodernist reading of literature means a departure from the linguistic turn of postmodernism where "fragmentation" is the watchword, which is replaced by "intensification" in post-postmodernism. Literature's privileged status in the postmodernist linguistic era and its "synecdochic role" (reading the literary "part" to grasp the "whole" context) are demolished, and a post-postmodernist reading instead involves understanding the whole (economic globalization) first (p. 150). At this point, I must state that it is the cosmopolitan novel that has the potential to install such a post-postmodernist reading practice as it primarily deals with globalizing conditions. As emphasized here, it provides a hyper-awareness in which contemporary political situations are responded to immediately. Nealon asks further: "*What* [...] *can poetics tell us about the workings of economics and culture, rather than* vice versa?" (p. 153; emphasis in original). It is also of significance to contextualize cosmopolitanism within this broader concept of post-postmodernism. This inquiry above can be taken as the central question in engaging particularly with the relation between cosmopolitan fiction and the economic dimension of globalization.

My approach to cosmopolitan fiction can partly be seen as a response to Nealon's demand that literature must be discussed in "socioeconomic terms" (p. 153). I argue here that the new cosmopolitan condition with its socioeconomic mechanisms has been evoked in the postmillennial cosmopolitan novel. This resonates with Binnie et al.'s assertion that cosmopolitanism is "an intrinsically classed phenomenon" (2006, p. 8). In this sense, one of the endeavors in this book is to show how this neo-capitalist attitude within contemporary cosmopolitanism is projected in the fiction that is under scrutiny here. In this respect, this book can be viewed as an attempt at a post-postmodernist reading of literature through grasping the whole (the context of economic globalization and cosmopolitanism) first. By so doing, it also aims to bring in renewed perspectives and insights to the scholarship of contemporary cosmopolitan fiction. I contend that the postmillennial cosmopolitan novel departs from pre-1990s discourses in two ways: firstly, it goes beyond positive connotations of multiculturalism mostly discernible in postmodernism, and secondly it assumes a suspicious stance toward the idea of universalism in cosmopolitan thinking itself.

Multiculturalism, as a response to cultural diversity within societies, is implicated in the idea of maintaining one's group affiliations, hence attachment to their own cultural community, while simultaneously living in a wider community of distinct cultures in mutual understanding and acceptance, though sometimes in dispute. Cosmopolitanism is, in contrast, not predicated on group dynamics, rather it has an individualistic dimension. Therefore, in multiculturalism, there is still an existence of collective identifications as well as an essentialist view of culture. In this view, cultures are regarded as distinct and self-sufficient, and individuals are contained within a well-defined cultural society alongside a multicultural one where distinctive cultures interact and exist side by side. By contrast, especially more recent understandings of cosmopolitanism reject a self-contained definition of cultural identity in favor of a cosmopolitan identity constituted by individualistic choices rather than collective associations. In the same vein, in cosmopolitanism, culture is seen as non-essential, and cultural boundaries dissolve, and hence, difference within a cosmopolitan society is viewed as an ordinary and everyday phenomenon. In the late twentieth-century novels of multiculturalism, cultural, and ethnic mix-ups lead to transformations of postcolonial societies, and thus diversity is embraced by and celebrated in novels like Rushdie's *Midnight's Children* (1984) and *The Satanic Verses* (1988), in which references to discrete cultures, in a blend with many others, still exist. Ian McEwan's *Atonement* (2001), likewise, celebrates a multicultural London with an optimistic vision. On the other hand, here I engage with cosmopolitan, rather than multiculturalist, conceptions in both Rushdie and McEwan's postmillennial novels to demonstrate how they depart from their earlier counterparts' celebratory stance.

Postmillennial cosmopolitan fiction not only challenges earlier multicultural understandings but also downplays the universalist attitude within cosmopolitanism. Classical meanings of the term imply that each and every citizen of the world is potentially equal and worthy of equal rights, and a society encompassing such tolerance for difference and solidarity among its people is capable of maintaining peace and providing possible solutions to the common problems of the world. This sense of oneness of the world as a universalist ideal is evinced as a too-optimistic and far-fetched view in the scope of contemporary cosmopolitanism. This universalist vision is also implicit in the idea of global communication, as well, which has been suspected, with too much hope invested in it, in the debates around contemporary issues as well as writing. Cosmopolitan fiction self-consciously disavows affirmative meanings attached to the notion of global communication by assuming a stance toward the awareness of the deficiencies of this universalist vision. Such a vision may be traced in twentieth-century writers who incorporate cosmopolitan themes and understanding into their oeuvre, yet in a different way from postmillennial cosmopolitan novels. In the twentieth-century, Dorothy J. Hale (2009) maintains, "[t]he novel gives authors and readers alike the opportunity, according to George Eliot, to forge an emotional relation with 'those who differ from themselves in everything but the broad fact of being struggling erring human creatures.'" (p. 15). Joseph Conrad, Iris Murdoch, and A. S. Byatt implement "the Eliotic project of 'enlarging' the spirit of the English citizen by expanding the capacity to respect and honor diversity, to 'extend the number and kind of people you are made to take account of.'" (p. 15). Obviously, sentiments such as diversity, solidarity, responsibility, and accountability show these writers' penchant for cosmopolitan sentiments, yet their cosmopolitan engagement remains universalist in orientation because of their lack in certain features that their postmillennial counterparts have: A global consciousness underlying these cosmopolitan sentiments, directness of response to the world, and its problems as well an acceptance of the complexity of allegiances within both global and local spheres. I must state, then, that the universalist understanding of cosmopolitanism in fiction as a general category implying a tendency in some novels from earlier periods toward cosmopolitan thought is abandoned in favor of a specific type of cosmopolitanism which is more implemental in comprehending twenty-first-century novels: particularism or vernacularism in cosmopolitanism. The following section captures cosmopolitanism from diverse angles, whereby probing into discrepant meanings and the broad scope of the concept as well as tracing the transition from universalist to particularist cosmopolitanism. Then, from the perspective of these conceptions of cosmopolitanism in general terms, the following chapter will explore how the intersecting areas of culture and economics become more visible in the defining elements of cosmopolitan fiction.

What Is Cosmopolitanism?: Diverse Points of Departure

With the proliferation of emerging theories of cosmopolitanism, it gets even harder to pin down a well-delineated definition for the notion. For some theorists, it corresponds to a worldview or a disposition while others see it as transnational politics to espouse global citizenship and human rights, or an identity politics beyond nation-bound definitions, or a new form of allegiance among countries to reconcile with each other to address currently moving people, commodities, capital, and information. Although these approaches vary considerably, one aspect is constant; cosmopolitanism emerges as an intellectual response to globalization. In Timothy Brennan's (2001) terms, "globalization bears on cosmopolitanism as structure to idea" (p. 662), that is the cultural and material reality of globalization gives rise to the idea of cosmopolitanism.

Cosmopolitanism originally consists of two related words used in Greek: cosmos (the world) and polis (political community), and in the crudest sense, it pertains to global politics conceiving humanity as a whole, as cosmopolitans, or citizens of the world, sharing common values and ethics. The term also evokes a sense of the global mobility of goods, information, and people, as well as communication between disparate cultures, communities, and individuals. Cosmopolitanism as a term can be traced back to the time of the Cynics in the fourth century BC, when they first referred to the "citizen of the cosmos" by the word "cosmopolitan". Every citizen belonging to a particular city, a polis, was also regarded as a part of the universe regardless of a division among communities. In the third century BC, the Roman Stoics' adoption of the notion emphasized the idea of the "oneness of humanity". Human beings' shared quality is, in Stoic philosophy, their reason, hence, owing to this, their right to moral value. This distinguishing feature of the human race is the underlying force that propels people toward their fellow citizens of the world. Cosmopolitan communication is, then, in its most ancient form, premised on the presumption that human beings are capable of reasoning, therefore, communicating with and understanding each other. This unifying and universalizing sense of cosmopolitanism has perpetuated since then, prevailing even in contemporary thinking.

The concept of cosmopolitanism came to the fore in philosophical debates during the Enlightenment, specifically in Kant's "Toward Perpetual Peace", "Idea for a Universal History with a Cosmopolitan

Purpose", and other writings. Kant's impact on the contemporary cosmopolitan debate cannot be denied. Kant's conception of cosmopolitanism seeks to establish a society that attains universal justice as well as moral and political unity, thereby enabling all humankind to enhance its capacities. The moral and normative framework of cosmopolitan order has come to unfold in cosmopolitan theories since Kant. As for human interaction, Kant (1795) asserts that it is the force of nature that brings about a "concord among men", a cosmopolitan unity which is guaranteed by nature through either war or trade between nations. This cosmopolitan interconnectedness is achieved by a "purposive plan of producing concord among men, even against their will and indeed by means of their very discord" ([1991], p. 109). Even wars inevitably culminate in cosmopolitan communication, which in turn, has ramifications for the ultimate good of humanity.

Modern cosmopolitanism seems to have not only ideological but also practical connotations. The ideological meaning of cosmopolitanism in general terms has been provided by Garrett Wallace Brown and David Held, in their Preface to *The Cosmopolitanism Reader* (2010): "In its most basic form, cosmopolitanism maintains that there are moral obligations owed to all human beings based solely on our humanity alone, without reference to race, gender, nationality, ethnicity, culture, religion, political affiliation, state citizenship, or other communal particularities" (p. 1). Conceiving humanity as a whole irrespective of such categories, this line of thought aspires to a universalism where common meanings and certain abstract values sustain. This conception of cosmopolitanism rests on pre-conceived notions of ethics, and "virtue" as Turner (2002) avers: "The revival of cosmopolitan idealism is in fact closely connected with the classical idea of virtue" (p. 49). Cosmopolitanism's classical moral meaning is still relevant, though with a change in its premises, in today's world struggling with numerous social, economic, and ecological challenges, whose solutions cannot be found solely in institutional cosmopolitanism. Brown and Held (2010) envision the transition from classical cosmopolitanism of moral orientation to institutional (thus, more concrete and practical) cosmopolitanism, which follows Kant and exhibits a degree of political engagement. In this sense, institutional cosmopolitanism without a moral basis is doomed to be nominal and impractical. This calls to mind the recent debates on Brexit, which accentuates the EU's lack of certain cosmopolitan tenets despite its status as an embodiment of institutional cosmopolitanism.

Cosmopolitanism is beyond being an abstract idea and it also has a practical or political dimension. As an example of the practical aspect of cosmopolitanism, Derrida addresses, in *On Cosmopolitanism and Forgiveness* (1997), the International Parliament of Writers. Derrida both delves into the concept of cosmopolitanism and the required hospitality in relation to it as well as the inherent contradictoriness within it. His idea of hospitality refers to welcoming all refugees and immigrants as residents of the "cities of refuge", yet this hospitality also involves certain conditions and restrictions that are imposed upon the newcomers. Derrida's cosmopolitanism has a political dimension demanding action, and this can be actualized with the coexistence of both, as Derrida suggests, "the Law of an unconditional hospitality, offered a priori to every other, to all newcomers, *whoever they may be*, and *the* conditional laws of a right to hospitality, without which *The* unconditional Law of hospitality would be in danger of remaining a pious and irresponsible desire" (pp. 22–3; emphasis in original). In his interrogation of the idea of cosmopolitan justice and equality, Derrida seems to emphasize both the realistic and implemental dimensions of cosmopolitanism. It is these aspects of cosmopolitan hospitality that are downplayed as a result of Brexit, and simultaneously brought into attention once more in the debate concerning cosmopolitanism in a post-Brexit climate.

Apart from this ideological-practical axis, the departure points in theorizing cosmopolitanism vary in significant ways. To start with, the cosmopolitan as a title may involve nations, states, governments, unions, smaller communities, cities, human/nonhuman agents, and even just attitudes. The fact that all these units may claim "cosmopolitan" before their names attests to the slipperiness of the term. What makes this title even more complicated is the ways in which it is approached as either positive or negative. Cosmopolitanism is regarded as positive by those who overemphasize its function as a promoter of global justice and contact, as well as human rights and tolerance for difference. Other approaches, on the other hand, expose it as a utopian ideal with certain negative and exploitative dimensions from which only the privileged communities benefit while the others become a victim of the workings of globalized economy.

Because of the variety of attachments, cosmopolitanism is naturally explicated within different terms: cultural, institutional, political, moral, ethical, economic, etc., depending on the discipline in which it is scrutinized: philosophy, anthropology, political science, cultural studies, sociology, economics, literary theory, and media studies. It has, therefore, wide-ranging dimensions and meanings, making it difficult to discern its limits; thus, this book adopts an eclectic and synthesizing approach in order to incorporate these theories into the literary analysis attempted here. S. Vertovec and R. Cohen, in *Conceiving Cosmopolitanism: Theory, Context, and Practice* (2002) have come up with a six-unit modality of cosmopolitanism with the aim of demonstrating diverse perspectives adopted by theorists of cosmopolitanism from different fields. This comprehensive typology of cosmopolitanism involves the following:

1. As a socio-cultural condition
2. As a philosophical worldview
3. As a political project to build transnational institutions
4. As a project for recognizing multiple identities
5. As an attitudinal or dispositional orientation
6. As a mode of practice or competence. (p. 9)

As can be discerned, these six modalities are linked to a variety of disciplines, such as sociology, political philosophy, economy, social theory, international relations, and cultural studies, thereby emphasizing the broad scope of the concept that cannot be apprehended within the realm of a single field of study. In this sense, it can be argued that cosmopolitan fiction represents all these propositions alternately, rather than projecting a single meaning of the term.

The first perspective argues that cosmopolitanism is a socio-cultural condition of a socially and culturally interpenetrated world that has emerged as an outcome of developments in transportation and telecommunications as well as migration, mass tourism, and resulting multiculturalism in "world cities" (Vertovec and Cohen 2002, p. 9). As the second viewpoint suggests, drawing on the idea of the "citizen of the world", cosmopolitanism is viewed as a commitment to a worldwide community with universal moral values (p. 10). As a political project to build transnational institutions, it aims to supplant nation-state systems that often fall short of addressing problems inflicting the whole globe. Another project of cosmopolitanism aspires to the recognition of human agents with "multiple affiliations" (p. 10). The fifth category, the cosmopolitan disposition or outlook, on the other hand, corresponds to a stance toward diversity and openness toward the other culture. Finally, cosmopolitanism is a competence representing one's ability to make sense of other cultures and a great number of global tastes.

Cosmopolitanism is often thought in relation with other conceptions, and there seems to be a tendency to study it in line or opposition with these related ideas. Positing the cosmopolitan in opposition to the national has been a common trend among the theorists who detect an aspect of repudiation of the parochial or local in favor of a broader, more inclusive vision within cosmopolitanism. Considering cosmopolitanism and nationalism in oppositional terms is a reductionist approach as the cosmopolitan and the national are not necessarily contradictory or mutually exclusive; on the contrary, these two seemingly adverse concepts are capable of coexisting with each other. Cosmopolitanism has traditionally been challenged by nationalist ideas, yet these two ideologies can now be observed to interact or even intertwine in recent thinking. It can be argued, thus, that the borderline between the national/local/parochial and the cosmopolitan has now been contested. Therefore, the cosmopolitan novel (and this book) evades such reductionist approaches to the concept. The following chapter will dwell on this complex relationship between nationality and cosmopolitanism in its reference to the ways cosmopolitan fiction exposes this complexity.

Another set of antitheses regarding cosmopolitanism pertains to the link between power and the potential to become a cosmopolitan. One view regards cosmopolitanism exclusively as an act of the privileged class, a mobility that can only be afforded by elite cosmopolitans while the other argues that not only dominant but also less privileged individuals or groups—migrants, international workers, refugees, and asylum seekers—can potentially be cosmopolitans. The approach in this book complies with the latter understanding above because it adopts an outlook which is in line with the latest theories of cosmopolitanism that are more relevant to the contemporary moment. To put it differently, as cosmopolitan fiction shows us, the unprivileged has an equal right to the title cosmopolitan in a society which is reigned by cosmopolitan ethos, and which necessitates "some degree of social equality", as Turner emphasizes (2006, p. 143). That is to say, for an ethical cosmopolitan community to sustain its existence, equality must take center stage in it. This is already recognized as an urgency in cosmopolitan fiction which increasingly articulates a concern with social and economic inequalities and gaps in the face of globalization's provision of more wealth for corporation classes. As Harvey (2009) avers, this planetary gap is already broad: "Neoliberalization has created a flat world for the multinational corporations and for the billionaire entrepreneur and investor class, but a rough, jagged, and uneven world for everyone else" (p. 58). In this case, the impact of globalization's economic dimensions must be investigated in a comprehensive analysis of cosmopolitanism. As Woodward and Skrbis (2012) aver, it is at times the cosmopolitan discourse itself that contributes to these exploitative mechanisms: "Global economic forces demand the marketization of products as ways of mobilizing hitherto untapped labour and resources, and of extracting economic value. As a fundamental part of this process, these goods can be produced and consumed through cosmopolitan frames" (p. 128). This complicity between globalization and cosmopolitanism becomes, explicitly or implicitly, manifest in contemporary cosmopolitan fiction.

Yet another trend in approaching cosmopolitanism is, then, to explore it in relation or in contrast to a very related concept, globalization. Globalization is in general terms considered within multiple dimensions, emphasizing the way economic, cultural, and political units (governments, states, corporations, businesses, people) become growingly interdependent. The way Roland Robertson (1992) defines it as "the compression of the world and the intensification of a consciousness of the world as a whole" (p. 8) resonates with cosmopolitanism. It is a highly agreed upon fact that cosmopolitanism shares many basic features with globalization, such as global interconnectedness, boundarylessness, and cross-borderline communication. Other views, on the other hand, tend to differentiate between the two while at the same time acknowledging their relatedness, regarding cosmopolitanism as the more positive side of globalization. For Pippa Norris and Ronald Inglehart (2009), at the root of the key concept of cosmopolitanism lies global interdependence in as many dimensions as economic, social, and political. As their starting point, they concede that: "Globalization is understood here to be multidimensional, encompassing *economic* aspects, such as the flow of trade, labor, and capital; *social* aspects, such as interpersonal contacts and mediated information flows; and *political* dimensions, including the integration of countries into international and regional organizations" (p. 6; emphasis in original). From this definition of globalization, it is apparent that the concept pertains to a sense of fluidity across geographical territories in multiple aspects of human life. The conception of the cosmopolitan, on the other hand, corresponds to "the idea that all humans increasingly live and interact within a single global community, not simply within a single polity or nation-state" (p. 8). In this respect, the concept of cosmopolitanism can be considered to be an inevitable culmination of globalization, a more general condition of the contemporary world. This relationship is both mutual and mundane, as Kendall et al. (2009) emphasizes: "In the global cultural economy there is an apparent confluence between global networks of capitalist exchange and the growth of cosmopolitan habits in a range of everyday fields" (p. 8).

Another attempt to distinguish between globalization and cosmopolitanism pays attention to their different motives to unite the world, globalization's to exploit through economic and cultural homogenizing; cosmopolitanism's to create worldwide communication: "[G]lobalization is a set of designs to manage the world", as Walter Mignolo (2000) argues, "while cosmopolitanism is a set of projects toward planetary conviviality" (p. 721). This distinction sees globalization as negative and cosmopolitanism as more promising for the achievement of world conviviality. Whether this optimistic ideal is attainable or not constitutes, more or less, the content of cosmopolitan novels, which most of the time retain their skepticism toward such conviviality. Cosmopolitanism then amounts to, as Paul Gilroy (2004) puts it, a condition in which "[t]he world becomes not a limitless globe, but a small, fragile, and finite place, one planet among others with strictly limited resources that are allocated unequally" (p. 83). In this sense, the idea that globalization impacts on diverse communities at different scales must be given further thought to understand cosmopolitanism better.

Cosmopolitanism has often been regarded as the general principle or the defining spirit of the contemporary world. Twenty-first-century discourse is largely determined by common concerns and conversation, rather than divisiveness, among cultures, states, and subjects. The departure point of the idea of one world and the ensuing communication among different communities and people is the existence of shared challenges that are faced globally. From this vantage point, cosmopolitanism is often accorded a rigorous mission to overcome such global difficulties. In "The Cosmopolitan Manifesto" (2010), Ulrich Beck attempts to distinguish between two paradigm-shifting phases of modernity: first modernity and second modernity. The former is "based on nation-state societies, where social relations, networks and communities are essentially understood in a territorial sense" and is characterized by "[t]he collective patterns of life, progress and controllability, full employment and exploitation of nature" (p. 217). However, these have all been contested by five related processes of second modernity: "globalization, individualization, gender revolution, underemployment and global risks (as ecological crisis and the clash of global financial markets)" (p. 217). It is the emergence of these risks that call all societies into collective action and communication. Therefore, Beck's version of the cosmopolitan world is a "world risk society" drawing on the sameness (not otherness) of Western and non-Western societies on the basis of sharing the same time and space as well as in the face of the same fundamental risks of the second modernity (p. 218). Thus, this risk regime is not premised on national, but on cosmopolitan cooperation. Most global threats are beyond borders and affect the whole world: climate crises, economic instability, geopolitical tensions, and global health risks. As a result of climate change, the world is witnessing the loss of biodiversity, which requires action and consciousness on a global level. Another world risk, the coronavirus pandemic that has caused the death of millions of people, menaces human health and proves how an originally local matter can be uncontrollable and unresolvable without global cooperation and collective action. It has also refreshed the common conviction in cosmopolitan urges of the age with the oft-articulated popular saying that "we are all in this together". This is a renewed call for cosmopolitan communication in essence.

The multifarious network of relations among the communities is predicated on, and simultaneously reinforcing, their interdependence and interconnectedness. Fundamentally, it is the underlying idea of cosmopolitanism that this interconnection can be key to the possibility of resolving ever-growing global problems, and the world can no longer be perceived in terms of polarity. Delanty's (2012) critical cosmopolitanism suggests a "concern with societal problems", which "animates the cosmopolitan imagination and gives to cosmopolitanism a critical edge" (p. 43). Critical cosmopolitanism involves communication, deliberation, and transformation of cultures as an outcome of cultural encounters (p. 42). For Held (2010), cosmopolitan cooperation can be significantly distinguished from the international cooperation that was extant in the past on the basis of its "rationale": "Cooperation between states is still important, if not more so, but what has changed is the rationale, which is now deeper and more complex. The old threat was the 'other'; the new threat is shared problems and collective threats" (p. 14). Held then comes to the conclusion that cosmopolitanism is the new defining social and political force: "[R]ealism is dead; long live cosmopolitanism!" (p. 14). In this celebratory statement, "realism" corresponds to older forms of cooperation in the global agenda, which is now discredited and can be contrasted with cosmopolitan cooperation with a more focused aim, that of dealing with contemporary global problems within collective action and solidarity.

Cosmopolitanism is concerned with not only the communication of societies but also that of individuals. Ulf Hannerz (1990) differentiates between "cosmopolitans" and "locals", establishing as the criteria the degree of openness to others, a quality that belongs distinctively to the cosmopolitan. For Hannerz, the cosmopolitan "needs to be in a state of readiness, a personal ability to make one's way into other cultures through listening, looking, intuiting, and reflecting" (p. 239). In this sense, cross-cultural interaction and openness, not cross-border mobility alone, is the prerequisite for being defined as cosmopolitan. With this formulation of Hannerz, migrancy, asylum-seeking, or traveling are not necessarily cosmopolitan activities unless they are accompanied by openness to the other culture. Interactive and communicative activity is once more emphasized in defining cosmopolitanism. Although the world is the ultimate site of these reciprocal activities in cosmopolitanism, very personal interactions that encapsulate openness, empathy, and several human feelings are also a part of cosmopolitan communication.

FROM UNIVERSALISM TO PARTICULARISM IN COSMOPOLITANISM

The progression of the cosmopolitan thought can be traced within the axis from universalism to particularism. Ancient and classical uses of the term have much to do with universalist meanings, values, attitudes, and concerns, but more recent approaches to cosmopolitanism seem to accept particularistic diversifications within parochial versions of cosmopolitanism. Bauman (1998) puts "universalization" in par with other key terms of modernity—"civilization", "development", and "consensus"— on account of their commonality, their "determination of order-making", "the order-*making* on a universal, truly global scale" while at the same time underscoring their ineffectiveness as concepts to define contemporary societies (p. 59). Within the framework of universalist cosmopolitanism, two dimensions—with an emphasis on commonness and emphasis on tolerance for difference—will be laid below, with a view to problems prevailing within both conceptions.

More ancient forms of cosmopolitanism tend to be universalist in their scope, regarding all humanity as a whole, all communities equal, hence deserving equal value and treatment with a universal set of ethical and legal rules. This also involves the question of whether it is possible to establish a system of world governance so that global matters can be addressed more efficiently. In terms of human subjectivity, universalist cosmopolitanism presupposes a sense of rootlessness, and a lack of patriotism, and a condition of belonging to a global human community, rather than a particular affiliation with a national, religious, ethnic, or racial group. Raised by Kant, the questions of transnational hospitality, which suggest feeling at home with all world communities regardless of any difference, also prevail in the debates over cosmopolitanism. It is the sheer state of being human, and shared morals and values that draw all humanity together, and it is upon this global solidarity that a more peaceful, less problematic human life can be attained. All these assumptions of classical and modern cosmopolitanism, however, have been thrown into question with the fostering number of recent theories inclining toward particularism in cosmopolitan thinking.

Traditional universalist-humanist cosmopolitans can be seen as advocates of a type of universal humanism. Martha Nussbaum's idea of cosmopolitanism in *For Love of Country* (1996) is universalist-humanist in that the cosmopolitan corresponds to "the person whose allegiance is to the worldwide community of human beings" (p. 4). Cosmopolitan agency is situated in concentric circles of identity, as suggested by Nussbaum, whereby the cosmopolitan subject "puts right before country, and universal reason before the symbols of national belonging" (p. 17). Nussbaum's cosmopolitanism is posited in a universalist perspective. Robbins (2012) asserts that "the older, singular cosmopolitanism in the mode of Nussbaum is now regularly dismissed as other-worldly, elitist, Eurocentric universalism in disguise" and has been "overwhelmed by the pluralizing tide of smaller, subuniversal cosmopolitanisms" (p. 31). It is impossible to think of a form of cosmopolitanism without the idea of openness to the other, not only on the international but also on an interpersonal level. Another definition of the concept by Kendall et al. (2009) has implications of transcending locality as it is "an ethical stance, in which the individual tries to go beyond the strong psychological and evolutionary pressures to privilege those nearest to him or her" (p. 1). Underscoring the universalist element in cosmopolitanism, this definition singles out the move "towards the possibility of connection and dialogue with the other" (p. 1). What makes this assertion universalist is the question of whether it is possible to achieve communication equally with those who are not as close to us as our immediate society.

One strand of cosmopolitanism involves the question of whether it is possible to talk of universal human traits that can be shared by all humanity regardless of nation, race, religion, and gender. Appiah (2006) claims that there are in fact certain universal traits of humanity, including "practices like music, poetry, dance, marriage, funerals; values resembling courtesy, hospitality, sexual modesty, generosity, reciprocity, the resolution of social conflict; concepts such as good and evil, right and wrong, parent and child, past, present, and future" (pp. 96–7). Universalist cosmopolitanism is grounded on the belief that human society can be governed by such common human ethics and values. However, there has been a gradual move away from the universalist claims of cosmopolitanism toward more specific, local, and parochial meanings surrounding the term, rendering it more efficient to be used in the plural, to talk of cosmopolitanisms in discrepant, and often contradictory senses rather than as a well-defined single concept. "Something has happened to cosmopolitanism", Bruce Robbins (1998a) rightly asserts, characterizing this radical shift in terms of a movement along a universalist-nationalist/particularist axis. In traditional view, "[u]nderstood as a fundamental devotion to the interests of humanity as a whole, cosmopolitanism has often seemed to claim universality by virtue of its independence, its detachment from the bonds, commitments, and affiliations that constrain ordinary nation-bound lives" (p. 1). This cosmopolitan ideal often tends to replace nationalist ethos on the grounds that being human precedes belonging to a specific nation-state, thereby calling forth universal norms and rules. This sense of cosmopolitanism views nationalism as restricting, limited in humanistic scope, hence detachment from it as emancipatory from any form of attachment. Seen as a fundamental responsibility to fellow humanbeings, cosmopolitanism is accorded greater value by these universalist-humanist cosmopolitans. In this universalist sense, cosmopolitanism is predominantly perceived as a concept in stark contrast to nationalism. The universalist line of cosmopolitanism is aligned with a premodern sense, an understanding transcending the nationalist tendencies of the modern era, which is rather compatible with the term's Greek origin as the citizen of the world.

This idea of the citizen of the world has also been challenged in multiple ways. In this respect, several questions emerge; yet sometimes remain unanswered: What are the connotations of the citizen of the world? Is it possible to be a citizen of the world? Are cosmopolitans able to put aside their devotion to their countries in favor of an allegiance to all humanity? Obviously, the universalist conception is not without problems. What Appiah (2006) calls "the impartialist version of the cosmopolitan creed" seems to be against patriotism and the idea of nation (p. xvi). This tendency to give up the local and the national in favor of universalism has also brought out animosity against cosmopolitanism. This kind of anti-cosmopolitanism is supported most fiercely by Hitler and Stalin in line with their fascist ideologies, and according to Appiah, this anti-cosmopolitan attitude is merely a euphemism for anti-Semitism (p. xvi). For Patell (2015), this "'[c]ounter-cosmopolitanism' is often linked to fundamentalisms of various kinds" because "[r]ather than embracing cultural difference and recognizing multiple points of view, fundamentalists insist on cultural purity" (p. 236). Even when the charges do not come from these extreme poles, due to its initial connotation as a detachment from roots and nation, cosmopolitanism is often accused of what Posnock (2000) calls "deracination": "The unsettling challenge of the cosmopolitan has historically incited the charge of deracination, especially by nationalists for whom blood and soil are sacred" (p. 803). Thus, an account of cosmopolitanism that is either too impartialist or too negligent of the nation is inconceivable.

The idea of universalism involves the supposition of commonness and sharing certain broadly accepted human values; yet the notion of difference is another constitutive element of the cosmopolitan vision, in which being different is not seen as a hindrance for communication. Contrary to the commonist-universalist orientation, the pluralist version of cosmopolitanism implies that difference rather than commonness properly defines the concept. For Appiah (1998), these two ideals of cosmopolitanism— the urge for commonness and respect for difference—often clash (p. xv). Whether emphasizing commonness or seeking tolerance for diversity in communities, this sense of cosmopolitanism follows a universalist orientation, which in turn remains a utopian vision that is difficult to actualize. As Tomlinson suggests, universalism is a "masquerade" (2002, p. 245) and in fact a sort of "moral foundationalism" (2002, p. 249), and thus must be reconciled with ideas of localism. Contemporary cosmopolitan fiction takes the view that cosmopolitanism is a concept that must be approached vernacularly or locally, rather than universally.

Particularist/Vernacular Cosmopolitanism: Emphasis on the Parochial/Local

With contemporary thought on cosmopolitanism, a shift from a universalist approach to a particularist one can be discerned. As Bruce Robbins (1998a) avers, "[b]ut many voices now insist, with Paul Rabinow, that the term should be extended to transnational experiences that are particular rather than universal and that are unprivileged—indeed, often coerced" (p. 1). Paul Rabinow (1986) stated before that cosmopolitanism is a state in which we live "in-between" local identifications and universal ones, thereby with a difficult task of balancing the two. Now, the emphasis on the universality of the human condition has shifted to include many particular notions of cosmopolitanism in reference to its versions that prioritize everyday and local experiences. As Robbins (2012) states elsewhere, "the term came to be modified by an ever-increasing number of adjectives—rooted, vernacular, discrepant, patriotic, actually existing, and so on—each insisting in its own way that cosmopolitanism was particular, situated, and irreducibly plural" (p. 12). "Cosmopolitanism is *local*", as Brennan (2001) puts it, "while denying its local character" (p. 660). The label "local"—however contradictory it may seem—is now considered side by side with cosmopolitanism. Cosmopolitanism need not be, as Skrbis and Woodward (2007) contends, "best imagined as an emergent world system that is borderless, utopian, and an expression of universal values, but rather a set of increasingly available cultural outlooks that individuals selectively deploy to deal with new social conditions" (p. 745). Going beyond universalism has implications of both taking into account local cosmopolitan existences and making choices for social and cultural attachments. In the same vein, as Delanty (2009) puts it, "cosmopolitanism loses its connection with simple notions of universalism", which means that "the only acceptable kind of cosmopolitanism today can be post-universal, that is a universalism that has been shaped by numerous particularism as opposed to an underlying set of values" (p. 9). Delanty's further argument is to distinguish cosmopolitanism from "relativistic postmodernism" with the "recognition that universal claims or normative principles are always limited and often context bound" and that "cosmopolitan orientations simply take different forms and can be found in many different cultural contexts and historical periods" (p. 9). Particularist orientations in cosmopolitan thinking can then be potentially more attentive to discrepant forms and contexts.

Robert J. Holton's *Cosmopolitanisms: New Thinking and New Directions* (2009) attempts at an extensive typology of cosmopolitanism and comes up with two lists of terms of cosmopolitanism as employed by major theorists, culminating in cosmopolitanism "from-above" or "top-down" cosmopolitanism and cosmopolitanism "from-below" or "bottom-up" cosmopolitanism (pp. 34–6). The first group includes the type of cosmopolitanisms given a specific name based on the power structure that mobilizes a certain group of cosmopolitans: bourgeois, colonial, corporate, despotic, forced, from above, hegemonic, *laissez-faire*, managed, market, merchant, military, of dependency, upper class, as well as capitalism, capitalists, state, and world order. (pp. 34–5). Types of bottom-up cosmopolitanism, on the other hand, are listed as follows: aboriginal, anti-colonial, anti-imperial, anti-proprietary, emancipatory, feminist, from below, marginal, migrant, minority, NGO, non-elite, oppositional, popular, non-Western, vernacular, working class, minoritarian, and subaltern (p. 36). Some of these categories seem to overlap, and others reject smooth divisions. However, defining all terms and probing into their distinguishing characteristics is beyond the scope of this book, which, therefore, selectively adopts certain terms for its specific aims. In the contemporary cosmopolitan novel, the concept of vernacular cosmopolitanism seems to predominate; thus, this term will be employed as an umbrella term by connecting it to certain other related terms, like working-class and non-elite cosmopolitanism.

Vernacular or everyday cosmopolitanism (and cosmopolitanism from below in a more general sense) is of significance for dealing with twenty-first-century fiction. Cosmopolitanism from below, in the most common understanding, refers to the transnational activities of social movement activists and non-governmental organizations to address global issues collectively. Such movements arise not only from global but also local initiatives as they pertain directly to the everyday problems of local peoples. Cosmopolitanism from below is usually born out of a "necessity" on the part of the everyday cosmopolitans who, according to Stuart Hall, "are driven by civil war, ethnic cleansing, famine, economic disaster, and search for economic benefits", and "'live a global life' by *necessity*, arising from 'the disjunctures of globalisation'", thus being "'in translation'" (cited in Werbner 2008, p. 18; emphasis in original). What renders vernacular cosmopolitanism distinctive is its attentiveness to class structures within a cosmopolitan society. Werbner (1999) calls for an urge to include considerations about class within cosmopolitan theory because "the class dimensions of a theory of global subjectivity have remained largely unexamined" (p. 18). However, it is observed in this book that the cosmopolitan novel does not put class issues aside in dealing with contemporary cosmopolitanism.

Vernacular cosmopolitanism implies locality, spatial particularity, and a sense of everydayness in many respects, including language, culture, and preoccupations. In this regard, cosmopolitanism ceases to be an abstract idea and a utopian ideal, rather it corresponds to what people actually do and how they interact transculturally within their everyday lives. According to Hiebert (2002), in "vernacular" or "everyday" cosmopolitanism, "men and women from different origins create a society where diversity is accepted and is rendered ordinary" (p. 212). This "actually existing cosmopolitanism", in Bruce Robbins's (1998a) words, is in fact what everyday, non-elite cosmopolitans, like refugees and migrants, experience in the very everydayness of their lives. This also resonates with Bhabha's (2017) notion of vernacular cosmopolitanism which is far from an "ideal" or "virtue" of "nomadism" and "miscegenation":

> Such an emancipatory ideal—so affixed on, so fetishizing of, the flowing, borderless, global world—neglects to confront the fact that the migrants, refugees, or nomads do not merely circulate just because the signifier suggests that they should. They need to settle, claim asylum or nationality, demand housing and education, assert their economic and cultural rights, and seek the status of some form of citizenship. (p. 144)

Emphasizing the necessity of particularism in cosmopolitan thinking, Bhabha (2004) asserts that globalization "must always begin at home" (p. xv) to grasp its local impacts prior to the global. Immigrants in metropolitan cities, as part of this kind of cosmopolitanism, resist complete assimilation to the dominant culture, or the perpetuation of their own cultural attachments to "home", rather they create a new set of juxtaposed attitudes and traditions (Diouf 2000; Appiah 2006). This amounts to what Stuart Hall (2002) means by:

> open space that requires a kind of vernacular cosmopolitanism, that is to say a cosmopolitanism that is aware of the limitations of any one culture or any one identity and that is radically aware of its insufficiency in governing a wider society, but which nevertheless is not prepared to rescind its claim to the traces of difference, which make its life important. (p. 30)

This sense of vernacular cosmopolitanism implies a sort of in-between position in which neither a complete erasure of difference nor imagining a society of a totalizing cultural structure can suffice to account for the current condition of the world; therefore, it is only this idea of vernacularism that sheds light on our contemporary global community. That is why vernacular cosmopolitanism comes to close attention in postmillennial cosmopolitan fiction.

In this sense, everyday or vernacular cosmopolitanism evinces a different form of cosmopolitan living, one which cannot be narrowly equated with the consumerist activities of the privileged or "elite" classes, what John Micklethwait and Adrian Wooldridge term as "cosmocrats", who are defined by their transnational attitude, traveling lifestyles, and global taste for culture (Vertovec and Cohen 2002, p. 6). In this "elite" version, diversity and difference in culture are not everyday phenomena, but rather such cosmopolitanism is a form of commodification and exoticism; therefore, it is not based on the ordinary but on the extraordinary. This elitist version of cosmopolitanism can be summed up in Calhoun's well-known definition aligning cosmopolitanism with the "class-consciousness of frequent travelers" as appears in his title "The Class Consciousness of Frequent Travelers: Toward a Critique of Actually Existing Cosmopolitanism" (2002). It is necessary, yet, to note that not everyone transported is a cosmopolitan of their own choice; an important portion of global mobility occurs by force, whether because of wars, unemployment, inadequate living conditions, asylum seeking, or environmental factors. Simon Gikandi (2010) argues that "global cultural flows are still dominated by those coerced migrants rather than the free-willing cosmopolitan subjects" (p. 28).

Pnina Werbner (2008) calls the term "vernacular cosmopolitanism" "an apparent oxymoron that seems to join contradictory notions of local specificity and universal enlightenment" (p. 14). Werbner suggests that vernacular cosmopolitanism proves more valid to make sense of the postmillennial context. Werbner (2006) also situates the term among other concepts that encompass evident oppositions: "cosmopolitan patriotism, rooted cosmopolitanism, cosmopolitan ethnicity, working-class cosmopolitanism, discrepant cosmopolitanism" (p. 496). Despite their contradictoriness and inclination toward the parochial, such concepts do not nullify universalist concerns of cosmopolitanism altogether, rather they attempt to shed light on the emerging sense of a less straightforward cosmopolitanism, by incorporating the original Greek and Kantian meanings of the term into "a more complex and subtle understanding of what it means to be a cosmopolitan at the turn of the twenty-first century" (2008, p. 15). For the sake of clarification, it is necessary to take a look at similar terms that posit cosmopolitanism in a more particularist fashion with the ideas of bottom-up cosmopolitanism: Appiah's "cosmopolitan patriotism" and "rooted cosmopolitanism", Clifford's "discrepant cosmopolitanism", Pnina Werbner's "working-class cosmopolitanism", Richard Werbner's "cosmopolitan ethnicity", and Robbin's "non-elite cosmopolitanism".

All of these terms pay attention to the specificities of the cosmopolitan experience within diverse contexts and reflect the rootedness of this seemingly universal disposition in highly parochial situations. Kwame Anthony Appiah (1998) implicates in the terms "cosmopolitan patriotism" and "rooted cosmopolitanism" that cosmopolitan ideals embark from smaller units of communal attachments (from families), and transcending ethnic and local bonds, move toward a global engagement with and open attitude toward the other. As a both/and perspective, this requires a renegotiation of multiple identities, between local affiliations and global responsibilities. Appiah (1998) concludes his position as follows: "[Y]ou can be cosmopolitans—celebrating the variety of human cultures; rooted—loyal to one local society (or a few) that you count as home; liberal—convinced of the value of the individual; and patriotic—celebrating the institutions of the state (or states) within which you live" (p. 106). Richard Werbner's (2004) "cosmopolitan ethnicity", too, intertwines both local and global commitments because it is "urban yet rural, at once inward- and outward-looking, it builds interethnic alliances from intra-ethnic ones, and it constructs difference while transcending it. Being a cosmopolitan does not mean turning one's back on the countryside, abandoning rural allies, or rejecting ethnic bonds" (p. 63). Here, the connotations of locality come to include ethnic specificity, and cosmopolitanism both respects and transcends such ethnic ties. All these terms have a common ground, that of acknowledging belongingness and affiliations within the concept of cosmopolitanism.

James Clifford (1992) draws attention to the shift in the characterization of the cosmopolitan. He adopts a totally different view of cosmopolitanism, expanding the definition of the cosmopolitan traveler. Now the title has come to include those servants who accompany their masters in the course of travel and who develop their own sense of cosmopolitan experience, as well as those "cosmopolitan workers" that emerge as the outcome of migrancy. "The notion that certain classes of people are cosmopolitan (travellers) while the rest are local (natives)" comes as "the ideology of one (very powerful) travelling culture" (pp. 107–8), thus "the project of comparing and translating different travelling cultures need not be class- or ethno-centric" (p. 107). Remarking on Clifford's idea of traveling culture, Bruce Robbins (1998b) states that "[q]uestions of power aside, 'they' and 'we' can no longer be divided as 'local' and 'cosmopolitan'" (p. 181). The title cosmopolitan can no longer be accorded only to the privileged class as it now has become more inclusive, containing the working class, and revoking the division between "local" and "cosmopolitan".

Pnina Werbner (1999) employs the term "working-class cosmopolitanism", drawing on Hannerz's distinction between "cosmopolitans", who willingly engage with the Other, and "transnationals"—migrants, settlers, refugees, and occupational travelers, who do not: "[E]ven working class labour migrants may become cosmopolitans, willing to 'engage with the Other'; and ... transnationals [...] inevitably must engage in *social* processes of 'opening up to the world', even if that world is still relatively circumscribed culturally" (p. 18). Cosmopolitanism is no longer regarded as a distinctively elite preoccupation through the inclusion of those "working-class cosmopolitans" in the definition of the term. The conditions that are normally attributed to Third-World elite intelligentsia—hybridity, in-betweenness—now pertain to "working-class cosmopolitans" as well, thereby making them as equally cosmopolitan as the elite, precisely because cosmopolitanism "does not necessarily imply an absence of belonging but the possibility of belonging to more than one ethnic and cultural localism simultaneously" (p. 34). Bruce Robbins (1998a), in the same vein, coins two useful terms—"actually existing cosmopolitanism" and "non-elite cosmopolitanism"—to draw attention to how the status, normally denied to immigrants and other "non-elites", actually includes multiple forms of cosmopolitanism which come to existence in various cosmopolitan spaces. Thus, the overall concern of cosmopolitanism from below is to give, as Holton (2009) suggests, "a response to cross-border processes and interdependencies which threaten the interests of those who [...] lie outside dominant social groups (classes and elites)" (p. 36). This can be concluded with the idea that "cosmopolitanism is", as Binnie et al. (2006) put it, "classed in multiple ways" (p. 9) and it is "an intrinsically classed phenomenon" (p. 8), and as argued in this book, contemporary cosmopolitan fiction demonstrates an awareness of this situation. Drawing on all these ideas on new cosmopolitanisms, the argument of this book is that the marriage between fiction and economics can be captured in the conception of vernacular cosmopolitanism, which in turn, appears in different forms in twenty-first-century novels.

The term "vernacular" or "everyday" cosmopolitanism has mainly appeared in the theories of 1. Homi K. Bhabha (1996); 2. Mamadou Diouf (2000); 3. Pnina Werbner (2006). Bhabha's (1996) version of the term "vernacular cosmopolitanism", in contradistinction to the universalism of Nussbaum's version of cosmopolitanism, seems cognizant of the particular conditions of migrants and refugees, who constitute a "cosmopolitan community envisaged in *marginality*" (pp. 195–6). These minorities keep moving back and forth between their local culture in the form of indigenous language, food, religion, and festivals and the culture of the metropole, in which they become a "part of a recognisable and shared sense of civic virtue": "It is this double life of British minorities that makes them vernacular cosmopolitans, translating between cultures, renegotiating traditions from a position where 'locality' insists on its own terms, while entering into larger national and societal conversations" (Bhabha 2000, p. 139). Vernacular cosmopolitanism, for Bhabha, comes to life in the liminal space between discrepant cultures:

> Aesthetic and cultural values are derived from those boundaries *between* languages, territories and communities that belong, strictly speaking, to no one culture; these are values produced in the on-going practices and performances of "crossing over," and become meaningful as cultures to the extent to which they are intricately and intimately interleaved with one another. (2000, p. 139)

Diouf's (2000) notion of "vernacular cosmopolitanism", likewise, refers to the everyday living realities of ordinary people, and their interactions with others who inhabit the same glocal territory. Pnina Werbner (2006) draws attention to the contradictory elements inhabited within the term by reminding us of the current debates in which the emerging question of "whether the local, parochial, rooted, culturally specific and demonic may co-exist with translocal, transnational, transcendent, elitist, enlightened, universalist and modernist" is asserted (p. 496). Lamont and Aksartova's (2002) term "ordinary cosmopolitanisms" (p. 1), likewise, pays attention to everyday cosmopolitan living in the belief that "they engage with difference perhaps just as often as the paradigmatic [elite] cosmopolitans, albeit on a local, as opposed to a global, scale" (p. 2). The vernacular dimension in cosmopolitan thinking pays attention to discrepancies in the particular versions of cosmopolitan lives irrespective of class, ethnicity, race as well as the potential for mobility. This is tantamount to claim that everyone can equally be a cosmopolite despite the diversity of their cosmopolitan experiences.

To wrap up all this debate around the conception of vernacular cosmopolitanism, it is necessary to restate all these connotations of the term. In concomitance with the broader concept of cosmopolitanism from below, vernacular cosmopolitanism opens up a possibility to consider divergences immanent within the term itself. Vernacular cosmopolitanism refers all at once to: (a) transnational activities as well as local initiatives on the level of everyday cosmopolitans; (b) a form of cosmopolitanism born out of "necessity" as a result of (civil) wars, economic and environmental disasters, unemployment, or other obligatory mobilities; (c) cosmopolitanism as acceptance of everyday difference which is made ordinary and vernacular; (d) attention to spatial particularity and the specific needs of local cosmopolitans; (e) a simultaneous attachment to and engagement with the universal and the parochial, the global and the local; (f) departure from a one-sided perception of cosmopolitanism as the cultural transposition of the privileged elite classes, acknowledging the existence of working-class cosmopolitans; (g) a state of opening up to the world irrespective of the possibility of mobility; (h) going beyond universalist ethicist idealism to considerations of economic dimension within the concept of cosmopolitanism complicit with neoliberal capitalism and neo-imperialism. In this sense, particularist or vernacular cosmopolitanism seems to respond to what universalist cosmopolitanism neglects to do, representing all types of cosmopolitans and cosmopolitanisms. These aspects of vernacular cosmopolitanism will be explored in the following chapters as a valid term that is able to reflect postmillennial fiction's thematic and aesthetic features.

Notes

1. Schultz, Nikolaj. 2020. New Climate, New Class Struggles. In *Critical zones: The science and politics of landing on earth*, ed. Bruno Latour and Peter Weibel, 308–311. Cambridge, MA: Cambridge MIT Press.

2. Stein Pedersen, J. V., Bruno Latour, and Nikolaj Schultz. 2019. A conversation with Bruno Latour and Nikolaj Schultz: Reassembling the Geo-Social. *Theory, Culture & Society* 36:215–230. https://doi.org/10.1177/0263276419867468.

REFERENCES

Appiah, Kwame Anthony. 1998. Cosmopolitan patriots. In *Cosmopolitics: Thinking and feeling beyond the nation*, ed. Pheng Cheah and Bruce Robbins, 91–114. Minneapolis: University of Minnesota Press.
Appiah, Kwame Anthony. 2006. *Cosmopolitanism: Ethics in a world of strangers*. New York: W. W. Norton & Co.
Ashcroft, Bill. 2010. Transnation. In *Rerouting the postcolonial: New directions for the new millennium*, ed. Janet Wilson, Sarah Lawson Welsh, and Christina Şandru, 72–85. London: Routledge.
Bauman, Zygmunt. 1998. *Globalization: The human consequences*. Cambridge: Polity.
Beck, Ulrich. 2010. The cosmopolitan manifesto. In *The cosmopolitanism reader*, ed. David Held and Garrett Wallace Brown, 217–228. Cambridge: Polity Press.
Beck, Ulrich, and Edgar Grande. 2007. *Cosmopolitan Europe*. Cambridge: Polity Press.
Bhabha, Homi. 1996. Unsatisfied: Notes on vernacular cosmopolitanism. In *Text and nation*, ed. Laura Garcia-Morena and Peter C. Pfeifer, 191–207. London: Camden House.
Bhabha, Homi. 2000. The vernacular cosmopolitan. In *Voices of the crossing: The impact of Britain on writers from Asia, the Caribbean, and Africa*, ed. Ferdinand Dennis and Naseem Khan, 133–142. London: Serpent's Tail.
Bhabha, Homi. 2004. *The Location of Culture*. London: Routledge.
Bhabha, Homi. 2017. Spectral sovereignty, vernacular cosmopolitans, and cosmopolitan memories. In *Cosmopolitanisms*, ed. Bruce Robbins and Paulo Lemos Horta, 141–152. New York: New York UP.
Binnie, Jon, Julian Holloway, and Steve Millington. 2006. Introduction: Grounding cosmopolitan urbanism: Approaches, practices and policies. In *Cosmopolitan Urbanism*, ed. Jon Binnie, Julian Holloway, Steve Millington, and Craig Young, 1–34. London: Routledge.
Braidotti, Rosi. 2016. Posthuman critical theory. In *Critical posthumanism and planetary futures*, ed. D. Banerji and M.R. Paranjape, 13–32. Springer. https://doi.org/10.1007/978-81-322-3637-5_2 2016: 13–32

Brennan, Timothy. 2001. Cosmo-Theory. *The South Atlantic Quarterly* 100: 659–691.
Brown, Garrett Wallace, and David Held. 2010. *The cosmopolitanism reader*. Cambridge: Polity Press.
Calhoun, Craig. 2002. The class consciousness of frequent travellers: Towards a critique of actually existing cosmopolitanism. In *Conceiving cosmopolitanism: Theory, context, and practice*, ed. Steven Vertovec and Robin Cohen, 86–109. Oxford: Oxford UP.
Calhoun, Craig. 2017a. A cosmopolitanism of connections. In *Cosmopolitanisms*, ed. Bruce Robbins and Paulo Lemos Horta, 189–200. New York: New York UP.
Calhoun, Craig. 2017b. Populism, nationalism and Brexit. In Brexit: Sociological Responses, ed. William Outhwaite, 57–76. Anthem Press. http://www.jstor.org/stable/j.ctt1kft8cd
Clifford, James. 1992. Traveling Cultures. In *Cultural Studies*, ed. Lawrence Grossberg, Cary Nelson, and Paula Treichler, 96–116. New York: Routledge.
Delanty, Gerard. 2009. *The cosmopolitan imagination: The renewal of critical social theory*. New York: Cambridge UP.
Delanty, Gerard. 2012. The idea of critical cosmopolitanism. In *Routledge handbook of cosmopolitanism studies*, ed. Gerard Delanty, 38–46. London: Routledge.
Derrida, Jacques. 1997. *On cosmopolitanism and forgiveness*. Trans. Mark Dooley and Michael Hughes. London and New York: Routledge.
Diouf, Mamadou. 2000. The Senegalese Murid trade diaspora and the making of a vernacular cosmopolitanism. *Public Culture* 12: 679–702.
Eaglestone, Robert. 2018. Introduction: Brexit and literature. In *Brexit and literature. Critical and Cultural Responses*, ed. Robert Eaglestone, 1–6. London and New York: Routledge.
Gikandi, Simon. 2010. Between roots and routes: cosmopolitanism and the claims of locality. In *Rerouting the postcolonial: New directions for the new millennium*, ed. Janet Wilson, Cristina Şandru and Sarah Lawson Welsh, 22–35. London: Routledge.
Gilroy, Paul. 2004. *After empire: Melancholia or convivial culture*. London and New York: Routledge.
Hale, Dorothy J. 2009. The art of English fiction in the twentieth century. In *The Cambridge companion to the twentieth-century English novel*, ed. Robert L. Caserio, 10–22. New York: Cambridge UP.
Hall, Stuart. 2002. Political belonging in a world of multiple identities. In *Conceiving cosmopolitanism: Theory, context, and practice*, ed. Steven Vertovec and Robin Cohen, 25–31. Oxford: Oxford UP.

Hannerz, Ulf. 1990. Cosmopolitans and locals in world culture. *Theory, Culture & Society* 7: 237–251. https://doi.org/10.1177/026327690007 002014.
Harvey, David. 2009. *Cosmopolitanism and the geographies of freedom*. New York: Columbia University Press.
Held, David. 2010. *Cosmopolitanism: Ideals and realities*. Cambridge: Polity Press.
Hiebert, Daniel. 2002. Cosmopolitanism at the local level: The development of transnational neighbourhoods. In *Conceiving Cosmopolitanism: Theory, Context, and Practice*, ed. Steven Vertovec and Robin Cohen, 209–223. Oxford: Oxford UP.
Holton, Robert J. 2009. *Cosmopolitanisms: New thinking and new directions*. Basingstoke: Palgrave Macmillan.
Ishiguro, Kazuo. 2021. *Klara and The Sun*. London: Faber & Faber.
Kant, Immanuel. 1795 [1991]. *Kant: Political writings*, ed. H. S. Reiss. Trans. H. B. Nisbet. Cambridge: Cambridge UP.
Kendall, Gavin, Ian Woodward, and Zlatko Skrbis. 2009. *The sociology of cosmopolitanism: Globalization, identity, culture and government*. Houndmills, Basingstoke, Hampshire and New York: Palgrave Macmillan.
Lamont, Michèle, and Sada Aksartova. 2002. Ordinary cosmopolitanisms: Strategies for bridging racial boundaries among working class men. *Theory, Culture and Society* 19: 1–26. https://doi.org/10.1177/0263276402019004001.
Mignolo, Walter D. 2000. The many faces of cosmo-polis: Border thinking and critical cosmopolitanism. *Public Culture* 32: 721–748.
Nealon, Jeffrey T. 2012. *Post-postmodernism or, the cultural logic of just-in-time capitalism*. Stanford: Stanford UP.
Norris, Pippa, and Ronald Inglehart. 2009. *Cosmopolitan communications: Cultural diversity in a globalized world*. Cambridge: Cambridge UP.
Nussbaum, Martha C., and Joshua Cohen. 1996. *For love of country: Debating the limits of patriotism*. Boston: Beacon Press.
Patell, Cyrus R. K. 2015. *Cosmopolitanism and the literary imagination*. New York: Palgrave Macmillan.
Posnock, Ross. 2000. The dream of deracination: The uses of cosmopolitanism. *American Literary History* 12: 802–818.
Rabinow, Paul. 1986. Representations are social facts. In *Writing culture: The poetics and politics of ethnography*, ed. James Clifford and George E. Marcus, 234–261. Berkeley: University of California P.
Robbins, Bruce. 1998a. Actually existing cosmopolitanism. In *Cosmopolitics: Thinking and feeling beyond the nation*, ed. Pheng Cheah and Bruce Robbins, 1–19. Minneapolis: University of Minnesota Press.

Robbins, Bruce. 1998b. Comparative Cosmopolitanisms. In *Cosmopolitics: Thinking and feeling beyond the nation*, ed. Pheng Cheah and Bruce Robbins, 246–264. Minneapolis: University of Minnesota Press.

Robbins, Bruce. 2012. *Perpetual War: Cosmopolitanism from the viewpoint of violence*. Durham, NC: Duke UP.

Robertson, Roland. 1992. *Globalization: Social theory and global culture*. London: SAGE Publications Ltd.

Schultz, Nikolaj. 2020. New climate, new class struggles. In *Critical zones: The science and politics of landing on earth*, ed. Bruno Latour and Peter Weibel, 308–311. Cambridge, MA: Cambridge MIT Press.

Shaw, Kristian. 2018. 'Brexlit'. In *Brexit and literature. Critical and cultural responses*, ed. Robert Eaglestone, 15–30. London and New York: Routledge.

Shaw, Kristian. 2019. Refugee fictions: Brexit and the maintenance of borders in the European Union. In *Borders and border crossings in the contemporary British short story*, ed. Barbara Korte and Laura M. Lojo-Rodríguez, 36–60. Basingstoke: Palgrave Macmillan. https://doi.org/10.1007/978-3-030-303 59-4_3

Shaw, Kristian. 2021. *Brexlit: British literature and the European project*. London: Bloomsbury Academic.

Skrbis, Zlatko, and Ian Woodward. 2007. The ambivalence of ordinary cosmopolitanism: Investigating the limits of cosmopolitan openness. *The Sociological Review* 55: 730–747.

Stein Pedersen, J.V., Bruno Latour, and Nikolaj Schultz. 2019. A conversation with Bruno Latour and Nikolaj Schultz: Reassembling the geo-social. *Theory, Culture & Society* 36: 215–230. https://doi.org/10.1177/026327641986 7468.

Tomlinson, John. 2002. Interests and identities in cosmopolitan politics. In *Conceiving cosmopolitanism: Theory, context, and practice*, ed. Steven Vertovec and Robin Cohen, 240–253. Oxford: Oxford UP.

Turner, Bryan S. 2002. Cosmopolitan virtue: Globalization and patriotism. *Theory, Culture & Society* 12: 45–63.

Turner, Bryan S. 2006. Classical sociology and cosmopolitanism: A critical defence of the social. *The British Journal of Sociology* 57: 133–151.

Vertovec, Steven, and Robin Cohen. 2002. Introduction: Conceiving cosmopolitanism. In *Conceiving cosmopolitanism: Theory, context, and practice*, ed. Steven Vertovec and Robin Cohen, 1–22. Oxford: Oxford UP.

Werbner, Pnina. 1999. Global pathways. Working class cosmopolitans and the creation of transnational ethnic worlds. *Social Anthropology* 7: 17–35.

Werbner, Pnina. 2006. Vernacular Cosmopolitanism. *Theory, Culture & Society* 23: 496–498.

Werbner, Pnina. 2008. Introduction: Towards a new cosmopolitan anthropology. In *Anthropology and the new cosmopolitanism*, ed. Pnina Werbner, 1–29. New York: Berg.

Werbner, Richard. 2004. *Reasonable radicals and citizenship in Botswana: The public anthropology of Kalanga elites*. Bloomington: Indiana UP.

Woodward, I.S., and Zlatko Skrbiš. 2012. Performing cosmopolitanism. In *Routledge handbook of cosmopolitanism studies*, ed. Gerard Delanty, 127–137. London: Routledge.

Žižek, Slavoj. 2020. *Pandemic! 2: Chronicles of a time lost*. New York and London: OR Books.

CHAPTER 2

New Intersections in Fiction: Cosmopolitanism, Culture, and Economics

Following the discussion on new forms of cosmopolitanism in Chapter 1, this chapter aims to capture the intersection of areas of culture and economics within postmillennial cosmopolitan fiction. This calls for a cultural and socioeconomic basis for understanding postmillennial fiction is precisely because cosmopolitanism is characterized by the vernacular in most postmillennial cosmopolitan novels, and inherent in the term vernacular is connotations of a redefined culture of everyday diversity as well as a neo-capitalist economic structure in which the local requires attention as much as the global. This chapter will, thus, show the general propensities in twenty-first-century cosmopolitan novels toward new considerations of culture and economic conditions. In fact, a renewal of interest in economics has been seen in the realm of literary studies, especially since the global economic crisis of 2008. The defining aspects of twenty-first-century cosmopolitan novels emerge at their intersection with culture and economics with the advent of several cosmopolitan themes and narrative features at this juncture. Below is a discussion of these distinctive features of the cosmopolitan fiction, which will be handled within six subsections, the first three of which mostly pertain to culture, and the last three to economic dimensions.

© The Author(s), under exclusive license to Springer Nature Switzerland AG 2024
E. Toprak Sakız, *Culture and Economics in Contemporary Cosmopolitan Fiction*, https://doi.org/10.1007/978-3-031-44995-6_2

Narrative Glocality: Interaction Between the Global and the Local

Culture in the cosmopolitan fiction can first be defined by the interplay between the global and the local. All global matters constitute the subject matters and themes of twenty-first-century cosmopolitan fiction. They include (but are not limited to) global wars, poverty, natural resources crisis, climate change, world terror, global economic crisis, and loss of biodiversity. All of these inform the cosmopolitan culture, which has both a domestic and global dimension, and I will show below how they are presented and represented in narrative. Rather than focusing on each of these contemporary issues separately, at the core of this section is the question of how postmillennial cosmopolitan novels approach them. To address this question, I suggest "narrative glocality" as a useful term, which summarizes the attitude in which vernacular cosmopolitan novels are oriented toward both the global and the local in considerations of culture. While glocality is one of the prevalent themes of postmillennial novels, narrative glocality represents the ways in which these novels engage with cosmopolitan culture.

Vernacular or everyday cosmopolitanism in the postmillennial novel reflects the transition from the universalist understanding of cosmopolitanism to the particularist one, with reference to the cosmopolitan conditions that are local, parochial, and quotidian. S. Vertovec and R. Cohen's definition of cosmopolitanism in terms of a capacity "to mediate actions and ideals oriented both to the universal and the particular, the global and the local" (2002, p. 4) applies well to the cosmopolitan fiction. Twenty-first-century cosmopolitan novels reflect the ability to negotiate between the universal and the particular, the global and the local in both thinking and actions. This seems to be an efficient response to Beck's call that "we must reorient and reorganize our lives and actions, our organizations and institutions along a 'local-global' axis" (1999, p. 11). Thematic diversity and most plot lines in cosmopolitan fiction are situated in the axis moving from the local to the global or vice versa. Yet, the distinction between the global and the local is not clear-cut since, as Gikandi puts it, "locality itself has been globalized" as a result of global movements of migrants (2010, p. 32). Accordingly, I argue that, in postmillennial cosmopolitan fiction, universalist ideals of the global are first interrogated and then reshaped with a view to the local. To put it more precisely, distinctively parochial interests of cosmopolitans are also represented and foregrounded. In

Anglophone fiction, as in cosmopolitan theory, there is an inclination toward intertwining the global and the local, propelling toward the "glocal" to inclusively represent both, thereby problematizing the borderline between the two seemingly distinct spheres. In Gerard Delanty's *Community* (2003), community is defined by a dual system simultaneously accommodating the local and the universal, and cosmopolitanism becomes central to this double understanding of community (p. 12). Cosmopolitan communities are, then, characterized by "glocalization", that is "the mixing of the local and the global" (p. 149). Calhoun emphasized the indispensability of our localities (including our cultural, national, and religious specificities) for our interactions with the world (2017, p. 191). Postmillennial cosmopolitan novels engage with the global and the local in their idea of contemporary culture and life. This is not to say that local cultures are foregrounded as much as a global culture in which they exist and communicate with each other. This is, rather, a radical change in the definition of contemporary culture which demolishes distinctions between the vernacular and the universal and creates new spaces for living in terms of everyday diversity.

This interconnected relationship between the global and the local is often reflected in cosmopolitan fiction in terms of space. Globalization connotes, according to Held (2010), a reorganization of the whole human activity in spatial terms with the boundaries between the local and the global dissolving as the impact of global events can be felt as forcefully in the local territories while a minor local event can have big influences beyond its boundaries (p. 29). This feature is discernible in the cosmopolitan novel where an event—global or local—has imbrications or consequences that are beyond its immediate territory, and has an impact on distant people, communities, and places. Thus, both of these territories seem to mutually impact upon each other; in other words, while globalization infiltrates and informs the vernacular, the local in turn comes up with ways of resisting and finding its own response to the world. The local is not passive nor has an inferior effect on our understanding of the contemporary world.

Now we have the themes of vernacular cosmopolitanism in the twenty-first-century novel. Primarily understood as an economic phenomenon, globalization implies trans-border economic processes such as transnational production, consumption, and capital flow. Despite its economic basis, globalization has come to encompass political, cultural, and religious interconnections in its definition, especially in the work of recent theorists. As such, it bears many affinities with cosmopolitanism on the basis of their common grounds of border-crossing and interconnectivity. Some scholars regard them as distinct phenomena with cosmopolitanism being only one dimension of globalization, often as the positive side of it. Cosmopolitanism has something to do with how the challenges created by globalization impact on our daily lives, on our real lived experiences as ordinary citizens and how we respond to socioeconomic inequalities and cultural crises of the century. It must be stated, then, that cosmopolitanism is, in a sense, vernacularizing the more far-flung concept of globalization. Gerard Delanty (2009), in the same vein, suggests that "the interaction of the global with the local […] opens up a range of considerations that bring globalization theory in the direction of a new conception of cosmopolitanism" (pp. 5–6). Rumford calls this new conception "critical cosmopolitanism [which] is engaged in a critique of globalization thinking, specifically the idea that we live in one world" (2008, p. 154). Globalization is a broader transnational occupation while its side-effect cosmopolitanism can be potentially more particular, involving the everyday experiences of a smaller local group or an individual in the face of a globalizing world. In contemporary cosmopolitan fiction, such particularities of cosmopolitan lives can be explored with a view to the concept of space. The concept of vernacular cosmopolitanism and its spatial focus is a relatively recent focus of study in contrast to the distant history of cosmopolitanism proper. The spatial focus of cosmopolitan fiction is in keeping with its attention to glocalization. I, thus, suggest that it is expedient, in the literary investigation of cosmopolitanism, to incorporate a spatial approach and give specific attention to spaces, possibly and sometimes less self-evidently cosmopolitan, to explore the particular cosmopolitan experiences of locals, which are nonetheless shaped not independently from the global. Far from encapsulating the cosmopolitan within strict boundaries of locales, this way of seeing the world is like a practice, as Sheldon Pollock perceives it, "of seeing the larger picture stereoscopically with the smaller" (2002, p. 12). Narrative glocality can then be likened to the working mechanism of a stereoscope, whereby multiple pictures of the cosmopolitan world create a whole vision which is characterized by depth, inclusion, and insight.

Vernacular cosmopolitanism emphasizes spatial positioning and the interface between the global and local spaces as a constitutive element of cosmopolitanism from below, or one lived by non-elite cosmopolitans. Everyday cosmopolitans are distant from cosmopolitan elites or "cosmocrats" in Micklethwait and Adrian Wooldridge's terms (Vertovec and Cohen 2002, p. 6). For Kristian Shaw, all cosmopolitan spaces as well as unprivileged positions are now subject to, and offer the potential for, cultural engagement, which makes cosmopolitanism more applicable as a social concept (2017b, p. 15). It is essential, then, that we "investigate how cosmopolitanism is formed and reformed in particular locales and everyday spaces", particularly in city spaces, in order to understand the relationship between the issues of class and commodification and the everyday practices of cosmopolitanism (Binnie et al. 2006, pp. 12–13). This approach is specifically fruitful in its inclusion of cosmopolitan everyday spaces in the analysis of contemporary fiction. We can, then, see more lucidly all spaces as well as all subject positions in interrelated and often complex networks of interaction.

For the purposes of spatial investigation in contemporary fiction and to manifest space as constitutive of a cosmopolitan culture, I will suggest a new term, narrative glocality, and resort to it in the analyses of fiction. Narrative glocality in postmillennial cosmopolitan novels corresponds to the idea of narrative space and the novel's consciousness as globally shaped and vernacularly specified, hence oriented toward, and premised on, the global and the local simultaneously. To put it more precisely, this term can be considered to be the application of the concept of glocality to narrative studies by focusing on the novel's both immediate and distant spatial activities. *Glocality* as a term to designate the contemporary condition is invented by Roland Robertson (1995), who defines it as "the simultaneity and the interpenetration of what are conventionally called the global and the local, or – in more abstract vein – the universal and the particular" (p. 30). Robertson, however, warns us against regarding all forms of locality as homogenized (p. 31). Paying attention to the interdependence of the global and the local as well to the heterogeneity of cosmopolitan experience, this term becomes relevant in the spatial discussion here. The cosmopolitan novel—either through the narrator or through the characters—often reflects on both near and distant people, situations and places, and by doing so, is characterized by an existence and consciousness which is glocal. To be more specific, the setting may be unique like *Saturday*'s London, but the narrative focus of attention is glocal with the constant wandering consciousness and the global political engagement of the protagonist. In this roaming narrative activity, the narrator often relates multifarious and often conflicting visions and perspectives equally and subsequently. *Saturday*, to illustrate, demonstrates a narrative strategy in which first the global voice is articulated, and then it is complemented by or often contradicted with the local perception. In this way, the narrator avoids being partial or narrow-minded by transcending characters' limited consciousness. I suggest, then, that narrative glocality represents the way in which the general term glocality is practiced in fiction through specific narrative activities, and the novel's political attitude as a whole.

What makes narrative glocality distinctive from other theories of space is its particular attention to the concept of vernacular cosmopolitanism informing a contemporary culture. By showing diversified perspectives, the novel seems to give the reader a message by showing the futility of very optimistic views of universal cosmopolitanism as well as the impossibility of collecting all under one ideal. Vernacular cosmopolitanism does not only refer to the type of cosmopolitanism experienced in local or non-central spaces, but also to the very centrality as well as everydayness of the cosmopolitan experience. In this respect, vernacular cosmopolitans can reside in central cities like London and New York, and still remain vernacular. This takes us to the definition of cosmopolitans "from below", those who can be mobilized not because they are elites but because they are migrants, workers, asylum-seekers, or cosmopolitans of choice. Furthermore, narrative glocality aspires, rather than distinguishing between cosmopolitanism and localism, or the global and the particular, to discover the interplay and mutuality between them as well as the re-enactment of vernacular cosmopolitanism in diverse forms and spaces.

What I have suggested here is that in the twenty-first century, there seems to be a mediation between the global and the local, a transition from universalism to vernacularism in cosmopolitan philosophy and culture. Spaces, stories, characters, and perspectives are manifested to be oriented toward connections that are informed by both globalism and localism. These thematic concerns of the cosmopolitan novel can be explored in the representation of space, and with a closer look at the notion of narrative glocality.

Allegiances as a Matter of Choice

Another element of cosmopolitan culture is optional forms of allegiances within it. Not only the approach to space but also the approach to the idea of belonging and allegiances is multidimensional in twenty-first-century novels. In Vertovec and Cohen's (2002) definition of the concept, cosmopolitanism "is capable of representing variously complex repertoires of allegiance, identity and interest" (p. 4). Cosmopolitan subjectivities are constructed in complex ways as affiliations are neither predictable nor compulsory. Cosmopolitanism has potential variances and complexities in forms of connectivities, identities, and belonging. Vernacular cosmopolitanism in contemporary cosmopolitan fiction renders connections based upon any forms of grouping problematic. Individual choices, rather than group dynamics, are defining elements of a cosmopolitan community. To be more specific, individuals give up defining themselves in connection with any racial, ethnic or cultural community or group. They also accept both the existence and difference of many others like themselves in the city. As a result, individuals with personal rather than communal specificities become the main constituents of a contemporary cosmopolitan society. In cosmopolitan novels, characters' non-identification with the locals with whom they cohabitate the cosmopolitan cities is in keeping with this idea of lack of group affiliations. This also undermines in these novels the utopian senses of universalist cosmopolitanism, involving the ideal of one community.

The cosmopolitan subject must be considered outside the restrictions of ethnic belonging without resorting to the language of plurality. The cosmopolitan is an individual who cannot simply be defined in terms of bearing the characteristics of a particular group; they make their own choices in the making of their subjectivity. It is necessary, then, to distinguish between "pluralist multiculturalists" and "cosmopolitan multiculturalists" in Hollinger's terms; the first group aims to preserve, and attach to, their well-defined group characteristics whereas the second longs to voluntarily establish new formations of communities (2017, p. 93). This difference resonates with the distinction between multiculturalism and cosmopolitanism in more general terms. It must also be noted that cosmopolitanism is a condition of, as Bruce Robbins puts it, "a density of overlapping allegiances rather than the abstract emptiness of non-allegiance" (1998b, p. 250).

Shaw (2016) underlines the distinction between late twentieth-century multiculturalism and twenty-first century cosmopolitanism: "While multiculturalism implies a form of homogeneity at the group level, cosmopolitanism explores heterogeneous forms of belonging both individually and culturally" (p. 171). Belonging becomes a matter of choice in cosmopolitanism in which identification with a specific culture—native or diasporic—is voluntary. In this sense, postmillennial fiction has more of heterogeneous forms of subjectivity and belonging than an insular view of such concepts. Transnationalism and the freedom to choose one's cultural associations have certain implications for literary and reading practices, too, allowing readers to construct their own individual responses to texts independent of any group affiliation (2016, p. 172). This approach is mostly concerned with how cosmopolitan identity is rendered individual rather than communal in the cosmopolitan novel, as opposed to pre-millennial multicultural novels. Shaw's example for this kind of mutability of allegiances is Teju Cole's *Open City* (2011), a contemporary cosmopolitan novel that "assumes a critical stance towards ethno-cultural allegiances to emphasise the creation of new and shifting affiliations within a transnational locale" (2017a, p. 5). The non-allegiant form of cosmopolitan identity is a fundamental characteristic of twenty-first-century narratives.

Contemporary cosmopolitanism is predicated on three models of attachment, as suggested by Walkowitz (2006): philosophical, anthropological, and vernacular. The philosophical model emphasizes "*detachment* from local cultures", and is thus universalist in scope while the anthropological is based on "multiple or flexible *attachments* to more than one nation or community" (p. 9), which is vernacularist. The last one, which is also vernacularist and the one relevant to the cosmopolitan novel, is "a vernacular or popular tradition that values the risks of social deviance and the resources of consumer culture and urban mobility" (2006, p. 9). This version is also attentive to the risks of consumer culture in the urban practices of *flânerie*: "vernacular cosmopolitanism has included such practices as *flânerie*, dance hall entertainment, department store shopping, and cultural exhibitions" (2006, p. 9). The conception of a city-wandering cosmopolitan and the idea of identity based on complex and mutable allegiances constitute the core of the cosmopolitan thought in the twenty-first-century fiction. The principle of complex models of attachment in cosmopolitanism has in its roots the interpenetration of the global and the local. Cosmopolitanism must, Patell (2015) proclaims, pay attention to the interconnectedness of the global and the local as a way of setting local attachments as the model for global attachments (p. 15). In this sense, in cosmopolitanism, allegiances can be based on the global as well as the local, constructed on an individual level, independent of one's positioning within a particular group. Robbins (1998a) avers that "instead of an ideal of detachment, actually existing cosmopolitanism is a reality of (re)attachment, multiple attachment, or attachment at a distance" (p. 3). Thus, both local and global attachments are always subject to reconstitution and renegotiation in contemporary cosmopolitanism. This feature of cosmopolitanism can emerge both as a theme and a narrative approach in the cosmopolitan novel.

Everyday Difference

Accepting everyday difference within culture is another common theme and attitude in postmillennial cosmopolitan novels. Not only there is a lack of group allegiances in cosmopolitan novels, but they also accept culture itself as devoid of boundaries. Individuals do not make attachments to culture inherently, nor do they define it in clear terms. In this sense, cosmopolitanism is, as Vertovec and Cohen put it, "culturally anti-essentialist" (2002, p. 4), a tenet that posits cosmopolitanism as vernacular. This refers to the absence of a monolithic definition and straightforward delineation of diverse cultures. Vernacular cosmopolitanism repudiates the idea of a unified global culture as well as a concrete division among disparate cultures. In fact, cultural hierarchies are no longer a defining element of the cosmopolitan community, where culture is regarded as a non-essential category. In contemporary cosmopolitan fiction, this aspect of culture is portrayed vividly with the employment of multiple cultural references without essentializing any of them. Thus, this type of novel also avoids cultural stereotypes and the exoticism of the other. In fact, it can be seen as a complete departure from the rhetoric of otherness. The term "other" has no longer credentials or validity in the cosmopolitan novel as cosmopolitan society is characterized by diversity, which is normalized. Everyone is accepted as different in the cosmopolis as well as the local territories, and this foregrounds one distinct element of the cosmopolitan novel: everyday difference. Cosmopolites make a contribution to the sense of everyday difference in cosmopolitan spaces where, as Hiebert puts it, "men and women from different origins create a society where diversity is accepted and is rendered ordinary" (2002, p. 212). Although diversity becomes an ordinary component of everyday cosmopolitan life, it does not necessarily mean an unproblematic coexistence. Everyday difference in contemporary cosmopolitan novels highlights economic inequalities and class divides while other forms of discrepancies are regarded as familiar and mundane.

A cosmopolitan community is composed of multiple nationalities, ethnicities, and races without recourse to the discourses of otherness. In fact, the idea of otherness is eliminated—even when national references are made, they are normalized, accepted, and made part of everyday life in Anglophone fiction. In this sense, it goes beyond the duality of us and others, yet in a distinct way from the postcolonial deconstruction of such binaries. What is suggested here is rather an acceptance of or vernacularizing of diversity without recourse to a process of othering. In these contemporary communities, no one is relegated to the position of the other, and everyone has a part (if not equal) in the constitution of the political and cultural community, which is in turn contingent upon a mutability of formations and reformations. It must be noted, however, that the cosmopolitan novel is concerned with representing other forms of threat to the cosmopolitan society where globally reinforced financial disparities predominate.

Unlike its universalist counterpart, vernacular cosmopolitanism does not desire to transcend cultural differences toward a unique culture; rather it acknowledges their existence, and exposes difference as an everyday phenomenon. In his review of Edward Said's *Orientalism*, Clifford (1988) reproaches "[t]he privilege of standing above cultural particularism, of aspiring to the universalist power that speaks for humanity", which is "a privilege invented by a totalizing Western liberalism" (p. 263). It is thus the main challenge in cosmopolitanism to avoid cultural universalism and at the same time to accept cultural differences without rendering them essentialist categories.

If culture is not an essentialist category and people cannot be grouped through this unsettled system, this raises significant questions regarding home and belonging. The notion of belonging is characterized by multiplicity and oscillation in cosmopolitan fiction. Caryl Phillips's cosmopolitan novels like *Higher Ground*, *The Nature of Blood*, and *A Distant Shore*, McCluskey (2015) claims, encourage the reader to assume a critical cosmopolitan vision by expanding the notion of home and making it "determined more by the material realities of the present rather than by an essentialist and mythical idea of the past", and hence "promot[ing] a more fluid, cosmopolitan idea of belonging" (p. 16). In cosmopolitanism, the implication of belonging nowhere must also be approached with suspicion, which is voiced by Bruce Robbins (1992) as he asserts that "[a]bsolute homelessness is indeed a myth, and so is cosmopolitanism in its strictly negative sense of 'free[dom] from national limitations or attachments'" (p. 173). Rather than erasure of or detachment from home and nation, cosmopolitanism is more implicated in the rendition of multiple attachments and belongings which are in no way stable and unmalleable. Therefore, I view the cosmopolitan sense of belonging as manifold and changeable as it appears in novels. Structured as a requirement of a non-essential culture, the conception of belonging to a community is predicated on the everyday materiality of cosmopolitan life, rather than cultural determinants and divisions.

Cosmopolitan identities also move away from a condition of hybridity to everyday difference. Hybrid subjectivities of multiculturalism contain and juxtapose various and often conflicting cultural, racial, and/or ethnical diversities although there is still a meaningful reference to the discreteness or distinguishability of culture, race, and ethnicity. Cosmopolitan identities, on the other hand, eliminate this condition of mix-up because these categories are deemphasized, and their difference is normalized or vernacularized. This kind of information about the characters' roots is rendered insignificant and even irrelevant in cosmopolitan fiction; references to culture, race, and ethnicity are slightly made, only to show their everydayness and normality. On the other hand, this departure from an idea of difference in terms of cultural and ethnical identity cannot be easily actualized in economic terms. In other words, the impact of globalization scaffolds an imbalanced economic structure within the cosmopolitan society. The cosmopolitan novel emphasizes these problems of the contemporary world while revealing that getting cosmopolitan does not mean eliminating inequality because it transcends the idea of otherness.

In fact, postmillennial cosmopolitan fiction is different from multicultural and cosmopolitan novels before 2000s. As Childs and Green (2013) maintain, both the content and form of contemporary fiction indicate a departure from the preoccupations of postmodernism and postcolonialism due to the "new patterns of human interaction, interconnectedness and awareness" (p. 4). Thematically, it goes away from a condition of mixing up to that of everyday difference. It is also more directly engaged with global, post-national, and cultural politics. Premillennial cosmopolitan novels, as observed by Brennan (1997), involve a juxtaposition of incompatible cultural elements for the purpose of displaying unity and harmony rather than cultural dissonance (p. 39). The cosmopolitanism of these novels has resonances with the multicultural novel, also overlapping with postcolonial fiction in many respects.

It is depicted as a harmonious amalgamation of multiple and contradictory cultural elements, which are somehow in a deconstructing interaction with each other. The contemporary cosmopolitan novel can rightly claim a transgression of the discourses of hybridity, mixture, and assumptions of simple categorizations in terms of national, ethnic, or racial belonging. It can be asserted, then, that the multicultural novel retains an essentialist idea of culture. On the other hand, in twenty-first-century cosmopolitan fiction, culture is seen as non-essential while difference is viewed as an ordinary and everyday phenomenon. Cosmopolitan identities eliminate the condition of ethnic hybridity since difference is deemphasized or normalized. Thus, in cosmopolitan fiction, information about the characters' roots is doomed to be an insignificant or unnecessary detail. This condition of everyday difference with a view to various cosmopolitans' lives is effectively reflected in cosmopolitan fiction. Cosmopolitanism in the twenty-first century is defined by difference in its ordinary sense, and accepts everyone as part of cosmopolitan city spaces.

Paralleling this idea of everyday difference, another idea regarding cosmopolitanism and culture is their plurality. Cosmopolitanisms and cultures in contemporary fiction are plural. The way characters experience cosmopolitanism and respond to the world differs significantly as they are economically as well as culturally divergent. The plurality of meanings, territories, and cultures in cosmopolitan thought can be reflected in postmillennial cosmopolitan fiction in various aspects of the narrative, including discrepant cosmopolitan characters, spaces, narrators, and themes. "Like nations", Robbins argues, cosmopolitan "worlds too are 'imagined'", or rather, localized and vernacularized precisely because they can be seen "in different sizes and styles" (1998a, p. 2). In cosmopolitan fiction, the very concept of cosmopolitanism, like nationalism, is also manifested as a construct, especially in its universalist sense.

The approach to nation as imagined is seen to be echoed in postmillennial novels' approach to cosmopolitanism and culture. In this sense, there is a complex relationship between nationalism and cosmopolitanism. Cosmopolitanism, though not replacing nationalism altogether, transcends nation-boundedness. In mainstream thinking, cosmopolitanism is viewed either in stark opposition, or at least as a challenge to the system of the nation-state. Cosmopolitan thinking has appeared in a great body of texts that respond to and interrogate the Westphalian state system, which was inaugurated by the Peace of Westphalia in 1648 and has constituted the primacy of the nation-state since then. Yet, vernacular cosmopolitanism suggests the idea that cosmopolitanism is far from being a system that aspires to completely superseding nation-bound governances, that it is neither possible nor desirable to get rid of the boundaries between nations, and that cosmopolitanism may coexist with ideas of national and territorial loyalties without necessarily replacing them altogether. In fact, the two are similar in certain respects, especially in terms of their multiplicity. Robbins draws an analogy between nations and cosmopolitanism in that "[l]ike nations, cosmopolitanisms are now plural, and particular. Like nations, they are both European and non-European, and they are weak and undeveloped as well as strong and privileged" (1998a, p. 2). Robbins' assertion that "cosmopolitanism is *there* –not merely an abstract ideal" but a concrete phenomenon "socially and geographically situated" (p. 2) also posits it as vernacular. This multiple and particularist form of cosmopolitanism is a defining feature of twenty-first-century fiction.

Another approach to culture which postmillennial cosmopolitan fiction adopts is, in Ulrich Beck's terms, a "cosmopolitan outlook" which also has a vernacularist attitude. In *The Cosmopolitan Vision* (2006), Ulrich Beck views cosmopolitanism as the defining concept of the contemporary era, of the second (reflective) modernity which is informed by a new standpoint, "the cosmopolitan outlook" (p. 2). Not only the cosmopolitan world but also cosmopolitan novels assume a cosmopolitan outlook in which they transcend a discrete imagination of the world in terms of boundaries. The most significant characteristic of this mode is its disengagement from nationalist discourses of society, such as dividing borders and exclusive identities. This new vantage point, the cosmopolitan outlook, reflects the interconnectedness between the global and local which is inherent in the idea of vernacular cosmopolitanism. Preceding this new vision was a "national outlook", in Beck's terminology, which dominated the social sciences and political studies by predicating societies on the assumption that they are organized through a nationalist structure. The national outlook, thus, regards the nation-state as constitutive of society and culture. Such an archaic view of society and sociology no longer holds as it requires revision in the face of irreversible changes in the globalized world. It is, thus, cosmopolitan outlook that provides a definitive tool for dealing with the representation of contemporary culture, society, subjectivity, and communication in cosmopolitan fiction. In general terms, then, we must regard it as an attitude or an approach through which we can analyze the contemporary cultures and identities in cosmopolitan fiction.

Cosmopolitanism's Veiled Ideologies: Relationship with Neoliberal Capitalism

Twenty-first-century fiction, especially in the form of cosmopolitan novel, is concerned with economics to a great extent and offers responses to economic instability of the contemporary era differently from economists. "Literary knowledge of economy", as Cristopher Newfield puts it, "will analyze and express the economy's internal contradictions and incommensurabilities without reducing them to linear or material causalities" (2019, p. 21). Cosmopolitan fiction's engagement with economics is far from being a scientific approach, yet is highly cognizant. This section is, thus, less an attempt at a theoretical discussion of economics than literary rendering of the themes currently relatable to dimensions of economics.

As capitalism is still the main aspect of the changes that take place in what is called "post-industrial society", Michael S. Miller sees the term "neo-capitalism" as more representative of the age in which the "neo" emphasizes the awareness that capitalism is now different from what Marx defined as capitalism, but despite certain shifts in its character, it retains its basic premises, so its effect does not wane altogether (1975, p. 2): "The post-industrial society does not transform social and power relations; the essential forms of capitalism, e.g., private property, could continue" (p. 31). Not only globalization and nationalism, but also capitalism has been evoked and rethought in the debates about cosmopolitanism as well as in the cosmopolitan novel. This is done mostly by cosmopolitan theorists and novelists who are critical of cosmopolitanism as an exploitative strategy that aims to facilitate the flow of capital beyond borders, commodification of cultural difference, as well as the fostering of global market growth. This "materialist" orientation in cosmopolitan thought brings to the fore what its "formalist" and "ethicist" counterparts fail to pay attention to: the bond between capitalism and cosmopolitanism, inequality among cosmopolitan citizens, and power relations in terms of dominating means of production as well as global markets. Drawing on Hardt and Negri's ideas, Kurasawa (2011) argues that "[w]hen devoid of a critique of capitalist forces, cosmopolitan ideology can complement the most recent global regime of exercise of power, a totalizing, deterritorialized and decentred network of economic and political relations designated as 'empire'" (p. 304). Considering this less emphasized aspect of cosmopolitanism, I emphasize here that cosmopolitan fiction assumes an overtly critical stance toward such shared interests of capitalism and cosmopolitanism.

The strict division between cosmopolitanism and nation, two concepts that have often been seen as mutually exclusive, is also erased in cosmopolitan fiction with a view to, and awareness of, neoliberal capitalism in contemporary cosmopolitan spaces. Brennan claims that these two concepts are far from being too distant. In fact, nationalism and globalism/cosmopolitanism are intertwined concepts which cannot, in turn, be separated from the concept of Americanization: "There can be no theorizing nationalism without theorizing globalism, and there can be no talk of globalism without Americanization" (1997, p. 125). In this sense, we can see certain forms of cosmopolitanism as a mask for new forms of Americanization, which evokes a link between capitalism and neoliberal capitalism. This kind of awareness is often represented in the postmillennial cosmopolitan novels that seem to have an inclusive attitude and a wide-angle vision in response to the political agenda of the contemporary world.

Seeing cosmopolitanism mostly as an imperialist instrument, such novels indicate an awareness of, and critique against, the utopian cosmopolitan ideology as the naïve idealization of a commitment to humanity as a whole and a shrinking world devoid of borders. According to Brennan (2001), one harsh critic of universalist cosmopolitanism, its function is to masquerade contemporary capitalism. Unlike universalist orientations, postmillennial cosmopolitan fiction is characterized by a hyper-awareness of such negative motivations hidden beneath the concept. In Ali Smith's cosmopolitan novel *Hotel World* (2001), the protagonist, the deceased hotel chambermaid Sara Wilby, as McCulloch (2012) puts it, "is merely one among many who will serve to boost the hotel's profit yet will remain insignificant to its global expansion" (p. 17). Drawing attention to the indifference within Global Hotel and beyond toward her unexpectedly early death, McCulloch argues that Smith's message is clear: "life's value must be acknowledged over global enterprise: in a scathing critique of capitalism, the text insists that life rather than wealth is the truly rare currency for citizens of the world" (p. 17). This kind of cosmopolitan worldview privileges the value of love over material ambitions, and this theme becomes an elemental constituent of cosmopolitan novels like *Hotel World*.

Contemporary cosmopolitanism can be regarded as the beginning of a new era in postcolonial thought and studies. Postcolonial fiction targets its criticism at divisions and discourses of first-world/third-world, of us/them, and shows the deconstructive dimension of such binary thinking. On the other hand, cosmopolitan theory and fiction both acknowledge the demolition of such polarities and at the same time call back considerations of colonialism and power inequalities that have emerged in a renewed form and veiled version. Drawing on George Simmel's the city/country antagonism as a source of capitalist modernity, Brennan concludes that cosmopolitanism functions as a justification of colonial expansion of urban/metropolitan centers over locally situated and powerless areas (2001, p. 666). According to this distinction, an aspect of cosmopolitanism, like colonialism, is a pretext to benefit the capitalist ventures on the part of the centrally positioned global powers.

In this vein of thought, as claimed by Brennan (1997), colonialism has not ended; on the contrary, the United States has overtaken England's place as the leading globally colonial force. Therefore, it is wrong to draw a sharp difference between the military expansion of former colonizers and the economically and culturally domineering contemporary "imperialists", precisely because what America does as the pioneering globalist is closer to previous forms of colonialist invasion although this is not perceived to be an invasion per se. In this sense, colonialism has not ended in the present era, nor is it a thing of the past as postcolonialism implies. Likewise, the nation-state does not lose power precisely because "[t]he United States continues to invade other countries, but the invasion is not now supposed to be an invasion: rather, the nation extends its shadow, *becomes* the elsewhere, decenters itself" (p. 6). In cosmopolitanism, the impact of nation-state becomes less discernible though it is not waning entirely. Rather, it emerges as another form of nation that consolidates this new version of cosmopolitan "empire". This version has much to do with corporation economies, and a "postindustrial" community where the mobility of capital is a salient feature of the transformation of the global economy.

In "The Class Consciousness of Frequent Travellers: Towards a Critique of Actually Existing Cosmopolitanism" (2002), Craig Calhoun also recognizes this side of cosmopolitanism by forcefully claiming that cosmopolitanism is "now largely the project of capitalism, and it flourishes in the top management of multinational corporations" involving preoccupations of elites while ignoring ordinary people in local territories (p. 106). Calhoun, as a solution, calls for a divorce between cosmopolitanism and neoliberal capitalism (2002, p. 106). It is, therefore, necessary to beware of a naïve commitment to cosmopolitanism as a universalist concept as such critical theorists of cosmopolitanism warn against "soft cosmopolitanism" in Calhoun's words, which is devoid of a contesting stance against capitalism and Western hegemony. By drawing on Calhoun's concept of "consumerist cosmopolitanism" in the volume they have edited, Vertovec and Cohen (2002) also draw attention to an aspect of cosmopolitanism informed by capitalism and consumerism: "Such [cosmopolitan] processes represent a multiculturalization of society, but also the advanced globalization of capitalism" (p. 14). In dealing with fiction, we must, then, take hidden or overt capitalist ideologies in cosmopolitanism into consideration.

In light of all these discussions, it is necessary to explore the reflections of all these ideas on the postmillennial fiction. I, thus, argue that the postmillennial cosmopolitan novel seems highly cognizant of the new "Americanism" suggested by Brennan (1997) regardless of the geographical setting of diverse novels (set in America or elsewhere), and it would be an incomplete analysis of contemporary fiction without reference to the workings of neoliberal capitalism. The novels in this book display attentiveness to the neo-imperialist project of American hegemony, though in disparate ways. The inscription of Iraq's invasion by America in McEwan's novel's mundane actions as well as what Rushdie calls the United States of Joker are both evocative of the ideology of "Americanism".

The "*Cosmoflâneur*": Existence in City Spaces

To put various aspects of the cosmopolitan character, and in some cases the narrator, in twenty-first-century novels in definitive terminology for the sake of preciseness and clarity, I will suggest the term—*cosmoflâneur*, and will try to explore its features in contemporary cosmopolitan fiction. A cosmopolitan character/narrator, I argue, can be named a *cosmoflâneur*, to adopt Charles Baudelaire and Walter Benjamin's conception of the *flâneur* and adapt it to the twenty-first-century context. In the first place, it is necessary to state that the two concepts differ in their cosmopolitan orientations: the *flâneur* is universalist while the *cosmoflâneur* is vernacular in that the first aspires a detachment from rootedness whereas the latter celebrates both global and local associations.

Baudelaire's *flâneur* as delineated below conjures images of a universalist cosmopolitan:

> For the perfect *flâneur*, for the passionate spectator, it is an immense joy to set up house in the hearth of the multitude, amid the ebb and flow of movement, in the midst of the fugitive and the infinite. To be away from home and yet to feel oneself everywhere at home; to see the world, to be at the centre of the world, and yet to remain hidden from the world— such are a few of the slightest pleasures of those independent, passionate, impartial natures which the tongue can but clumsily define. (1863 [1995], p. 9)

A celebrated sense of diversity, mobility, homelessness, fascination with the world, impartiality, and independence from any kinds of attachment are among the defining elements of universalist cosmopolitanism. However, contemporary forms of cosmopolitanism characterized by vernacularism centralize novel ways of experiencing the city, which are embodied, I argue, in the practices of *cosmoflânerie*. To draw further distinctions between the two concepts, it is important to note that the top-down cosmopolitan activity of *flânerie* is a sphere of the exclusively privileged liberal citizen—of upper-middle-class, male, white, and Western, whereas *cosmoflânerie* allows space for diversity in terms of class, gender, race, and ethnicity. In this sense, it is this inclusiveness that also aligns it with vernacular cosmopolitanism.

What is constant, on the other hand, in each conception of a city-wandering individual is a degree of mobility, which is, yet, defined by distinct experiences as well as reactions, and triggered by different motivations. The *flâneur* is exposed to modernity through this mobility while the *cosmoflâneur* experiences second modernity, in Ulrich Beck's (2010) terms, in its most material urban forms. As for their motivations, the first is propelled to movement with the enchantment of the colors of the city, out of attraction to cultural diversity. The latter, on the other hand, is mobilized for several, often contradictory, reasons, including not only fascination by diversity but also necessity and compulsion. Both Baudelaire and Benjamin portray the figure of the *flâneur* in terms of a self-motivated mobility. Drawing on Baudelaire's concept of the *flâneur* as an everyday street wanderer or a nineteenth-century aesthete who strolls Paris's streets and arcades in order to observe and experience the modern city, Benjamin dwells on the concept in his incomplete text, *The*

Arcades Project, a compilation of quotations and reflections, pointing at its functionality to discover urban modernity. There, the *flâneur* refers to a modern urban citizen who is characterized by instant and continuous mobility, not able to occupy one place for long, and by loitering or aimlessness in this constant activity of city strolling. It is this perpetual mobility that evokes cosmopolitanism in the figure of the *flâneur*, too. The reader also participates in *flânerie* by wandering through the city alongside this cosmopolitan character. Drawing attention to the city-like design of Benjamin's segmented text with headings like Filling Station, No. 13, and Optician, Featherstone argues that "*flânerie* is a method for reading texts, for reading the traces of the city" (1998, p. 910). Reading through Benjamin's textual city is an act of *flânerie* on the part of the reader. In the same vein, a contemporary experience of reading cosmopolitan fiction makes us experientially a *cosmoflâneur* in that we perceive the world from miscellaneous cosmopolitan perspectives intertwining the global and the local, and experience multiple ways of world-making through this virtual experience. Unlike the detached, aimless, and reactionless existence of the *flâneur* in city spaces, this experiential *cosmoflânerie* potentially calls the reader to actively respond to the world with its very purposefulness.

In cosmopolitan novels, what I call *cosmoflânerie* is a way of opening up to the world through the lens of a strolling character/narrator or her/his consciousness that roams freely through a gaze throughout the city, a form of virtual mobility that keeps functioning even when the beholder remains physically immobile. As mobility is not the unique requirement in this act of *cosmoflânerie*, what distinguishes it from its earlier counterpart *flânerie* is the capacity to encompass both global and local outlooks, to engage with the city as a site of class consciousness and economic disproportions, and to respond to the world with an urge to take an active role in its formation, or at least its preservation. These three features of the *cosmoflâneur*—outlook, consciousness, and activity—are mostly discernible in the aspects of characterization and narration in twenty-first-century cosmopolitan fiction. These critical aspects of postmillennial novels, however, call forth a reconsideration of the ancient senses of the term *flânerie*. In other words, the processes of *cosmoflânerie* in the contemporary cosmopolitan city involve observing the global and local diversity, recognizing commodification in cityscapes, and ultimately taking active steps in world-making with particular attentiveness to the world's economic and ecological exigencies. To further this discussion on a more solid ground, all these features of cosmopolitan outlook, consciousness, and activity that characterize the *cosmoflâneur* will be illustrated in the textual analysis in the following chapters, especially in McEwan and Ishiguro's protagonists' urban experiences.

Cosmopolitan outlook that espouses the interconnectivity of the global and the local is the first defining characteristic of the *cosmoflâneur*. To put it succinctly, this is a way of looking at the city, and the world by extension, through an inclusive lens, and seeing global and local connections simultaneously. As the initial step of a cosmopolitan existence in the city, this involves an act of observation. This metaphoric sense of the *cosmoflâneur* as a seer is reinforced by a kaleidoscopic vision of the world. In other words, the *cosmoflâneur*'s observations of the city are like gazing through a kaleidoscope, which potentially yields as diverse images of the world as possible. Installation of multiplicity in the object of kaleidoscope evokes connotations of cosmopolitanism in its definition. "Kaleidoscopic metaphors", as Helen Groth puts it, suggest "positive associations with a self-consciously cosmopolitan gaze open to diversity" (2007, p. 218). Baudelaire likens the *flâneur* to "a kaleidoscope gifted with consciousness, responding to each one of its movements and producing the multiplicity of life and the flickering grace of all the elements of life" (1863 [1995, p. 9).

In cosmopolitan novels, the narrator's inclusive and wide-angle vision creates a picture of the world in quick, direct yet changeable pieces. In this sense, this echoes Schoene's idea of compositeness as a kaleidoscopic representation in cosmopolitan novels in which we see "a momentarily composite picture of the world – quite like a child's kaleidoscope held still for only a second before collapsing into new, equally wondrous, yet perfectly plausible constellations" (2010, p. 27). In this way, cosmopolitan representation creates composite pictures similar to contemporary cinema which makes use of montage, focus, and perspective changes, multiple story lines, and contrasting images (2010, p. 14). Cosmopolitan representations in the novel are mostly kaleidoscopic, and this is guaranteed by the perpetual act of observation of the *cosmoflâneur*. "The kaleidoscope", as Groth puts it, "immersed the observer in a visual field that never allowed the eye to rest, producing a visual effect that tested the limits of verisimilitude" (2007, p. 217). In this sense, the *cosmoflâneur* sees the world through a kaleidoscopic lens.

Another characteristic of the *cosmoflâneur* is her/his lack of group allegiances, which is based on a propensity toward the global and the local simultaneously and toward personal choices in defining affiliations. Kristian Shaw (2017b) exemplifies, in his analysis of Cole's *Open City*, another urban *flâneur*, Julius, who is detached from ethnicity and group identification in favor of individuality (p. 22). The *cosmoflâneur* avoids any forms of group allegiances in favor of individual forms of identity-making strategies. The act of moving through the city facilitates multiple formations and reformations of affiliations. Therefore, cosmopolitan characters are frequently depicted in an act of walking or other forms of mobility, and it is through this mobility that their individualistic choices compose their cosmopolitan agency. Breaking with group allegiances, constantly being in physical or mental mobility, and engaging inevitably in overconsumption of information (sometimes provided by media) and commodities are the main features of a *cosmoflâneur*, a type of character often visible in twenty-first-century novels.

The second tenet of the *cosmoflâneur* is a consciousness in the sense of an awareness of the working mechanisms of capitalism and a classed society, which is manifested in contemporary city spaces. Benjamin's *flâneur* is involved in this footloose wandering as a resistance to consumerism and commodification imposed by the arcade-like design of modern cities full of attractive commodities. The *flâneur* is positioned in the system of commodification in the way Benjamin explicates below:

> To be sure, in sofaras a person, as labor power, is a commodity, there is no need for him to identify himself as such. The more conscious he becomes of his mode of existence, the mode imposed on him by the system of production, the more he proletarianizes himself, the more he will be gripped by the chilly breath of the commodity economy, and the less he will feel like empathizing with commodities. (Benjamin 2006, pp. 88–89)

The *cosmoflâneur*, despite referring to the older term for its foundation and formulation as well as having certain affinities with it, departs from Benjamin's *flâneur* in this. The *flâneur* suggests a city-dweller that is always in flux and on the go, and whose connection with the world and other people is usually superficial and transient. Yet, a *cosmoflâneur* is far from a state of idleness or resistance to consumerism; this cosmopolitan individual is inevitably subject to a world of over-engagedness, exposure, and activity. Emily Johansen revisits the *flâneur* to designate the territorialized mobility of local cosmopolitans: "if the movement typically associated with cosmopolitanism [...] is compelled by capital and its demands, *flânerie* resists this compulsion through its very aimlessness, positing other ways of engaging physical space" (2014, p. 44). Unlike the *flâneur*'s reaction to capitalism by her/his anti-consumerist loitering, the *cosmoflâneur*'s experience of the city is implicated in the mechanisms of neoliberal capitalism, which is the hallmark of the contemporary cosmopolitan city. Thus, a *cosmoflâneur*, as suggested here, differs fundamentally from the original meaning describing its aimlessness and defiance against capital consumption because a *cosmoflâneur*'s positioning in the consumption places makes her/him highly aware of the repercussions of urban spatial mobility and neoliberal capitalism. It is through this awareness that the cosmopolitan novel assumes a more responsive attitude toward the contemporary situation. This reactive attitude of the *cosmoflâneur* opens up some possibilities for cosmopolitan attention to class disparities. The new form of the *flâneur* below shows a degree of optimism in this sense:

> The consciousness of latter-day *flânerie* thus balances somewhere on the cusp of hope and hopelessness, with the optimism that alternative routes do exist perpetually tempered by suspicion as to the iron grip of consumerism and the inexorable nature of multi-national capitalism. (Biron 2014, p. 33)

The state of awareness in fact has a political dimension, which goes beyond an act of seeing and involves an element of interpreting: "Walking, as an everyday practice – as opposed to marching or a street gathering and demonstrating – can also be seen as a political practice that determines our frames of seeing as well as our conceptualisation and interpretation of space" (Pusca 2008, p. 375).

The *cosmoflâneur* is, in one sense, a highly class-conscious member of what Binnie et al. call "the so-called 'new' middle classes" (2006, p. 14) consisting of, as David Ley suggests, the "residents of gentrified inner-city neighbourhoods that have multiple points of openness to cosmopolitanism" (qtd. in Binnie et al. 2006, p. 14). Rather than resisting consumption, these cosmopolites are located in the locales characterized by consumption, in what Rofe calls "consumptionspaces" (qtd in Binnie et al. 2006, p. 15). These urban territories also resonate with the definition of glocal spaces mentioned earlier: "the gentrifying neighbourhood is […] the global grounded in the local" (2006, p. 15).

In this sense, a contemporary *cosmoflâneur* is distinguished by hyperawareness, partly due to the advance of information networks and overconsumption (of information as well as commodities). To exemplify, Ian McEwan's London-based protagonist, Henry Perowne, is a middle-class *cosmoflâneur* in ways in which he is situated within several "consumption-spaces". "[A] cosmopolitan *flâneur*", as Walkowitz suggests, "is a rather different experience for those who have full access to the city than it is for those – women, migrants, colonial subjects – who do not" (2006, p. 16). Acknowledging these distinctive forms of city-wandering activity, contemporary cosmopolitan fiction generates variants of *cosmoflâneurs*, which is evocative of cosmopolitanism from below.

The *cosmoflâneur* overlaps with certain aspects of Bruce Robbins's figure of "the beneficiary" that is defined as "the relatively privileged person in the metropolitan center who contemplates her or his unequal relations with persons at the less-prosperous periphery and feels or fears that in some way their fates are linked" (2017, p. 5). In their consciousness of the global economics and its impact on both the victims as well as the metropolitan cosmopolitans themselves, both the beneficiary and the *cosmoflâneur* struggle to negotiate their feelings for the other with self-interest. In this sense, *Saturday*'s Perowne is a typical character of the beneficiary as well as the *cosmoflâneur*. Robbins writes that "the discourse of the beneficiary refers to something between a recognition of global economic injustice and a denunciation of it" (2017, p. 6). Similarly, there is an element of repudiation in the idea of *cosmoflâneur* in facing class inequalities and global financial exploitations. On the other hand, like the beneficiary, the *cosmoflâneur* is not always very harsh in their criticisms which may come "in a range of tonalities, not all of them political, some perhaps more rueful than indignant" (2017, p. 7). Political awareness does not guarantee active political engagement or repudiation, as in the case of Perowne. Nevertheless, the *cosmoflâneur* is a highly responsive character—both direct and aware—in engagement with the world.

Thirdly, being an active citizen of the world is celebrated in the character of the *cosmoflâneur*. The principle of activity implies participating actively in the act of world-making, responding to the world, and its ever-growing problems. In this sense, this is one step further than the previous two features of the *cosmoflâneur*—cosmopolitan outlook and consciousness. To observation, understanding, empathy, analysis, and insight as relatively passive elements of being a cosmopolitan are added decision-making, action, interrogation, participation, directness, and resistance, which are, on the other hand, characterized by activeness.

City spaces are where cosmopolitanism and cosmopolitan activity become tangible and concretized, as testament to Kendall et al.'s argument that "cosmopolitanism is something that can be observed in objects, settings and social spaces, and that it is something – to suggest it is a set of values, attitudes and practices is sufficient for the present – that should be identifiable in individuals as forms of cosmopolitan subjectivity" (2009, p. 100). Cosmopolitanism's down-to-earth definition is in fact embodied in the figure of the *cosmoflâneur*. Drawing on Hannah Arendt's notion of "worldliness", which means "a particular mode of being in the world, a heightened care for the world", William Smith demands that a cosmopolitan citizen "promotes a world which is more reflective of cosmopolitan aspirations" as well as "aspire to a degree of skill and excellence in our worldly performances and judgements" (2007, p. 38). The *cosmoflâneur* is quite skillful in such Arendtian practices of world-making. The city is a site of consumerist capitalism where labor is constant, yet a *cosmoflâneur* can also generate endurable cosmopolitan products rather than sheer consumables.

Bart van Leeuwen interrogates the connection between *flânerie* and cosmopolitanism in that "the *flâneur* embodies the city both as a centre of modernity and as a site of encounter with the socially strange and unfamiliar", which "gives his or her outlook a distinctive cosmopolitan flavour" (2019, p. 302). However, being interested in the other only in cultural terms does not equal to being a cosmopolitan, as van Leeuwen accentuates: "The modern city dweller as *flâneur*, in order to become a cosmopolitan in the moral sense, needs to go beyond transcendence fetishism to establish some kind of subject-subject relationship" (2019, pp. 310–11). This requires then an active preoccupation in a moral sense with others and with the world. As van Leeuwen emphasizes, "the *flâneur* is essentially preoccupied with the practice of observing, with the role of passive spectator" (2019, p. 307), and this is where the *cosmoflâneur* departs from an earlier version of a city-dweller. Not only observant and captivated by the city's diversity, the *cosmoflâneur* is also active and respondent in numerous ways. This activity does involve opening up to both global and local others as well as attending to the healing of the world itself, especially in ecological terms.

Going beyond sheer cultural fascination and appeal, activity is a genuine form of cosmopolitanism even if it is in the form of passive resistance to the economic as well as ecological ills of the world.

Narrative Immediacy and Political Hyper-awareness

With the turn of the century, cosmopolitan fiction comes to create novel paradigms and techniques for narration, mostly inclined toward directness and quickness in dealing with contemporary events and economic issues. A significant change in twenty-first-century fiction is the employment of a cosmopolitan vision, one that can be aligned with broader concerns of cosmopolitan thought like directness, speed of responsiveness, and high level of attentiveness. In line with these motives of the cosmopolitan attitude, the cosmopolitan novel invokes forms of narrative immediacy—direct yet constantly changing responses—to the contemporary world.

Narrative immediacy is one of the essential principles of contemporary cosmopolitan narration. Directness emerges as a new attitude in narration which is distinguished by postmodernist techniques of the late twentieth century. Postmodernism has used subversion, parody as well as indirect and deconstructing devices. Twentieth-century cosmopolitan fiction is, likewise, characterized by, as Walkowitz (2006) puts it, "artful idiosyncrasies", that is the use of such literary techniques as evasion, naturalness, triviality, and others by modernists to generate a cosmopolitan "posture" because "the idiosyncratic vision of modernism is congruent to and necessary for the *critical* aspect of today's critical cosmopolitanism" (p. 15). In other words, mannerism or the use of particular modernist writing styles contribute to the critical cosmopolitanism of the century. Rather than engaging directly with politics, these artful idiosyncrasies are indirect ways of responding to the world. However, with the turn of the century, these styles fall short of explaining the cosmopolitanism of contemporary novels. Although McEwan, Smith, and Rushdie's novels in this book may have their own artful mannerism or literary styles to some extent, a more characteristic formal aspect can be observed in all: directness and immediacy. Thus, I argue here that postmillennial fiction is also concerned with style, but with one different from modernist or postmodernist examples through the prioritization of directness and the immediacy to act politically. Walkowitz (2006) detects a tendency of negation or indirectness in each of the tactics of artful idiosyncrasies: Naturalness suggests pretense, and triviality implies pettiness; mix-up and vertigo revoke a lack of agency or efficacy; evasion and treason hint at negligence and intentional bad faith (p. 8). However, I will show that twenty-first-century fiction differs from these tendencies of negation and implication by developing more direct ways of responding to the contemporary world. Narrative immediacy seen in postmillennial fiction, on the other hand, is characterized by directness and engagement.

Narrative immediacy refers to the speed and directness of response to contemporary cosmopolitics as a narrative strategy. This often requires a new type of cosmopolitan narrator, an outspoken and attentive third-person heterodiegetic narrator or a more inclusive homodiegetic one, both of whom seem to reflect not only global but also local consciousness and vision. Not beating around the bush, this cosmopolitan narrator proves a tendency toward directness of criticism, rather than parodic dismantling. This directness is in fact of critical importance for the success of, in Nealon's words, "literature's engagement with the superfast world of capital" (2012, p. 154). In other words, if the cosmopolitan world is fast, the speed of response to it must also be high. The pace of global mobility acts as a determinant or catalyst for the responsiveness of a contemporary narrator who is preoccupied with this world of speed. In a cosmopolitan novel, the narrator's priority is to interact with the world, to comment upon cross-cultural communication, to be aware of the intersection of the global and the local as well as the economic dimension of cosmopolitanism. These features of narration reflect the cosmopolitan novel's preoccupation with providing immediate responses to the challenges of the world.

Twenty-first-century cosmopolitan fiction is also more conscious and politically engaged. It shows hyper-awareness toward neo-capitalism and veiled Americanism in contemporary cosmopolitan thought. This aspect of fiction can be discerned in forms and concerns specific to the cosmopolitan novel. It is, thus, different from its twentieth-century counterparts. Twentieth-century cosmopolitanism, for Walkowitz (2006), contains "political ambiguities", contradictory or suspicious attitudes toward politics. Rushdie's engagement with antiracism involves playfulness and confusion. Similarly, Woolf's tactic of evasion or "refusal to think" independently is a negation of autonomous thinking (p. 4). Different versions of suspicious attitudes toward social projects are a feature of critical cosmopolitanism in the twentieth century while twenty-first-century cosmopolitanism predominantly diverges from postmodern suspicion and ambivalence. Therefore, I put forward that postmillennial cosmopolitan fiction is characterized more by directness and awareness rather than ambiguities. The authors analyzed in this book implement new ways of attentiveness to the cosmopolitan world especially in the second decade of the twenty-first century. The term "political ambiguities" falls short of explaining contemporary cosmopolitanism in the fiction of Smith and Rushdie with their more hyper-aware and engaged attitude responding to global economic and cultural relations. Critical cosmopolitanism's affiliation with political responsiveness is also valid for twenty-first-century fiction, but with a difference: The postmillennial novel is politically more open and cognizant rather than ambiguous or suspicious—hence, "politically hyper-aware".

Political hyper-awareness, as a revision of "political ambiguities", to be more precise, corresponds to a direct engagement with ideology and contemporary politics by the cosmopolitan novel without recourse to a naïve approach to, and acceptance of, cosmopolitan conviviality. This amounts to aligning the cosmopolitan novel with the idea of vernacular cosmopolitanism, thereby assuming a hyper-aware stance toward the multifaceted dimensions of global connections as well as the veiled ideology of neoliberal capitalism within cosmopolitan thinking. This aspect of these novels also provides the means to see cosmopolitanism as a classed phenomenon and complicit with economic exploitative mechanisms of globality as well as Americanism. From this vantage point, the cosmopolitan novel of the twenty-first century becomes more and more politically engaged and globally focused. I will elaborate these concerns and attitudes further with reference to the way McEwan, Smith, Rushdie, and Ishiguro's novels take up a cosmopolitan attitude.

All in all, this chapter has aimed to discover the ways in which the postmillennial cosmopolitan novel, together with the specificities of its rendering of spatiality, characterization, and identity, intersects with both culture and economics. In the course of this endeavor, I have suggested some new terminology in order to provide precise definitions and tools to deal with different aspects of the cosmopolitan novel. The rendering of culture in city spaces in contemporary cosmopolitan fiction can effectively be explicated by the concept of narrative glocality, which corresponds to the inseparability of the local spaces from a global consciousness. This interconnectedness is also demonstrated in the portrayal of cosmopolitan characters, *cosmoflâneurs*—those who wander around the city and take an active part in the world and in some cases its preservation. Cosmopolitan identities are shaped by a cosmopolitan outlook, an identity-making process defined by choice and inclusiveness. Finally, cosmopolitans cannot be contained in a monolithic definition. To put it more precisely, cosmopolitan identity is constituted by everyday difference as well as a lack of collective allegiances.

References

Baudelaire, Charles. 1995. *The painter of modern life and other essays*, trans. and ed. Jonathan Mayne. London: Phaidon.
Beck, Ulrich. 1999. *What is globalization?* trans. Patrick Camiller. Cambridge: Polity.
Beck, Ulrich. 2006. *The cosmopolitan vision*, trans. Ciaran Cronin. Cambridge and Malden: Polity Press.
Beck, Ulrich. 2010. The cosmopolitan manifesto. In *The cosmopolitanism reader*, ed. David Held and Garrett Wallace Brown, 217–228. Cambridge: Polity Press.
Benjamin, Walter. 2006. *The writer of modern life: Essays on Charles Baudelaire*, ed. Michael W. Jennings, trans. Howard Eiland and Edmund Jephcott. Cambridge, MA and London: The Belknap Press of Harvard University.
Benjamin, Walter, and Rolf Tiedemann. 1999. *The arcades project*. Cambridge, MA and London: Belknap Press of Harvard University.
Binnie, Jon, Julian Holloway, and Steve Millington. 2006. Introduction: Grounding cosmopolitan urbanism: Approaches, practices and policies. In *Cosmopolitan urbanism*, ed. Jon Binnie, Julian Holloway, Steve Millington, and Craig Young, 1–34. London: Routledge.
Biron, Dean. 2014. Benjamin, Adorno and the modern day *flânerie*. *Thesis Eleven* 121: 23–37. https://doi.org/10.1177/0725513614528782.
Brennan, Timothy. 1997. *At home in the world: Cosmopolitanism now*. Cambridge, MA and London: Harvard University Press.
Brennan, Timothy. 2001. Cosmo-theory. *The South Atlantic Quarterly* 100: 659–691.
Calhoun, Craig. 2002. The class consciousness of frequent travellers: Towards a critique of actually existing cosmopolitanism. In *Conceiving cosmopolitanism: Theory, context, and practice*, ed. Steven Vertovec and Robin Cohen, 86–109. Oxford: Oxford University Press.
Calhoun, Craig. 2017. A cosmopolitanism of connections. In *Cosmopolitanisms*, ed. Bruce Robbins and Paulo Lemos Horta, 189–200. New York: New York University Press.

Childs, Peter, and James Green. 2013. *Aesthetics and ethics in twenty-first century British novels: Zadie Smith, Nadeem Aslam, Hari Kunzru and David Mitchell*. London and New York: Bloomsbury.
Clifford, James. 1988. *The predicament of culture: Twentieth-century ethnography, literature, and art*. Harvard University Press. https://doi.org/10.2307/j.ctv jf9x0h.
Delanty, Gerard. 2003. *Community*. London: Routledge.
Delanty, Gerard. 2009. *The cosmopolitan imagination: The renewal of critical social theory*. New York: Cambridge University Press.
Featherstone, Mike. 1998. The *Flâneur*, the city and virtual public life. *Urban Studies* 35: 909–925.
Gikandi, Simon. 2010. Between roots and routes: Cosmopolitanism and the claims of locality. In *Rerouting the postcolonial: New directions for the new millennium*, ed. Janet Wilson, Cristina Şandru and Sarah Lawson Welsh, 22–35. London: Routledge.
Groth, Helen. 2007. Kaleidoscopic vision and literary invention in an "age of things": David Brewster, Don Juan, and "a lady's Kaleidoscope". *ELH* The Johns Hopkins University Press 74: 217–237. https://www.jstor.org/stable/30029552.
Held, David. 2010. *Cosmopolitanism: Ideals and realities*. Cambridge: Polity Press.
Hiebert, Daniel. 2002. Cosmopolitanism at the local level: The development of transnational neighbourhoods. In *Conceiving cosmopolitanism: Theory, context, and practice*, ed. Steven Vertovec and Robin Cohen, 209–223. Oxford: Oxford University Press.
Hollinger, David A. 2017. Cosmopolitanism and the problem of solidarity. In *Cosmopolitanisms*, ed. Bruce Robbins and Paulo Lemos Horta, 91–101. New York: New York University Press.
Johansen, Emily. 2014. *Cosmopolitanism and place: Spatial forms in contemporary Anglophone literature*. New York: Palgrave Macmillan.
Kendall, Gavin, Ian Woodward, and Zlatko Skrbis. 2009. *The sociology of cosmopolitanism: Globalization, identity, culture and government*. Houndmills, Basingstoke, Hampshire and New York: Palgrave Macmillan.
Kurasawa, Fuyuki. 2011. Cosmopolitanism's theoretical and substantive dimensions. In *Routledge international handbook of contemporary social and political theory*, ed. Gerard Delanty and Stephen P. Turner, 301–311. London: Routledge.
McCluskey, Alan. 2015. *Materiality and the modern cosmopolitan novel*. Houndmills, Basingstoke, Hampshire and New York: Palgrave Macmillan.
McCulloch, Fiona. 2012. *Cosmopolitanism in contemporary British fiction: Imagined identities*. Houndmills, Basingstoke, Hampshire and New York: Palgrave Macmillan.

Miller, S. Michael. 1975. Neo-Capitalism. *Theory and Society* 2: 1–35.
Nealon, Jeffrey T. 2012. *Post-postmodernism or, the cultural logic of just-in-time capitalism*. Stanford: Stanford University Press.
Newfield, Christopher. 2019. What is literary knowledge of economy? In *The Routledge companion to literature and economics*, ed. Matt Seybold and Michelle Chihara, 15–26. London: Routledge.
Patell, Cyrus R. K. 2015. *Cosmopolitanism and the literary imagination*. New York: Palgrave Macmillan.
Pollock, Sheldon. 2002. Cosmopolitanisms. In *Cosmopolitanism*, ed. Carol A. Breckenridge, Sheldon Pollock, Homi K. Bhabha, and Dipesh Chakrabarty, 1–14. Durham: Duke University Press.
Pusca, Anca. 2008. The aesthetics of change: Exploring post-communist spaces. *Global Society* 22: 369–386. https://doi.org/10.1080/13600820802090512.
Robbins, Bruce. 1992. Comparative cosmopolitanism. *Social Text* 31: 169–186. https://doi.org/10.2307/466224.
Robbins, Bruce. 1998a. Actually existing cosmopolitanism. In *Cosmopolitics: Thinking and feeling beyond the nation*, ed. Pheng Cheah and Bruce Robbins, 1–19. Minneapolis: University of Minnesota Press.
Robbins, Bruce. 1998b. Comparative cosmopolitanisms. In *Cosmopolitics: Thinking and feeling beyond the nation*, ed. Pheng Cheah and Bruce Robbins, 246–264. Minneapolis: University of Minnesota Press.
Robbins, Bruce. 2017. *The beneficiary*. Durham: Duke University Press.
Robertson, Roland. 1995. Glocalization: Time-space and homogeneity—Heterogeneity. In *Global modernities*, ed. Mike Featherstone, Scott Lash, and Roland Robertson, 25–44. London, Thousand Oaks and New Delhi: Sage.
Rumford, Chris. 2008. *Cosmopolitan spaces: Europe, globalization, theory*. New York and London: Routledge.
Schoene, Berthold. 2010. *The cosmopolitan novel*. Edinburgh: Edinburgh University Press.
Shaw, Kristian. 2016. Teaching contemporary cosmopolitanism. In *Teaching 21st century genres*, ed. Katy Shaw, 167–185. Basingstoke: Palgrave Macmillan.
Shaw, Kristian. 2017a. 'A passport to cross the room': Cosmopolitan empathy and transnational engagement in Zadie Smith's *NW (2012)*. *C21 Literature: Journal of 21st-century Writings* 5 (1): 1–23. https://doi.org/10.16995/c21.15.
Shaw, Kristian. 2017b. *Cosmopolitanism in twenty-first century fiction*. Basingstoke: Palgrave Macmillan.
Smith, William. 2007. Cosmopolitan citizenship: Virtue, irony and worldliness. *European Journal of Social Theory*. 10: 37–52.
van Leeuwen, Bart. 2019. If we are *flâneurs*, can we be cosmopolitans? *Urban Studies* 56: 301–316. https://doi.org/10.2307/26621553.

Vertovec, Steven, and Robin Cohen. 2002. Introduction: Conceiving cosmopolitanism. In *Conceiving cosmopolitanism: Theory, context, and practice*, ed. Steven Vertovec and Robin Cohen, 1–22. Oxford: Oxford University Press.

Walkowitz, Rebecca L. 2006. *The cosmopolitan style: Modernism beyond the nation*. New York: Columbia University Press.

CHAPTER 3

Narrative Glocality and the *Cosmoflâneur* in Ian McEwan's *Saturday*

Ian McEwan's *Saturday* (2005), as part of its cosmopolitan agenda, comes as a conspicuous response to 9/11 terror attacks, the aftermath of which has noteworthy global repercussions. It engages with the world on a global level in a less direct way precisely because the world is mostly focalized and refracted from the vision of the 48-year-old protagonist, Henry Perowne, who seems to have a limited sense of involvement in world politics than everyday routines. The novel takes place in London on a single day, February 15, 2003, which is a significant date when thousands of UK citizens gathered in Hyde Park to protest at the prospect of a war in Iraq. Even though London's massive anti-war march against the imminent Iraq invasion by the USA government sets the background scene in the narrative, the physically and professionally superior, white, English, middle-class neurosurgeon, Henry Perowne remains preoccupied with personal and familial issues throughout the narrative. His distant engagement with this world event has been regarded as a sign of detachment and failure to participate politically in the global agenda by some critics. McEwan's novel is characterized by "political aloofness", "self-detachment" (Schoene 2010, p. 41), and recognition of "a multicultural and cosmopolitan society with which it resists engagement" (Wallace 2007, p. 467). The relationship between the powerful and intellectual Perowne and his antagonist, a petty city vagrant, Baxter, is even considered in terms of "British nationalism and imperialism", whereby Perowne

© The Author(s), under exclusive license to Springer Nature Switzerland AG 2024
E. Toprak Sakız, *Culture and Economics in Contemporary Cosmopolitan Fiction*, https://doi.org/10.1007/978-3-031-44995-6_3

is "the obvious embodiment of this imperial authority" (Wells 2010, p. 113). My analysis is different from the ones that upbraid the main character, and through him the novel in general for lack of cosmopolitan stance and engagement.

Saturday draws on conceptions of vernacular cosmopolitanism, paying attention to more parochial forms of the concept and the subsistence of neoliberal capitalism in the contemporary city as well as to the inseparability of the global from the local. The novel's modernist reflections have predominantly been the focus of many critics who prioritize a temporal approach in references to the novel's treatment of "monumental time", "private time", "public time", "modernist time", as seen in the readings of Mark Currie (2007), Laura Marcus (2009), and Sebastian Groes (2009). I assume, on the other hand, a cosmo-spatial, rather than a temporal, approach to underpin the novel's cosmopolitan, rather than modernist, dimensions. The novel is marked by its attention to the contemporary moment in a way to bestow it the label "*cosmopolitan*" as Michael L. Ross (2008) also emphasizes for the grounds that the novel can be categorized as a Condition of England novel (p. 76). Childs (2006) rightly observes that the novel represents ways in which "the liberal Western citizen can engage with the contemporary world" (p. 146). Wallace asserts that "*Saturday* evokes an all-encompassing cosmopolitanism that it then paradoxically marginalizes" (2007, p. 467). Perowne is a cosmopolitan character rather than a modernist one that is engrossed in his inner world and personal experiences while remaining partially engaged with global politics. Ulrike Tancke (2015) suggests that the novel's preoccupation with the protagonist's small-scale concerns, nevertheless, offers important commentary on a post-9/11 world (p. 20). Central to the novel's agenda is, then, its juxtaposition of the personal and public crises, and through this, its display of a contradictory, yet common form of world engagement typifying twenty-first-century citizens.

It is necessary to distinguish the implied author's treatment of global matters from that of the protagonist, which will shed light upon the politics of the novel that lies beneath the surface. The limited cosmopolitan engagement of the protagonist and his transformation toward the end is contrasted with the more engaged world beyond his own, which also has certain inconsistencies and deviation from its ideals. It is then unequivocal that in the novel, McEwan manages to manifest the deficiencies in Perowne's perceptions (Estévez-Saá and Pereira-Ares 2016, p. 273). Schwalm suggests that "Perowne assimilates everything and everyone into his view of the world", yet we cannot say that "the implied author remains invisible (or inaudible) behind him" (cited in Tancke 2015, p. 29). According to Magali Cornier Michael, the narrating voice diverts from that of the protagonist's by "subtly criticizing Perowne as symptomatic of and complicit with the problems Western cultures and human beings face in the contemporary moment" (2009, p. 28). Viewed as a catalyst for social inequality and global problems, Perowne is often regarded as a figure disengaged from the world outside his own; however, the narrator, looking through Perowne's eyes reveals the moments of ambiguity when the self-seeking protagonist suffers from feelings of guilt as well as self-knowledge as to his incapacity to resolve matters beyond his own immediate surrounding. It is this revelation of Perowne's moments of hesitation that primarily define the ambivalence of the protagonist toward cosmopolitan commitment. Distinct from later cosmopolitan novels written in the second decade of the twenty-first century, the narrative's treatment of cosmopolitics remains somehow latent. Yet, the purposefully drawn self-interest of the protagonist can in fact be seen as a narrative strategy to manifest his flawed perspective. As a result, a gap occurs between the protagonist's and the implied author's engagement with global politics. However, through the transformation of the protagonist in the end, this gap gets narrower. Reading the novel involves recognizing such a distance, and as Tancke puts it, "the cracks and fissures in Henry's point of view" as well as "questioning Henry's perception of himself and the world" (2015, p. 29). McEwan uses free indirect discourse in his narrative for the purposes of blurring the borderline between narrator and character voice in order to encourage the reader to, as Green maintains, "simultaneously [inhabit] Henry's mind while remaining critical and more knowing than him" (2010, p. 62), and to, as Gauthier puts it, "prevent the reader from identifying uncritically with the protagonist" (2013, p. 9). Considering this distance between Perowne's worldview and that of the novel, I suggest here that it is through revealing Perowne's perspective and the mistakenness of his position that the implied author communicates the novel's more subtle cosmopolitical engagement with the contemporary world to the reader. Despite being positioned apart from the implied author and the reader initially, Perowne is transfigured toward the end, and eventually gets closer to the cosmopolitics of the novel.

Narrative Glocality and Vernacular Cosmopolitanism

Narrative glocality as a significant aspect of the novel can be explored with a view to both the protagonist and the narrator's consciousness and the relayed details of the narration that is roaming glocally. It thus underscores the impossibility of divesting oneself of contemporary politics, disentangling the local from the global in cosmopolitan living spaces. The novel relates a single day in the life of Henry Perowne, tracing his daily mobilities as well as his roaming global consciousness throughout February 15, 2003, Saturday. Whatever happens during the day involves both the mundane and the extraordinary, the local and the global. The progression of his day is ordinary with the exception of a few unanticipated events and encounters. Awakened very early in the morning while everyone is still asleep, the middle-aged neurosurgeon, Henry Perowne, sees from his bedroom window a plane in flames struggling to land in Heathrow; unable to go back to sleep, he goes downstairs and drinks coffee with his son, Theo, who is a jazz singer and just back from a performance. Again, in his bedroom, he makes love with his wife, Rosalind; gets ready to go out for a squash match with his anaesthetist colleague; has a minor car crash, and a culminating altercation with the other driver on the way; takes a visit to the suburban neighborhood where his old mother is cared for mental loss and old age; makes his way to see his son's jazz performance. Back at home, he cooks for the evening's dinner gathering, and welcomes his daughter, Daisy, an award-winning poet living in Paris. With the arrival of Daisy and her grandfather, old poet John Grammaticus, the family reunites in the evening, but Baxter, the other driver in the morning's accident punctuates this joyous meeting as he forces the family with a knife poised in his hand to act in accordance with his wishes for a few threatening hours. Eventually, his aggression is counteracted as Henry and Theo throw him down the stairs. The family rejoices around the dinner table as Baxter is defused in the end. But later that night, Perowne is summoned to the hospital to operate on Baxter, who has put him and his family under duress early on. The narrative comes to an end in a circular pattern when the neurosurgeon returns from hospital and contemplates further at his bedroom window before going to sleep, echoing his musings when he saw the burning plane. McEwan's day-in-the-life narrative explores, as quoted from the novel's epigraph from Saul Bellow's 1964 novel, *Herzog*, "what it means to be a man. In a city. In a century. In transition" (Epigraph). Although the doctor goes through some of the day's hardships with triumph, his seemingly secure private life and elated mind are intermittently intruded into by the public and global realms. The omnipresent third-person narrator describes the world through Henry's focalization, articulating the neurosurgeon's ponderings about what is unfolding not only in his immediate locality but also on a global scale, and by so doing, the narrative voice somehow transcends the protagonist's limited vision to consolidate a broader cosmopolitan perspective.

The novel deals with contemporary cosmopolitan politics since the narrator does not limit his vision only to Perowne's by relating simultaneously both immediate incidents taking place around the protagonist and more remote events informed by global realities that are beyond him. It is to say that "*Saturday* includes dimensions that broaden the scope of the novel beyond what Henry, and by implication, his intellectual commitments, are willing or able to consider" (Root 2011, p. 64). Perowne avoids assuming supernatural explanations when he is woken up at night for some unknown reasons, and denounces too much subjectivity in human beings which is "[a]n excess of the subjective, the ordering of the world in line with your needs, an inability to contemplate your own unimportance" (McEwan 2005, p. 17). For Perowne, such subjective inclinations are nothing less than "psychosis" (p. 17). Broadening its perspective, then the narrative connects the topic of subjectivity to the famous quantum thought experiment called the Schrödinger's Cat, designed by the Austrian-Irish physicist Erwin Schrödinger in 1935. In this imaginary experiment, a cat is placed in a box with a small amount of radioactive substance. There is fifty percent chance for the cat to be dead or alive. It basically demonstrates that until one opens the box, the cat is both dead and alive, which implies that the result is not independent of the observer's contemplation. Viewing this as an excessive form of subjectivity, Perowne finds this quite senseless:

> Until the observer lifts the cover from the box, both possibilities, alive cat and dead cat, exist side by side, in parallel universes, equally real. At the point at which the lid is lifted from the box and the cat is examined, a quantum wave of probability collapses. None of this has ever made any sense to him at all. No human sense. […] [A] result, a consequence, exists separately in the world, independent of himself, known to others, awaiting his discovery. (pp. 18–19)

Commencing with his own beliefs regarding the plane crash incident, Perowne carries on with the general, the well-known experiment that he remembers as a result of what he has personally experienced. The unfolding of the narrative like concentric circles widening continuously provides the reader with a spectrum of perspectives and visions, which at times complement and at others contradict each other.

At the center of the novel's engrossment with the global, alongside its very parochial setting of a circle of London streets, lies the inseparability of the global from the local and the interplay between them on a daily basis, in the everyday activities of cosmopolitan characters. In other words, Perowne's personal existence is inevitably informed by the global. This complies with cosmopolitanism's ability "to mediate actions and ideals oriented both to the universal and the particular, the global and the local" (Vertovec and Cohen 2002, p. 4). As Ross puts it, "the protagonist Henry Perowne's customary private composure is repeatedly tested by tremors from the public realm" (2008, p. 76). The global intermittently intrudes into the local space in *Saturday* mostly in the form of daily news reports. Both the narrative of the day's local events and the flow of Perowne's Saturday activities are interrupted at almost every point with a view to the news from the world as well as the global perspective provided by the narrator. The narrative strategy of juxtaposing the immediate or local happenings with the distant or global events and perspectives—and by doing so, sharing multifarious positions and attitudes of vernacular cosmopolitanism—can be defined as narrative glocality.

Perowne's reaction to the news is ambiguous. In some cases, Perowne listens to the news reports voluntarily, or switches them off abruptly after a few attentive moments, and in others, he catches a glimpse of TV news as a passer-by. With the hope of finding out more about the particular news story of the plane, he watches the TV news in the kitchen with his son, Theo, at 04.00, but instead hears about Hans Blix, the assigned UN weapon inspector during the Iraq invasion, and preparations for anti-war demonstrations in London and worldwide:

> 'Hans Blix – a case for war?' the anchor intones over the sound of tomtoms, and pictures of the French Foreign Minister, M. de Villepin, being applauded in the UN debating chamber. 'Yes, say US and Britain. No, say the majority.' Then, preparations for anti-war demonstrations later today in London and countless cities around the world; a tennis championship in Florida disrupted by woman with a bread-knife ....

He turns the set off and says, 'How about some coffee?' (McEwan 2005, p. 29)

Switching off the news channel impulsively is an indicator of Perowne's faltering attitude characterized by neither total indifference nor full engagement. Nonetheless, curious about the local news like the burning plane, with which he is more concerned than with more distant crises, he gives up listening with nothing to hear about relevant to himself. Obviously, there is a marked change in the postmillennial concerns as a result of 9/11 attacks.

The narrative progressively begins to include other viewpoints than the doctor's in order to broaden its angle of response to global realities as a part of its vernacular cosmopolitanism. Theo, now old enough to talk about world politics with his father, interrogates about the plane accident: "You reckon it's terrorists?" (p. 31). The narrator then introduces Theo's position: "The September attacks were Theo's induction into international affairs, the moment he accepted that events beyond friends, home and the music scene had bearing on his existence" (p. 31). Contrary to his father, as a member of the younger generation, Theo finds politics as part of his life: "International terror, security cordons, preparations for war – these represent the steady state, the weather. Emerging into adult consciousness, this is the world he finds" (p. 32). Unlike his father, Theo scans the news usually on the Internet without giving much attention to details while Perowne, on the contrary, reads printed news stories "with morbid fixation" on every single detail. Perowne's feelings about the status of the world shifts from optimism to hopeless acceptance:

> Despite the troops mustering in the Gulf, or the tanks out at Heathrow on Thursday, the storming of the Finsbury Park mosque, the reports of terror cells around the country, and Bin Laden's promise on tape of 'martyrdom attacks' on London, Perowne held for a while to the idea that it was all an aberration, that the world would surely calm down and soon be otherwise, that solutions were possible, that reason, being a powerful tool, was irresistible, the only way out; or that like any other crisis, this one would fade soon, and make way for the next, going the way of the Falklands and Bosnia, Biafra and Chernobyl. But lately, this is looking optimistic. Against his own inclination, he's adapting, the way patients eventually do to their sudden loss of sight or use of their limbs. No going back. The nineties are looking like an innocent decade, and who would have thought that at the time? (p. 32)

This changing mindset is also in keeping with Henry's hesitant cosmopolitanism in which he is mentally occupied with the world's welfare, yet too disillusioned to take an active part. Remembering the previously unsolved global matters mentioned above, his attention to the current catastrophes does not sustain. Perowne in fact suffers from feelings of inertia and guilt as he fails to go beyond his partial engagement and remains inactive.

The two generations' difference in their response to cosmopolitanism can be explicated by their approach to world disasters; Theo finds them an ordinary part of twenty-first-century life while Perowne is nostalgic about better times than the present moment. Not compatible to his sense of orderliness, a tenet that can be seen in his familial and professional life, the contemporary chaos makes him confused and indecisive. As a result, he remains often ambivalent in his response to the overwhelming state of the world. Theo's "initiation, in front of the TV, before the dissolving towers, was intense but he adapted quickly", and as he scans the newspapers, "[a]s long as there's nothing new, his mind is free" (p. 32). However, the neurosurgeon cannot get rid of his state of global anxiety, adopting the view in a book he has read before that: "the New York attacks precipitated a global crisis that would, if we were lucky, take a hundred years to resolve. *If we were lucky*. Henry's lifetime, and all of Theo's and Daisy's. And their children's lifetime too. A Hundred Years' War" (pp. 32–33; emphasis in original). Henry Perowne and his family, like millions in the world, are regarded as part of this global "we" community on the whole, yet at the same time, fall short of fully engaging with global matters if they are distant enough. This is the paradox Henry experiences as a twenty-first-century subject.

As stated earlier, as a narrative technique, the narrator opens up possibilities for looking at the events from variously diverse positions transcending the protagonist's. Upon Theo's questioning about the reason for the plane crash ("You think it's jihadists …?") (p. 33), there occurs a narrative gap between the query and the doctor's answer that "I don't know what I think" (p. 34). In this gap, the narrator voices as different views as those of "the Arabic world" and "a Londoner" (pp. 33–34). Opposing outlooks on Islamic terrorism are provided; on the one hand, the prevalent paranoia about the ambitions of jihadists for an Islamic state is articulated: "In the ideal Islamic state, under strict Shari' a law, there'll be room for surgeons. Blues guitarists will be found other employment. But perhaps no one is demanding such a state. Nothing is demanded.

Only hatred is registered, the purity of nihilism" (p. 33). On the other, the view that this is more than mere paranoia is thought by Henry: "But that's not quite right. Radical Islamists aren't really nihilists – they want the perfect society on earth, which is Islam" (p. 34). From these two positions, the narrator makes it explicit that "Perowne takes the conventional view" (p. 34). The one-sidedness of his view is also revealed when Perowne contemplates on another radical reaction, but one supported by the Western citizens: "As a Londoner, you could grow nostalgic for the IRA. Even as your legs left your body, you might care to remember the cause was a united Ireland" (pp. 33–34). Through Perowne's two examples—one from Western and another from Eastern radicalism—the narrative seeks to look at the cosmopolitan world as a whole. Eventually, the narrator does not come up with a resolution and instead the reader is provided with an encompassing cosmopolitan perspective.

Narrative glocality in the novel is incarnated mostly through the reflection of distant or global perspectives with the news broadcast alongside the immediate or local occurrences. Always on the move, a journalist seeking new pieces of news throughout the city is regarded as a *flâneur* in Benjamin's theory. Perowne also almost always grapples with the news, but as a *cosmoflâneur*, not limiting himself to the local, he is globally preoccupied with the rolling news from all over the world. Reading or listening to the news stories allows Perowne to step out of his parochial environment and confront the bigger world outside. In fact, his situatedness in his very insular locality is not a hindrance for opening up to the global; he becomes a cosmopolite precisely because he resides in glocal spaces, which can be specified to be "the spaces of the shopping street and the home as sites for the construction of an imaginative cosmopolitanism and a practised globality" (Binnie et al. 2006, pp. 12–13). The narrated single day in Perowne's life is spent in very local urban spaces like his home and the shopping streets, but there he practices to be a cosmopolitan by imagining being one.

Perowne's house becomes a glocal space where the very locality of the place is always intervened by the global. Suspecting the aircraft accident to be a possible terror attack, Theo and Perowne talk about a number of global issues at their kitchen table while drinking their coffee:

> They discussed Iraq of course, America and power, European distrust, Islam – its suffering and self-pity, Israel and Palestine, dictators, democracy – and then the boys' stuff: weapons of mass destruction, nuclear

fuel rods, satellite photography, lasers, nanotechnology. At the kitchen table, this is the early-twenty-first-century menu, the specials of the day. (McEwan 2005, p. 34)

A very local place opens up to the global through their daily exchanges. The interior of the house is almost always susceptible to the public sphere. These world problems are treated as part of everyday life in distant parts of the world, but their real effects are felt only where they take place. In this way, it is emphasized that the way cosmopolitanism is really experienced is not totalizing or monolithic, rather there are cosmopolitanisms in plural. Theo's response to this conversation or his recently-found "aphorism" demonstrates this plurality and the vernacular tendencies in contemporary cosmopolitanism: "the bigger you think, the crappier it looks" (p. 34). His explanation echoes with particularist perspectives: "When we go on about the big things, the political situation, global warming, world poverty, it all looks really terrible, with nothing getting better, nothing to look forward to. But when I think small, closer in [...], then it looks great. So this is going to be my motto – think small" (pp. 34–35). No longer deluded by the utopian ideals of universalist cosmopolitanism, vernacular cosmopolitans seek particular ways of interacting with the world. Perowne, on the contrary, adopts and reiterates the universalist view voiced by Darwin in his *On the Origin of Species*: "There is grandeur in this view of life" (p. 55), in a way to contrast Theo's particularism. The two generations represent different orientations in cosmopolitanism at this stage: Perowne the universalist and Theo the particularist while Perowne is disillusioned in the end and reconsiders his vision, Theo's approach, like his father's, is also indeterminate, and characterized by only partial involvement. Both of them are alert to the local plane news once again when the radio begins. Relieved that the incident is simply a Russian cargo plane whose engine has been on fire, rather than a terror venture, Theo comments, "not an attack on our whole way of life then" (p. 35), to which Henry agrees: "A good result" (p. 35). The other two news stories about the demonstrations and Hans Blix get subordinated now as the two characters remain non-responsive. As self-seeking Western subjects, they both seem more interested in threats to their own lives than in world disasters in general.

The over-protected double front doors of the Perowne's with its Banham locks, iron bolts, tempered steel security chains, spyhole, Entry-phone system, red panic button, and alarm pad fail to guard the inside from the invasion of the outside. As Alexander Beaumont puts it, "the family's attempts at spatial fortification" prove ironically inefficient in that "Perowne thinks that the security hardware makes him safe, but McEwan knows that he is fooling himself and quietly communicates this to the reader" (2015, p. 141). The centrality of the white, upper-middle class protagonist in the novel puts all the others that are not white nor wealthy in a marginalized position, yet they keep intruding into his well-protected life and consciousness (Butler 2011, p. 102). Once more, the implied author's broader vision becomes eligible by the comment: "beware of the city's poor, the drug-addicted, the downright bad" (McEwan 2005, p. 37). Obviously not belonging to Perowne himself, this ironic remark is the narrative's cleavage to the outside world otherwise unseen by the protagonist. It is also made clear that Perowne seeks detachment from other people in the shelter of his home, and thus cannot be aligned with the type of cosmopolitanism which is defined as one's willing openness to the world outside her/himself.

In a like manner, the most private space in the house, his bedroom, is also prone to the global; he first mulls over his own desires, and then compares them to those of despotic kings and ancient gods. Transferring Perowne's deliberations from the personal to the general is the narrator's common tendency of comprehensiveness that is a movement from the particular experience to the general outlook in order to be more inclusive. Even while he is in erotic thoughts beside his wife in bed, he begins to speculate about Saddam and how he looks like "an overgrown, disappointed boy" (p. 38) and wonders: "But how quickly he's drifted from the erotic to Saddam – who belongs in a mess, a stew of many ingredients, of foreboding and preoccupation" (p. 39). Nevertheless, his attempt to separate this chaotic world of Saddam from his orderly inner life proves fruitless. This ever-growing chain of reflections ends up in more and more musings, which reflect Perowne's "wild unreason" (p. 39) as he blames himself for his mistake about the plane accident. Striving to give explanations for his delusion, he generalizes: "This trick of dark imagining is one legacy of natural selection in a dangerous world. [...] Misunderstanding is general all over the world. How can we trust ourselves?" (p. 39). Evidently, his attempt to postulate his own deception is a general inclination among his fellow cosmopolitans. His pessimism is a result of the contemporary world risks where he inevitably chooses, in reference to Schrödinger's imaginary experiment, the dead cat rather than the alive (p. 39). Therefore, the novel demonstrates the need to understand many

Westerners' fears after the 9/11 trauma while simultaneously showing a consciousness that irrationality and prejudice complement these fears (Estévez-Saá and Pereira-Ares 2016, p. 272). The 9/11 trauma is functional in twenty-first-century subjects' ambiguous, and mostly pessimistic, attitude in the face of negative events.

Another glocal space is the city square upon which Perowne keeps glaring from a distance and muses about the wider world outside his own, yet his attitude is mostly ambivalent. From his superior position at his window, his gaze wanders around the people in the square and diagnoses their problems, like the young couple that, he decides, suffers from drug addiction. Once more he is curious about others' problems and yet aware that he cannot do anything for them. Speculating about people's attraction to the square, he draws a parallel between the vast space below him and the Iraqi desert: "A desert, it is said, is a military planner's dream. A city square is the private equivalent" (McEwan 2005, p. 60). This interconnectedness between these local and global spaces is reinforced by the next analogy, one between himself and Saddam once more, as he "imagines himself as Saddam, surveying the crowd with satisfaction from some Baghdad ministry balcony" (p. 62). The function of this analogy can be explained through its perspective-changing impact on the readers who are propelled to "try on" characters' standpoint and consequently revise that of their own (Caracciolo 2013, p. 73). The narrative focal broadening occurs here to the effect of presenting a different viewpoint. In the shoes of Saddam, he acknowledges his misconception as he eventually understands that the war is impending and in fact necessary to preserve Iraqi people from the subjugation, arrests and tortures overwhelming the country. Having listened to the story of one of his former patients, an Iraqi professor, Miri Taleb, who had also been under arrest in Baghdad for a while and tormented for some unknown reason by Saddam's soldiers, Perowne is introduced to a different perspective than that of Londoners. Perowne's view of the war seems to be shaped by Taleb's testimony: "it's only terror that holds the nation together, the whole system runs on fear, and no one knows how to stop it. Now the Americans are coming, perhaps for bad reasons. But Saddam and the Ba'athists will go" (McEwan 2005, p. 64). The neurosurgeon is, as a result, likely to assume a position for war in support of his patient's opinions stemming from his first-hand experience of Iraqi government's domination, and detaches himself from the anti-war protestors in the square. In this way, an antithesis for the anti-war position, presupposed by Taleb and possibly followed by many others like Perowne, is provided by the inclusive narrator. Yet another perspective, that of an American, regarding the war is laid open through the narrative's wide focus. Joy Strauss, Henry's American colleague, as "a man of untroubled certainties" is in the opinion that "Iraq is a rotten state, a natural ally of terrorists, bound to cause mischief at some point and may as well be taken out now while the US military is feeling perky after Afghanistan. And by taken out, he insists he means liberated and democratised" (p. 100). This pro-war positioning of his colleague makes Perowne even more agitated, yet more indecisive: "Whenever he talks to Jay, Henry finds himself tending towards the anti-war camp" (p. 100). His position in reference to the Iraq war remains indeterminate as he vacillates between several contradictory opinions that belong to both for and against groups. Nevertheless, he is involved in all this international politics either from the interior of his bedroom or inside his car, wandering his thoughts across the world and remaining neither responsive nor active politically. It is through this narrative strategy of inclusiveness that the novel presents a myriad of outlooks in which various responses to the world exist simultaneously as in Schrödinger's experiment. The protagonist's indecisiveness in response to the contrasting views about the war is in line with the novel's representation of the general tendency of twenty-first-century cosmopolitans.

The narrator's widening angle makes it possible to see many contradictions within the cosmopolitan ethos itself. Observing the preparations for the anti-war march from his bedroom window, Perowne witnesses the "happiness" of the crowd in the street:

> Placards are already piled high, and folded banners and cards of lapel buttons and whistles, football rattles and trumpets, funny hats and rubber masks of politicians – Bush and Blair in wobbling stacks, the topmost faces gazing blankly skywards, ghastly white in the sunshine. [...] A small crowd round the cart wants to buy stuff before the vendors are ready. The general cheerfulness Perowne finds baffling. (p. 61)

For Perowne, this joy is not compatible with the aim of the meeting, and "[t]he scene has an air of innocence and English dottiness" (p. 62). Despite his detachment from the crowd, the doctor is in fact highly conscious of this international conflict: "The one thing Perowne thinks he knows about this war is that it's going to happen. With or without the UN" (p. 62). He is convinced that, despite the demonstrations or the peace supporters, the war is inevitable. When he is in the streets later that day trying to go to his squash match, he sees the same protestors he has seen in the news, "tens of thousands of strangers converging with a single purpose conveying an intimation of revolutionary joy" (p. 72). He does not seem to be sharing beliefs in common action, in what David Held (2010) summarizes as "a framework of political and moral interaction in order to coexist and cooperate in the resolution of our shared (and pressing) problems" (p. 19). He often articulates his deeply-rooted suspicions about this communal spirit:

> All this happiness on display is suspect. Everyone is thrilled to be together out on the streets – people are hugging themselves, it seems, as well as each other. If they think – and they could be right – that continued torture and summary executions, ethnic cleansing and occasional genocide are preferable to an invasion, they should be sombre in their view. (McEwan 2005, pp. 69–70)

This familiar contemporary picture seems to promise cosmopolitan conviviality where humanity is brought together by a sole aim, which is, nevertheless, unattainable. Yet, it is also made precise that it is more of self-interest and fear of revenge than of a genuine global engagement, Perowne suspects, because millions of marchers gather out of "concerns for their own safety" rather than "a passion for Iraqi lives" because "none of the people now milling around Warren Street tube station happens to have been tortured by the regime, or knows and loves people who have, or even knows much about the place at all" (p. 73). The overtones of vernacular cosmopolitanism are manifest in this self-revelation while the ethical ground of universalist cosmopolitanism is revealed to be far-fetched and questionable by the narrator: "Self-interest is a decent enough cause, but Perowne can't feel, as the marchers themselves probably can, that they have an exclusive hold on moral discernment" (p. 73).

Narrative glocality reverberates throughout the novel, characterizing the local places in inevitable connection with the global. As Shaw (2017) maintains, "all [local, parochial and quotidian] spaces are now subject to, and offer the potential for, cultural engagement" (p. 15). Another example of a glocal space is the squash court where Perowne and Jay Strauss regularly meet for a squash game. In the court, during the short interval between the sets, Perowne catches a glimpse of the silent TV through the mirror and understands that the two Russian pilots of the burning plane have been arrested on suspicion of a terror attack. Regretful that the news also arrests him even in his supposedly very private occupation, he wonders: "Isn't it possible to enjoy an hour's recreation without this invasion, this infection from the public domain?" and claims his "right [...] not to be disturbed by world events, or even street events" (McEwan 2005, p. 108). The answer becomes self-evident as Perowne gets more and more involved in world issues regardless of where he is. His desire to free this private space from the intrusion of the public proves unfulfilled.

Later that day, again in the kitchen to cook for the evening's family reunion, Perowne feels he is driven to hear the news because "[i]t's a condition of the times, this compulsion to hear how it stands with the world, and be joined to the generality, to a community of anxiety" (p. 176). This impulsive preoccupation with the news has emerged, Henry speculates, because of the terror induced upon people expecting the news of an impending attack in a European or American cosmopolis. His acts of cooking and the unfolding pieces of news are interchangeably presented in this kitchen scene as if they are blended into each other only to show the entangled relationship between the local and the global:

> Onto the softened onions and garlic – pinches of saffron, some bay leaves, orange-peeled gratings, oregano, five anchovy fillets, two tins of peeled tomatoes. On the big Hyde Park stage, sound-bite extracts of speeches by a venerable politician of the left, a pop star, a playwright, a trade unionist. Into the stockpot he eases the skeletons of three skates. (p. 177)

These easy transitions between the inside and the outside world are a significant narrative strategy in which the glocal is interwoven into each line. He intermittently catches a glimpse of the TV news, but intolerant to hear it, he keeps the volume off. He only wants to hear more about "his" aircraft story, a local detail rather than a distant event. It is finally revealed that the burning plane had nothing to do with a terrorist attempt, but was carrying a cargo of American child pornography. Rather than relief, this news gives him a sense of anxiety in the belief that he can sometimes be fooled by the overpowering impact of the media upon the global issues, and that such manipulating media with its act of presenting "ungrounded certainties" (p. 180) can even deteriorate the global crisis. His delusion, he senses, is "part of the new order, this narrowing of mental freedom" and a ramification of his "becoming a dupe, the willing, ferbile consumer of news fodder, opinion, speculation and of all the crumbs the authorities let fall" (p. 180). "For Henry Perowne", as Ferguson puts it, "the news does not push us in the direction of agreement, does not prompt debates that end in a resolute decision about public affairs" (2007, p. 49). Regretting the subjective opinions presented alongside the news as well as his earlier illusion, he is now convinced that the ambiguity of his feelings regarding the global issues is an inevitable culmination of this imposing attitude of the authorities that rid the cosmopolitans of their freedom to think and consequently interact with each other. Whether he opts for the war or against it, he feels he is not free. "Either way", he muses, "it amounts to a consensus of a kind, an orthodoxy of attention, a mild subjugation in itself. [...] His nerves, like tautened strings, vibrate obediently with each news 'release'. He's lost the habits of scepticism [...] and just as bad, he senses he isn't thinking independently" (McEwan 2005, p. 181). These self-revelations say a lot about the condition of contemporary cosmopolitan subjects who, like Perowne, are driven into such contradictory forms of interacting with the world.

During kitchen-table conversations, this time with his daughter, Daisy, who has just arrived from Paris, he expresses his opinions freely, sometimes sounding pro-war to the disgust of his political activist and poet daughter. Henry believes Daisy's speech about the danger awaiting the world if the war happens is "a collation of everything she heard in the park, of everything they've both heard and read a hundred times, the worst-case guesses that become facts through repetition, the sweet ruptures of pessimism" (p. 186). He blames the news reports for the deception about cosmopolitics since they cause such prosaic remarks as his daughter's, which are far from facts. Nevertheless, Perowne summarizes this kitchen dialog: "the world matters" (p. 189). At the end of their long debate about the case for or against the war, he recognizes "how luxurious [it is] to work it all out at home in the kitchen, the geopolitical moves and military strategy, and not be held to account, by voters, newspapers, friends, history" (p. 193). He has his own response to global issues, and he is aware that his is a remote involvement with the world, and thus an unencumbered one. After much debate, the conversation ends peacefully in music, a blues song about "reunion and friendship", proving Henry's belief in its universality. In the security of their home, world matters are discussed safely, not harming anyone; it is also in this sheltered state that they finalize their conversation over the war politics with the music that evokes peace. In this sense, Perowne's self-evaluation as to his and many other contemporary cosmopolitans' limited engagement with the distant world events proves true in this scene where they offer solutions to global threats within their privileged circumstances.

THE *COSMOFLÂNEUR* AS A GLOBALLY CONSCIOUS CITY-WANDERER

Saturday's protagonist remains ambivalent regarding global politics while simultaneously beginning to commit himself to the concerns of the vernacular cosmopolitans inhabiting his local world. In fact, the novel seems to present an alternative approach to cosmopolitanism through its attentiveness to neoliberal capitalism and the particular versions of cosmopolitan life in the city. The rest of the chapter will demonstrate that the protagonist can also be characterized as a *cosmoflâneur*, one that is self-aware of his non-involvement in global issues, but still cannot bring himself to a state of active engagement. It is the narrative's glocal awareness, inclusiveness, as well as the contrasting manifestation of the protagonist's ambivalence and reluctance to engage the global more than the local that marks the novel's cosmopolitics. In the novel, not only the protagonist himself in physical form, but also his mind is involved in *cosmoflânerie*, moving along the streets and far beyond both locally and globally.

As I argued in Chapter 2, the three principles of *cosmoflânerie* involve discerning the global and the local simultaneously in cityscapes, recognizing class and commodification whose impact is prevalent there, and last but not least, taking active steps in world-making with a view to the world's economic and ecological emergencies. In an attempt to demonstrate these particularities of the figure of the *cosmoflâneur* in *Saturday*, I argue here that Henry Perowne's daily wandering in London's streets encompasses these three cosmopolitan aspects—outlook, consciousness, and activity to a certain extent. Obviously, he has both a global and local outlook from the outset, as well as a consciousness of the city as a site of class divides and economic disproportions. However, the third feature of the *cosmoflâneur*, activeness or responding to the world with an urge to take an active role in its formation, develops in Perowne only in the end when he undergoes a transformation, in which he comes to engage with others in a more active way.

Perowne's mentality can be depicted as indeterminate and fluctuating in response to life and the world. Even though Perowne's self-definition is marked by a sense of contentment in every aspect of his life, including his loving relationship with his wife, his professional success and his pride in the artistic talents of both of his children, a paradox still exists, a kind of "dissatisfaction in his own life" or "the missing element" which is reminded to him especially as he listens to his son Theo's jazz music (p. 28). He cannot fully escape from the global trauma inflicting the spaces he occupies, even his own house, seemingly safe enough to keep the inside exempt from the turmoil and dangers of the outside. He begins the day with "a pleasurable sensation" (p. 3) and energy, which he loses to a great extent by the day's ending. When he wakes up at 3.40 on Saturday, Perowne is extraordinarily delighted with no identifiable reason, feeling "inexplicably elated" and "unusually strong" (p. 3). He finds "sustained, distorting euphoria" wherever he looks as he gazes over the city out of his bedroom window: the Post Office Tower is "memorial to more optimistic days"; "[t]he overfull litter baskets suggest abundance rather than squalor"; their house is located in a "perfect square" and in the "perfect circle of garden", in which benches expect "cheerful lunchtime office crowds" in the morning (p. 5). This celebration of city spaces becomes even more explicit as he muses: "the city is a success, a brilliant invention, a biological masterpiece – millions teeming around the accumulated and layered achievements of the centuries" (p. 5). At this stage of his interaction with the city, he assumes an overlooking and detached position, whereby he watches cityscapes from his bedroom window without fully being present within them. Gazing at the city from this position, Perowne lacks activeness in this initial phase.

In fact, the economic dimension of contemporary living is always implemental to understanding vernacular cosmopolitanism. As a second step, the *cosmoflâneur* shows a consciousness of the classed structure of society imposed by neoliberal capitalism. The opening scene, the reader is seeing through Perowne's focalization, reveals his materialistic mindset. This is elucidated in his reflections on the surplus of materials that end up in the rubbish bin, the abundance in the city square of both the wage-earning population as well as the food consumed by them. All these mean for him that the city is full of such consumption spaces. Rather than castigating this consuming urban community, he feels perfectly at home with its materialist practices. However, this overwhelming sense of exhilaration gradually gives way to other feelings as if he is waking up from a dream as he keeps standing at the window: "the elation is passing, and he's beginning to shiver" (p. 13). His elevated mood is totally disturbed by "this nightmare" (p. 15), by the siren of the passing ambulance and the extraordinary sight of a burning plane. Seeing the flaming plane seems to contribute to this sense of vertigo and discontent on his part. At first, he mistakes the plane for a comet, one which is "too extraordinary not to share [with Rosalind]", and thinks of waking her up; however, as soon as he is assured that it is a burning airplane rather than a celestial object, he revises his decision: "Why wake her into this nightmare?" (p. 15). His initial optimism is now far gone, which is manifest in his new reflections on the air travel sector which is "a stock market" and his conclusion that "[t]he market could plunge" (p. 15). His change of mood at the end of the scene also stems from his focus on the negative financial impact caused by the plane crash. He emphasizes the economic consequences of the accident, which would be otherwise regarded as a fatalistic catastrophe for human life. Not involved emotionally, he also makes it clear that "deaths per journey" (p. 15) is a matter of statistics. His choice of an economics term ("market") to express his concerns for a plane that he sees on fire evinces his materially-oriented mind as well as the narrative's attentiveness to the prevalence of neoliberal capitalism within contemporary societies.

I view *cosmoflânerie* as a way of opening up to the world through the outlook of a strolling character, of Henry Perowne in this instance, or through the narrator's roaming consciousness throughout the city. This is also a form of virtual mobility that goes on functioning even when the beholder remains physically immobile. At its core, the *cosmoflâneur* is characterized by the juxtaposition of global and local perspectives as well as an engagement with the city by conceiving it as a site of class consciousness and economic disproportions. The conception of the *cosmoflâneur* is able to bear out the idea of vernacular cosmopolitanism by foregrounding its economic dimension together with its global effect. It has commonalities with Benjamin's concept of *flâneur* to some extent, especially in terms of city-wandering, yet becomes its contemporary counterpart due to their divergences which are made explicit in Benjamin's definition of the latter concept: "The flâneur is a man uprooted. He is at home neither in his class nor in his homeland, but only in the crowd. The crowd is his element" (1999, p. 895). The cosmopolitan orientation of the *flâneur* is universalist while that of the *cosmoflâneur* is vernacular as the former is detached from specified associations and remains attached to a universal crowd, whereas the latter celebrates both global and local ties. In other words, the *cosmoflâneur* transcends communal associations by making individual choices for her / his affiliations, yet is more class conscious than a *flâneur*, who can forget his class while walking within the crowd, with which he identifies. Unlike a *flâneur*, Perowne denounces an identification with the greatest mass of walkers that constitute the crowd in the city. He is not an integral part of this community, preferring to drive safely in his Mercedes, rather than walk among the people rallying against the war. Benjamin views "[t]he flâneur as *bohémien*. [...] He lacks political schooling. Uncertainty of class consciousness" (1999, p. 895). In contrast, Perowne's experience of *cosmoflânerie* complies with Calhoun's (2002) idea of cosmopolitanism as the "class consciousness of frequent travellers" in his article with the same name. He is perfectly at home in his class, in fact proud that he is an accomplished member of the middle class, seeing himself more superior than many non-elite cosmopolitans of the city as well as Baxter, his antagonist. Neither is he a bohemian nor a connoisseur of art, rather he is accused of "his astounding ignorance" and "poor taste and insensitivity" in relation to literature (McEwan 2005, p. 6) by his poet daughter because he dismisses creativity, deeply rooted in pragmatic materialism. By drawing his protagonist as a *cosmoflâneur*, McEwan goes beyond Benjamin's conception of the *flâneur*, and becomes more politically-concerned as part of the novel's cosmopolitan agenda. Benjamin's *flâneur* is marked by a resistance to consumerism and commodification encouraged by the arcade-like design of modern cities. By highlighting and involving in capitalist consumerism in the city, Perowne becomes a contemporary counterpart to the modernist city-dweller.

It is on the level of observation and awareness that Perowne is initially defined as a *cosmoflâneur*, and his responsiveness remains to be developed in the course of the narrative. In criticisms of the novel, Perowne is usually blamed for his political detachment, indifference to the external world, smugness, naïve optimism, pro-war positioning, support for social hierarchy, and self-assertion about the superiority and the outstanding talents of all the family members including himself. He may have all these flaws, yet this does not stop him from responding to the world though this response mostly remains ambiguous. Not totally indifferent to the world, Perowne ponders continuously: "And now, what days are these?" (p. 4). He sometimes gets even "comfortably nostalgic for a verdant, horse-drawn, affectionate England" (p. 6), lamenting these contemporary times. This nostalgia for good old times occurs to him the moment he hears the UN weapon inspector Hans Blix speak on the radio about the Iraq war, and inattentively he switches the radio off. This only partial attention to global news reiterates throughout the narration. Perowne is not alone, the narrator implies, in his callous attitude toward "words like 'catastrophe' and 'mass fatalities', 'chemical and biological warfare' and 'major attack' [which] have recently become bland through repetition" as the hospital's Emergency Plan keeps changing in par with the authorities', not the doctors', view of the definition of emergency (p. 12). Global concerns like these are among the committees' negotiation list, yet they remain unresolved and cannot avoid the risk of banality. Not actively involved, he is both politically ambiguous and self-conscious of his own detached approach to contemporary world issues.

Perowne is in fact highly familiar with global consciousness, if not an active participant or an activist in the way London protestors assert their fierce opposition to the Iraq War. Millions of Londoners join the anti-war march that is considered to be the most crowded gathering that London has seen thus far. Perowne is passive in cosmopolitan practice, but the implied author endows his protagonist with a global consciousness which he cannot separate from the mundane activities of his everyday life. By doing so, the implied author also reveals the common propensity of ambivalence among contemporary cosmopolitans in response to the world with the incompatible feelings of inertia and resulting guilt due to their disdain. Henry is a typical example of this ambiguous position, and his cosmopolitan posture is characterized by incertitude. Having closed his bedroom's shutters to avoid further involvement with the outside world and return to his comfort zone, he still encompasses these incompatible feelings: "He feels culpable somehow, but helpless too. These are contradictory terms, but not quite, and it's the degree of their overlap, their manner of expressing the same thing from different angles, which he needs to comprehend. Culpable in his helplessness" (p. 22). Perhaps, these are feelings not specific to the doctor only as the twenty-first-century cosmopolitan subject seems to be posited similarly toward world events, highly aware of cosmopolitics, yet unable to engage with them adequately. This is also "a peculiarly modern mix of self-consciousness and loss of self-control" (Holland 2017, p. 392). Perowne now regrets not having called the emergency services to offer his assistance for the air crash sufferers, contemplating "[h]is crime [...] to stand in the safety of his bedroom, wrapped in a woollen dressing gown, without moving or making a sound, half dreaming as he watched people die" (McEwan 2005, pp. 22–23). Like many others, he is self-conscious of not only his communal responsibility but also his helplessness in the face of the need to take real action. The narrator makes it explicit that Perowne, as a typical Western cosmopolitan, cannot totally disengage himself from the global, but at the same time fails to free himself from self-indulgence and give his full attention to others.

Perowne is a *cosmoflâneur* in that he wanders the streets of London mentally from his bedroom window, attending to the specificities of the unique experiences of others. Awake in his bedroom, he looks down at the city square and his vision traverses as in *cosmoflânerie* as his gaze moves with the burning plane in the sky, which propels him into further thoughts. For Perowne, "the spectacle has the familiarity of a recurrent dream" (p. 15). Reminiscent of the 9/11 terror attacks, the image of the plane over the Post Office Tower is a local experience informed by the global. To put it differently, the global becomes familiar in this local scene. As a ramification of collective trauma, the image of the burning plane approaching a tall public building is "familiar" even "from the outside, from afar like this" for the post-9/11 world:

> It's already almost eighteen months since half the planet watched, and watched again the unseen captives driven through the sky to the slaughter, at which time there gathered round the innocent silhouette of any jet plane a novel association. Everyone agrees, airlines look different in the sky these days, predatory or doomed. (p. 16)

These universal feelings that have been reinforced after the 9/11 attacks are also reflected by Perowne's own thoughts. Yet, the idea of cosmopolitan cooperation is annulled as Perowne distantly views the plane's engines in flames and ponders:

> That is the other familiar element – the horror of what he can't see. Catastrophe observed from a safe distance. Watching death on a large scale, but seeing no one die. No blood, no screams, no human figures at all, and into this emptiness, the obliging imagination set free. (p. 16)

The ambivalence of his reaction is also evinced by his contradictory senses of horror and familiarity which exist simultaneously. He sustains his undisturbed position in the face of outside terror. Perowne feels glad that he is only an observer rather than a sufferer of the disaster, yet he is equally afraid that the plane might be a terror attempt over the city.

Hesitant in the face of threat, yet concerned about a possible local attack, Perowne remains indecisive. Perowne's attitude is marked by vagueness rather than total negligence: "It occurs to Perowne that there's something he should be doing" (p. 17). He thinks only momentarily of calling the hospital in case they need him after the aircraft disaster, yet decides not to do so as Heathrow is outside the borders of his hospital's emergency action area. Feeling only parochially responsible, yet empathizing with his colleagues, he thinks beyond his own situation widening his angle of focus: "Elsewhere, further west, in darkened bedrooms, medics will be pulling on their clothes with no idea of what they face" (p. 17). Yet, when it comes to taking action, he fails in this incident as he also does during the day's anti-war rallies. He closes his windows to the outside, ending this experience by "quietly unfold[ing] the shutters to mask the sky" (p. 18). His refusal to get involved in this event and in others is subtly criticized by the narrator and is also shown as symptomatic of the twenty-first-century world where the prospect of a common solution is seen as a too optimistic view. This is a narrative hint of Perowne's flawed cosmopolitanism, evincing that the novel is away from ideals of universalism yet dissatisfied with the contemporary Western subject's engagement with cosmopolitics.

Far from identifying with the crowd, Perowne also adopts a resentful stance toward the protestors, who in fact serve capitalism and contribute to social injustice, even while they fight for a better cause, by purchasing consumerist products like McDonalds and coca cola, and polluting the streets with these consumables, and in turn deteriorating the environmental pollution as well as contributing to the unequal share of wealth influencing the least lucky in the community, namely the street wipers: "What could be more futile than this underpaid urban scale housework when behind him, at the far end of the street, cartons and paper cups are spreading thickly under the feet of demonstrators gathered outside McDonald's on the corner" (p. 74). With this hyper-awareness on the part of Perowne, it is made unequivocal that contemporary cosmopolitan fiction departs from the naïve idealism of soft cosmopolitanism, and by contrast pays attention to the often neglected aspects of economic, environmental, and social ramifications of globality and global movements. Paterson's conception of "McDisneyfication" leads to, as John Horton and Peter Kraftl put it, "the homogenisation of consumption opportunities, the ubiquity of global brands, and the prevalence of particular kinds of highly 'stage-managed' consumption spaces" (2013, p. 60). London streets in the narrative are represented in terms of such "McDisneyfication" and as examples of consumption space. It is toward the end of the day that his recognition begins to emerge as he sees these local scenes of consumption spaces.

Perowne gets more and more locally concerned as he recalls an environmental disaster, a daily blizzard of litter across the metropolis. Convinced of the significance of the local to attain global happiness, he believes that "[t]he world must improve, if at all, by tiny steps" (McEwan 2005, p. 74), which are in this case the steps of the non-elite cosmopolitans like, for example, the street cleaner who sweeps the mess caused by the protestors. Empathizing with the "unlucky" street cleaner, Henry achieves a moment of cosmopolitan interaction, which is local rather than global, by looking at the man's eyes: "The whites of the sweeper's eyes are fringed with egg-yellow shading to red along the lids. For a vertiginous moment Henry feels himself bound to the other man, as though on a seesaw with him, pinned to an axis that could tip them into each other's life" (p. 74). Perhaps, cosmopolitan communication begins, for him, with such "tiny" pieces of vernacular interaction first. At the end of the day, on his way back home from a night surgery, he sees the same sweeper and identifies with him as they both do overtime at this time of the day, which perhaps makes him more of a vernacular cosmopolitan than actively participating in the day's demonstrations: "a whole day behind the broom, and now, courtesy of untidy world events, some serious overtime" (p. 244). Henry also subtly criticizes the overconsumerist tendencies of the demonstrators that are unseen beneath their political activism:

> [M]ounds of food, plastic wrappings and discarded placards […]. And the debris has a certain archaeological interest – a Not in My Name with a broken stalk lies among polystyrene cups and abandoned hamburgers and pristine fliers for the British Association of Muslims. On a pile he steps round are a slab of pizza with pineapple slices, beer cans in a tartan motif, a denim jacket, empty milk cartons and three unopened tins of sweetcorn. (p. 243)

All types of commercial products, which are also detrimental for the environment, are cleaned away by the sweepers who are working overtime. It is again made clear that Henry is not inattentive to the global challenges, but he seems to hesitantly interrogate the ways in which possible solutions are sought for. The gathering crowd is composed of as diverse groups as "the British Association of Muslims", "the Swaffham Women's Choir", and "Jews Against the War" (p. 72), yet remains ineffective in solving problems. The community composed of millions of marchers is evinced to come together only arbitrarily and temporarily, lacking a sustaining value that holds them together.

In mobility in the streets of London, Perowne mentally goes far beyond this local surrounding through his speculations on global crises:

> The world has not fundamentally changed. Talk of a hundred-year crisis is indulgence. There are always crises, and Islamic terrorism will settle into place, alongside recent wars, climate change, the politics of international trade, land and fresh water shortages, hunger, poverty and the rest (p. 77).

He vacillates between such optimistic beliefs in solving these global problems and human progress at times and dejection at the state of the world at others: "The world probably has changed fundamentally and the matter is being clumsily handled, particularly by the Americans" (pp. 80–81). He seems to be the typical cosmopolitan who is aware of the global state of affairs, yet hesitant about the ways in which such affairs must be handled. Perowne's concept of progress is not without hesitation in the face of world catastrophes, an idea which echoes Benjamin's (1999):

> The concept of progress must be grounded in the idea of catastrophe. That things are "status quo" is the catastrophe. It is not an ever-present possibility but what in each case is given. [...] hell is not something that awaits us, but this life here and now. (p. 473)

Perowne does not turn his back to this catastrophic state of the world altogether; this is the "life here and now", rather than a distant future. In other words, global problems are inevitably everywhere, and he thinks the way in which they are dealt with is inadequate to create a cosmopolitan world. Perhaps he also feels responsible, as a twenty-first-century citizen, for this insoluble global state. Ulrich Beck, in "The Cosmopolitan Manifesto" (2010), like Benjamin, draws on Marx in his reference to the world risks that are "here and now". The underlying basis in his postmillennial Manifesto is an understanding that the central human worries are "world" problems, and not only because in their origins and consequences they have outgrown the national schema of politics. They are also "world" problems in their very concreteness, in their very location here and now in this town, or this political organization. (2010, p. 226)

Cosmopolitan novels engage in world-creation with a similar understanding described by Schoene: "[t]he most crucial skill of the cosmopolitan novelist is not to map or navigate the world, [...] but start mingling among the world's vast, inoperative being-in-common, that is, the world as such rather than any one of its projected models or interpretations" (2010, p. 29). It is the world's current state that is the subject of examination in the cosmopolitan novel, as in *Saturday*. Unlike the arcades traversed by Benjamin's *flâneurs*, the city is reflected in the cosmopolitan novel in its most realist, and in fact catastrophic state. For Benjamin, arcades' utopian dimension reflects "anticipation and imaginative expression of a new world" (1999, p. 237). McEwan's London streets, on the other hand, rather than creating a utopian living space, project a world that is catastrophic and consumptive.

As an act of *cosmoflânerie*, Perowne moves along the city independently, within his silver Mercedes, from the turmoil of street crowds, yet even the privacy of his car is not exempt from exposure to the public sphere. He listens to the news on the radio about the enormous mass of anti-war marchers as he drives, and rebukes a peace demonstrator for quoting "a warrior king", Henry the Fifth from Shakespeare's play, in his public speech: "Those who stay in their beds this Saturday morning will curse themselves they are not here" (McEwan 2005, p. 125). On the way back home, Perowne once more gets exposed to silent news inside his car while passing by a television shop, and "his attention is caught" by the identical image on the numerous screens: the close-up sight of the Prime Minister's mouth, which is zoomed in as if people need to test if he is lying or not when he has asserted in the past that "if we knew as much as he did, we too would want to go to war" (p. 141). The multiplicity of the TV screens showing the current news is indicative of the inescapable invasion of the private by the public, local by the global. This image reminds him of a memory when he had met the Prime Minister of the time, Tony Blair, at the opening party of the Tate Modern. Followed by a group of journalists, the politician had come to meet Perowne and expressed his admiration for his work, only to learn a few minutes later that he was making a mistake by assuming Perowne to be an artist, yet failing to acknowledge his mistake in front of the public and the media. Relaying this memory after his exposure to the manifold screens, Perowne re-evaluates the possibility of the Prime Minister's mistaken treatment of international politics by supporting the war, and seeks, on the screen, a sign of the same facial expression of hesitancy as he had witnessed in the politician's face before: "Henry looks out for an awareness of the abyss, for that hairline crack, the moment of facial immobility, the brief faltering he privately witnessed. But all he sees is certainty, or at worst a straining earnestness" (p. 145). In his diagnostic look at Blair, the doctor assumes a general and all-knowing stance, certainly doubting the politician's treatment of the international affairs and seeking a sign of self-awareness in his face. However, it is Perowne himself who hesitates, not the politician, in reaction to the war; he recognizes "his own ambivalence as a form of vertigo, of dizzy indecision" (p. 141).

Benjamin deals with the urban shopping centers in *The Arcades Project* (1999), paying attention to the allure they create to attract wanderers, or *flâneurs*, who move quickly from one shop window to another. Such consumption spaces are evoked in *The Arcades Project*, in the passage quoted from the *Illustrated Guide to Paris* (1852):

> These arcades, a recent invention of industrial luxury, are glass-roofed, marble-panelled corridors extending through whole blocks of buildings, whose owners have joined together for such enterprises. Lining both sides of the corridors, which get their light from above, are the most elegant shops, so that the arcade is a city, a world in miniature, in which customers will find everything they need. (p. 15)

The novel echoes the existence of such consumption spaces in contemporary London, yet underscores the conflict between this consumerist tendency and the simultaneous global awareness that prevails in the narrative. It is Marylebone High Street, where "[t]he largest gathering of humanity in the history of the islands, less than two miles away, is not disturbing Marylebone's contentment" and "[s]uch prosperity, whole emporia dedicated to cheeses, ribbons, Shaker furniture, is protection of a sort. This commercial wellbeing is robust and will defend itself to the last" (McEwan 2005, p. 126). The protagonist seems to suggest that economic ramifications of cosmopolitanism are more visible in this street, and considered to be the harbinger of peace: "It isn't rationalism that will overcome the religious zealots, but ordinary shopping and all that it entails – jobs for a start, and peace, and some commitment to realisable pleasures, the promise of appetites sated in this world, not the next" (p. 126). This attention to the economic dimension of the globalized world has much to do with contemporary cosmopolitanism. Marylebone Street seems to epitomize what Binnie et al. call a "gentrifying neighbourhood" where "[t]he new middle and gentrifying classes are definable through their particular combination of economic and cultural capital that enables them to distinguish themselves from other classes" (2006, p. 14). The residents of Marylebone, just as Perowne himself, are sometimes "selective in [their] mercies" (McEwan 2005, p. 127), withdrawn from the concerns of ordinary cosmopolitans. What Perowne calls "the growing complication of the modern condition, the expanding circle of modern sympathy" (p. 127) is aligned, as the narrator wittily demonstrates, with the paradox prevailing in the concept of vernacular cosmopolitanism: "Not only distant peoples are our brothers and sisters, but foxes too, and laboratory mice, and now the fish. Perowne goes on catching and eating them, and though he'd never drop a live lobster into boiling water, he's prepared to order one in a restaurant" (p. 127). This nicely put analogy attests to the paradoxical self-centered inclination in the cosmopolitan idea, which is made visible in this simultaneous interest in both preserving the world and consuming its sources, or caring for spreading democracy in other parts of the world without regard to the damage that will be caused by wars under this excuse. The twenty-first-century novel's engagement with vernacular cosmopolitanism is evinced in the narrator's treatment of protestors fighting for humanity globally, but also disrespecting their local environment as well as in the revelation about "gentle Marylebone [where] the world seems so entirely at peace" because of prosperity (p. 127).

Benjamin's reflections on the condition of the *flâneur* within a city seem to be epitomized in the cosmopolitan London of *Saturday*:

> The phantasmagoria of the flâneur. The tempo of traffic in Paris. The city as a landscape and a room. The department store as the last promenade for the flâneur. There his fantasies were materialized. The flânerie that began as art of the private individual ends today as the necessity for the masses. (1999, p. 895)

This passage from *The Arcades Project* summarizes the contemporary cosmopolitan situation in which the "phantasmagoria" of the global crises haunts the individuals even in very private spaces. The indistinguishability of the local and the global is pervasive throughout the city, which in turn functions either as a public ("landscape") or a private ("room") territory. Yet, it is the consumption spaces in the city that not only the *cosmoflâneur* but also the "masses" are drawn to owing to the prevailing impact of neoliberal capitalism.

Perowne's mood changes considerably by the end: "His sense of separation from the violence of the world has been shattered and Perowne ends the book a still contented but now anxious man" (Childs 2006, p. 147). His anxiety is predominantly rooted in the fact that he fails to divorce his own quotidian life from the global menace imminent in the everyday incidents. Perowne's vulnerability does not only pertain to the personal:

> Despite the seemingly circular structure of these events, there is a discernible trajectory to Perowne's thinking in the course of the day. He moves from an initial state of contentment and reasonable complacency to a far more sombre and complex mood at the end, as he has been forced to confront the frailty of happiness, whether at the level of the personal or the global. (Foley 2010, p. 141)

As a source of his misery, he laments God's indifference to human suffering in this world; the earlier celebration of the city life has also now disappeared:

> Cities and states beyond repair. The whole world resembling Theo's bedroom. A race of extraterrestrial grown-ups is needed to set right the general disorder, then put everyone to bed for an early night. God was once supposed to be a grown-up, but in disputes He childishly took sides. Then sending us an actual child, one of His own – the last thing we needed. A spinning rock already swarming with orphans .... (McEwan 2005, p. 122)

Referring to the world and the ruthless existence in it, Perowne is pessimistic. Vacillating between different states of mind, he cannot decide whether this sense of progress must be really celebrated. In another instance, he strives to look at the city from the lenses of the scientists of the English Enlightenment, like Newton, Boyle, Hooke, Wren, and

Willis, who, he predicts, would have been "awed" upon seeing this much progress of the modern life. Yet, he remains doubtful: "Mentally, he shows it off to them: this is what we've done, this is commonplace in our time. All this teeming illumination would be wondrous if he could only see it through their eyes. But he can't quite trick himself into it" (p. 168). This style of Henry's to aspire to the vision of others is in keeping with the narrative inclusiveness in which the narrator reflects thoughts and viewpoints beyond the protagonist himself. Henry self-consciously acknowledges that "he's a realist, and can never escape" into utopian visions regarding his age (p. 168). Henry's mindset, as a result, has undergone modifying processes that culminate in his now somewhat changed approach to cosmopolitanism.

The third stage of *cosmoflânerie* helps us to distinguish between the self-absorbed attitude of the contemporary Western citizen and the inadequacy of this to create true cosmopolitan engagement. Perowne's ambivalence in terms of his cosmopolitan stance gives way to his transformation toward the end, and only then he takes this ultimate step toward vernacular cosmopolitanism.

Perowne's Transformation and the Vernacular Feelings

Marking his passage from universalist to particularist cosmopolitanism, Perowne is seen to undergo great mental transformations toward the end. Initially, unlike his daughter, Perowne does not celebrate literature for the reason that "it interests him less to have the world reinvented; he wants it explained. The times are strange enough. Why make things up? He doesn't seem to have the dedication to read many books all the way through" (p. 66). The doctor is deeply rooted in scientific explanations rather than fictional imagination. In the eyes of his daughter, he is an "unredeemable materialist" (p. 134). He hardly completes the literary readings Daisy assigns to him, and especially the magical realist writers are in stark contrast to his reading tastes and understanding. He finds it senseless that although written for adults rather than children, in these books, some "heroes and heroines were born with or sprouted wings", or "[o]thers were granted a magical sense of smell, or tumbled unharmed out of high-flying aircraft" (p. 67). For Perowne, such escapes to the supernatural are in fact "the recourse of an insufficient imagination, a dereliction of duty, a childish evasion of the difficulties and wonders of the real, of the demanding re-enactment of the plausible" (p. 68). His misconception is a result of his rationalist and universalist beliefs that the world can solely be saved by a singular cosmopolitan truth which is often informed by various totalizing thought systems. For the neurosurgeon, the "notion of Daisy's, that people can't 'live' without stories, is simply not true. He is living proof" (p. 68). However, this conviction is bound to be recanted as their own story unfolds unexpectedly.

Perowne is primarily epitomized by the priority of reason, science, brain, and progress, and as a rationalist is disconcerted in his cosmopolitan beliefs. What sets apart his position from those of his children is his rejection of the power of feelings, human interaction, and art in a general sense. He is indignant that Daisy and her professors at university consider "the idea of progress old-fashioned and ridiculous", and contrary to them, Perowne is celebrating the modern city life and the idea of progress it represents: "The street is fine, and the city, grand achievement of the living and all the dead who've ever lived here, is fine too, and robust" (McEwan 2005, p. 77). One of the lectures in Daisy's school finds "our consumerist and technological civilisation" disenchanting while Henry thinks that "[t]his is an age of wondrous machines" (p. 78). But his "spirit of aggressive celebration of the times" in which "everyone he's passing now along this pleasantly down-at-heel street looks happy enough, at least as content as he is" is later contradicted by himself: "Perhaps he isn't really happy at all, he's psyching himself up" (p. 78). Eventually, he discovers the reason for his negative feelings, acknowledging to himself that "it is in fact the state of the world that troubles him most" (p. 80).

Perowne's notion of literature is repudiated by the end of the novel where the salvation of the family is guaranteed inadvertently by the buttress of literature as Baxter, their aggressor, is neutralized when Daisy recites a poem and triggers his deep-seated emotions. Earlier that day he has insulted Baxter, with whom he is mixed up in a minor car crash on his way to the squash court, by diagnosing and mentioning his genetic illness in front of his other two friends. Perhaps, the most significant interruption of his contentment with the security of his house occurs when Baxter breaks into it for revenge in the evening, threatens Rosalind with a knife, forces Daisy to undress and read a poem she has written, and breaks his father-in-law John Grammaticus's nose. With her poet grandfather's directions, Daisy reads Matthew Arnold's "Dover Beach" instead of her own poem to the effect that Baxter, in a state of self-revelation and fascination, wants her to read again. Remembering his love for life, he is now persuaded that the doctor can help him to recover from Huntington's disease. Abandoning his encroachment on the family, he goes upstairs to the neurosurgeon's study to see the details of the recent articles about his illness. Finally, pulled down to the stairs by Theo, in an attempt to protect his father, he is wounded and faints. The family is, in the end, reunited by the dinner table after the ambulance and the police leave them alone, and discuss this scene of poem-reciting. Appreciating the poem trick by Daisy and Grammaticus, Perowne is now bound to reconsider his approach to literature. Katherine Wall (2008) suggests that Perowne recognizes, through Daisy's reciting of "Dover Beach", both that he is "human, not animal" (p. 785) and that poetry "reveals how beauty can disarm anger and incite hope" (p. 761). Perowne is incredulous for this fortuitous impact of literature: "Could it happen, is it within the bounds of the real, that a mere poem of Daisy's could precipitate a mood swing?" (McEwan 2005, p. 221). This realization incites an alternative way of seeing things on his part: "The effect of sustained focalisation through Henry, the scientist, emphasises the gulf between his way of thinking and an alternative but complementary way of knowing found through the arts" (Green 2010, p. 63). Just like his obsession to see things from others' eyes, this time he strives to hear the lines through Baxter's ears in an attempt to fathom its significance better. The immensity of the poem's reception on the part of Baxter is confirmed when he takes the book for himself with great satisfaction. It is understood by the end of the narrative that not only Baxter but also Perowne himself is not without feelings, of which the rationalist doctor accuses himself: "What weakness, what delusional folly, to permit yourself sympathy towards a man, sick or not, who invades your house like this" (McEwan 2005, p. 230). Despite regretting having given his enemy a first-aid care, the neurosurgeon cannot pass over his responsibility altogether, and fixes upon going to his hospital, upon the urgent call, to operate on Baxter. It is made clear that perhaps for the first time he is so unambiguous in his cosmopolitan attitude: "[D]espite various shifts in his attitude to Baxter, some clarity, even some resolve, is beginning to form" (p. 233). After the operation, he interacts with Baxter, in a state of disorganized thoughts, by holding his hand (p. 263). It is only when he accomplishes this human accountability that he feels "profound happiness" and "deep, muted joy": "[H]e's happier than at any other point on his day off, his valuable Saturday" (p. 258). With this ending, the narrative appears to display once more the importance of what people can do for their fellow locals first, and take a responsible step toward the problems of their immediate environment. Such human feelings are possibly evoked when Perowne understands the impact of literature for the first time in his life as he sees the alteration in Baxter's attitude toward life. Like his antagonist, he has also undergone a change which coincides with this recognition about the effect of literature on his part. His previous conviction about progress is now reconfigured in a way to acknowledge the significance of affect, empathy, and artistic creation in human life. All these shifts in his mindset and outlook trigger the steps he takes toward cosmopolitanism in its vernacular sense. Hillard points to the protagonist's final recognition: "Baxter becomes the catalyst for Perowne recognizing, if not realizing, a wider community from which he has shielded himself. The dawning sense of mutuality comes ever more insistently in the final scene of the novel" (2008, p. 192). Perhaps, Perowne opts for a form of cosmopolitanism in which he remains globally reticent, yet locally more attentive. This kind of cosmopolitanism, it is suggested, begins with small steps. This is in line with his precaution that "a culture obsessively preoccupied with global, large-scale risks and threats all too easily loses sight of the seemingly banal manifestations of violence and the individual human predisposition to harm and inflict hurt on others" (Tancke 2015, p. 39). It is as a result of this recognition that he makes a stride toward a cosmopolitan realm even if he commences with small-scale contributions.

Perowne is transformed in the end, changing his form of interaction with other people; rather than assuming a superior medical look diagnosing them from afar, he now participates in their problems. His novel attitude attests to the idea that "[t]o conceive of *flânerie* as a step towards moral cosmopolitanism requires a change in the practice of *flânerie*, namely from detached, uncommitted observation of 'the other' to more meaningful modes of interaction" (van Leeuwen 2019, p. 302). With the self-satisfaction he feels when he takes care of Baxter, he then communicates with the young African female patient, who is normally considered troublesome by the doctors, showing his understanding for her secret love for one of the assistant doctors. Coming to the end of his circularly structured day culminating in his bedroom as in the beginning, Perowne is now more concerned with how other people's problems must be handled within the community:

> No amount of social justice will cure or disperse this enfeebled army haunting the public places of every town. So, what then? [...] You have

to recognise bad luck when you see it, you have to look out for these people. Some you can prise from their addictions, others – all you can do is make them comfortable somehow, minimise their miseries. (McEwan 2005, p. 272)

Remaining in this mental state for a while, he reaches perhaps the ultimate point in his insightful and curious look at the world, and "feels himself turning on a giant wheel, like the Eye on the south bank of the Thames, just about to arrive at the highest point – he's poised on a hinge of perception, before the drop, and he can see ahead calmly" (p. 272). It is significant that his attempts to wander into others' minds and perceptions peak at the very moment he gets closer to people. His cosmopolitanism can, thus, be characterized by insight rather than activism, by tiny steps rather than great contributions to the good of humanity. His aspiration to seep into diverse worlds and lives is evinced once more as he imagines himself in the place and mental state of a doctor who lived a hundred years ago, in February 1903, and was wondering about the next century. He desires to warn this imaginary doctor against what he is to encounter:

> If you describe the hell that lay ahead, if you warned him, the good doctor – an affable product of prosperity and decades of peace – would not believe you. Beware utopianists, zealous men certain of the path to the ideal social order. Here they are again, totalitarians in different form, still scattered and weak, but growing, and angry, and thirsty for another mass killing. A hundred years to resolve. But this may be an indulgence, an idle, overblown fantasy, a night-thought [...]. (pp. 276–277)

In his pursuit to transcend into other minds and generations, Perowne is still pessimistic about the condition of the world, but retains his belief in the colossal effect of a small portion of goodness for others, a thought that reinforces his decision to persuade his family not to pursue charges on Baxter as he has little time to live because of his genetic illness. He is now engaged emotionally more than he has ever done. As Gauthier asserts, "[t]he novel illuminates a desire to empathize, to recognize its importance, and expresses an assuredness in the civilized individual's capacity for forbearance, understanding, and magnanimity" (2013, p. 8). In fact, these feelings are also necessary in a global sense. As suggested in the novel, the impact of a good behavior even on a small scale can be felt elsewhere. The novel is, thus, full of images related to healing and comforting, which are, for Foley, necessary in a world suffering from many forms of violence

(2010, p. 154). As a doctor, he seems to find alternative ways to offer his cure for the ills of the century, for the trifling problems of his fellow cosmopolitans. This local cosmopolitan ethos can widen further as the global community acts vernacularly.

By way of conclusion, this chapter accentuates that these considerations about neoliberal capitalism as well as responding to the world in its very quotidian way render McEwan's postmillennial narrative a representative of the vernacular cosmopolitan novel. In particular, the representation of city spaces in terms of narrative glocality as well as the rendering of the cosmopolitan protagonist a *cosmoflâneur* are testament to the endeavor to posit the novel within contemporary cosmopolitanism. The transformation the protagonist has gone through attests that it is the real, albeit trivial, interactions within the community, rather than the high-brow ambitions which are irreconcilable with the lived experiences of cosmopolitans, that ensure the sustainability of twenty-first-century cosmopolitanism. In the end, having lost his faith in universalist ideals, Henry steps toward a realm where he is engrossed with the local problems and people more, toward what can be described as an altruistic form of vernacular cosmopolitanism. Despite the limitedness of his engagement, it must also be acknowledged, with Perowne, that this kind of everyday cosmopolitanism can be inaugurated with tiny steps, which in turn may make a world of difference.

REFERENCES

Beaumont, Alexander. 2015. *Contemporary British fiction and the cultural politics of disenfranchisement: Freedom and the city*. Basingstoke: Palgrave Macmillan.

Beck, Ulrich. 2010. The cosmopolitan manifesto. In *The cosmopolitanism reader*, ed. David Held and Garrett Wallace Brown, 217–228. Cambridge: Polity Press.

Benjamin, Walter, and Rolf Tiedemann. 1999. *The arcades project*. Cambridge, MA and London: Belknap Press of Harvard University.

Binnie, Jon, Julian Holloway, and Steve Millington. 2006. Introduction: Grounding cosmopolitan urbanism: Approaches, practices and policies. In *Cosmopolitan urbanism*, ed. Jon Binnie, Julian Holloway, Steve Millington, and Craig Young, 1–34. London: Routledge.

Butler, Heidi. 2011. The master's narrative: Resisting the essentializing Gaze in Ian McEwan's *Saturday*. *Critique: Studies in Contemporary Fiction* 52: 101–113. https://doi.org/10.1080/00111610903380063

Calhoun, Craig. 2002. The class consciousness of frequent travellers: Towards a critique of actually existing cosmopolitanism. In *Conceiving cosmopolitanism: Theory, context, and practice*, ed. Steven Vertovec and Robin Cohen, 86–109. Oxford: Oxford University Press.

Caracciolo, Marco. 2013. Phenomenological metaphors in readers' engagement with characters: The case of Ian McEwan's *Saturday*. *Language and Literature* 22: 60–76. https://doi.org/10.1177/0963947012462948.

Childs, Peter. 2006. And now, what days are these?: *Saturday* (2005). In *The fiction of Ian McEwan*, ed. Peter Childs, 144–151. Basingstoke: Palgrave Macmillan.

Currie, Mark. 2007. *About time: Narrative, fiction and the philosophy of time*. Edinburgh: Edinburgh University Press.

Estévez-Saá, Margarita, and Noemí Pereira-Ares. 2016. Trauma and transculturalism in contemporary fictional memories of 9/11. *Critique: Studies in contemporary fiction* 57: 268–278. https://doi.org/10.1080/00111619.2015.1078765

Ferguson, Frances. 2007. The way we love now: Ian McEwan, *Saturday*, and personal affection in the information age. *Representations* 100: 42–52. https://doi.org/10.1525/rep.2007.100.1.42.

Foley, Andrew. 2010. Liberalism in the new millennium: Ian McEwan's *Saturday*. *JLS/TLW* 26: 135–162. https://doi.org/10.1080/02564710903495461.

Gauthier, Tim. 2013. 'Selective in your mercies': Privilege, vulnerability, and the limits of empathy in Ian McEwan's *Saturday*. *College Literature* 40: 7–30. https://doi.org/10.1353/lit.2013.0020.

Green, Susan. 2010. Consciousness and Ian McEwan's *Saturday*: 'What henry knows.' *English Studies* 91: 58–73. https://doi.org/10.1080/00138380903355114.

Groes, Sebastian. 2009. Ian McEwan and the modernist consciousness of the city in *Saturday*. In *Ian McEwan. Contemporary critical perspectives*, ed. Sebastian Groes, 99–114. London: Continuum.

Held, David. 2010. *Cosmopolitanism: Ideals and realities*. Cambridge: Polity Press.

Hillard, Molly Clark. 2008. When desert armies stand ready to fight': Re-reading McEwan's *Saturday* and Arnold's 'Dover Beach.' *Partial Answers* 6: 181–206.

Holland, Rachel. 2017. Reality check: Ian McEwan's rational fictions. *Critique: Studies in contemporary fiction* 58: 387–400. https://doi.org/10.1080/00111619.2017.1313720.

Horton, John, and Peter Kraftl. 2013. *Cultural geographies: An introduction*. London: Routledge.

Marcus, Laura. 2009. Ian McEwan's modernist time: *Atonement* and *Saturday*. In *Ian McEwan: Contemporary critical perspectives*, ed. Sebastian Groes, 83–98. London: Continuum.
McEwan, Ian. 2005. *Saturday*. London: Vintage.
Michael, Magali C. 2009. Writing fiction in the Post 9/11 world: Ian McEwan's *Saturday*. In *From solidarity to schism: 9/11 and after in fiction and film from outside the US*, ed. Cara Cilano, 25–51. Amsterdam and New York: Rodopi.
Root, Christina. 2011. A melodiousness at odds with pessimism: Ian McEwan's *Saturday*. *Journal of Modern Literature* 35: 60–78. Re-assessing, Breaking, Transcending Genres. https://doi.org/10.2979/jmodelite.35.1.60.
Ross, Michael L. 2008. On a darkling planet: Ian McEwan's "Saturday" and the condition of England. *Twentieth Century Literature* 54: 75–96.
Schoene, Berthold. 2010. *The cosmopolitan novel*. Edinburgh: Edinburgh University Press.
Shaw, Kristian. 2017. *Cosmopolitanism in twenty-first century fiction*. Basingstoke: Palgrave Macmillan.
Tancke, Ulrike. 2015. *Deceptive fictions: Narrating trauma and violence in contemporary writing*. Newcastle upon Tyne: Cambridge Scholars Publishing.
van Leeuwen, Bart. 2019. If we are *flâneurs*, can we be cosmopolitans? *Urban Studies* 56: 301–316. https://www.jstor.org/stable/10.2307/26621553.
Vertovec, Steven, and Robin Cohen. 2002. Introduction: Conceiving cosmopolitanism. In *Conceiving cosmopolitanism: Theory, context, and practice*, ed. Steven Vertovec and Robin Cohen, 1–22. Oxford: Oxford University Press.
Wall, Kathleen. 2008. Ethics, knowledge, and the need for beauty: Zadie Smith's *On Beauty* and Ian McEwan's *Saturday*. *University of Toronto Quarterly* 77: 757–788.
Wallace, Elizabeth K. 2007. Postcolonial melancholia In Ian McEwan's *Saturday*. *Studies in the Novel* 39: 465–480.
Wells, Lynn. 2010. *Ian McEwan*. New York: Palgrave Macmillan.

CHAPTER 4

Vernacular Cosmopolitanism, Cosmopolitan Culture, and Economics in Zadie Smith's *NW*

At the center of Zadie Smith's postmillennial cosmopolitan novel, *NW*, lies the everyday concerns of the characters residing in the northwest of London. Contrary to the privileged status of *Saturday*'s accomplished, English, white, and middle-class protagonist, *NW* bears on diversity and particularity in its portrayal of characters as well as spaces. Revolving around the life struggles, economic problems, and identity crises of four protagonists, the novel explores the issues of twenty-first-century cosmopolitanism. Not only the number of the main characters but also the narrative voices and perspectives are diverse in Smith's novel. As demonstrated in the previous chapter, in *Saturday*, the narrative mostly unfolds through the focalization of Perowne while the narrative glocality in the novel enables the inclusion of broader perspectives beyond the protagonist. In *NW*, in contrast, focalization is not limited to a unique character only as the narration alternates between various focal points as well as shifting first and third person narrators. In this sense, the novel redefines the concept of narrative glocality by comprising it in ways different from McEwan's narrative. As an example of a cosmopolitan narrative in the second decade of the twenty-first century, *NW* proves to be politically firmer and less ambivalent as well as stylistically more innovative in its response to contemporary concepts of cosmopolitan identity and communication.

© The Author(s), under exclusive license to Springer Nature Switzerland AG 2024
E. Toprak Sakız, *Culture and Economics in Contemporary Cosmopolitan Fiction*, https://doi.org/10.1007/978-3-031-44995-6_4

Class consciousness is at the center of Smith's *NW* in ways that will be unfolded below. Preoccupation with contemporary culture is highly relevant to issues of class inequalities as well as new paradigms of individualistic identity-formation involving choice-making beyond group affiliations, which also informs communicative practices of vernacular cosmopolitans in *NW*. In fact, cosmopolitan novels in the second decade of the twenty-first century incapsulate a markedly important shift in their engagement with neoliberal capitalism and globalization which loom large in world politics and global economic inequalities. As Binnie et al. put it, cosmopolitanism is "an intrinsically classed phenomenon" (2006, p. 8). "In twenty-first century London", as Carbajal states in reference to *NW*, "differences in class are all the more relevant, and characters are encouraged to think about these lines when pondering the meaning of their existence in the postcolonial metropolis" (2016, p. 86). Especially "[a]fter 2008 [when the global economic crisis peaked]", as Knepper and Deckard argue, "class, capital, and inequality re-emerged as terms of critique in public discourse" (2016, p. 12). This change can be conspicuously observed in Smith's new trajectory in *NW*, which distinguishes this novel from her earlier oeuvre. Shaw bases this propensity on Smith's renewed concentration in her fourth novel: "Although instability of ethnic identity was noticeable in *White Teeth*, identity politics in *NW* develop outside of this framework, placing an emphasis on class and personal idiosyncrasy away from collective grouping" (2017, p. 83). In this novel, Smith departs both aesthetically and thematically from her earlier work on account of her "more profound interrogations of class and identity" (Arnett 2018, p. 1).

Revolving around the intersecting lives of four inhabitants of northwest London in their mid-thirties, Zadie Smith's *NW* depicts the subtle details of urban everyday life in a non-central and diversified area of the cosmopolis that is notorious for crime and poverty. Each part in the novel mostly pertains to one of the main characters: Leah Hanwell in "visitation"; Felix Cooper in "guest"; Natalie (born Keisha) Blake in "host"; and Nathan Bogle in company with Natalie in "crossing"; and a final "visitation" where they all ironically come together, if not physically. The narrative combines a third-person narrator assuming different perspectives with occasional passages to a homodiegetic narration. The characters are of mixed origins: Leah Hanwell was born to Irish and English parents and is married to an Algerian-French hairdresser; Natalie is of Jamaican heritage with a well-off African-Italian husband and two children. Felix

Cooper is a Caribbean-descent car mechanic who was born in a poor circle of the city called Garvey House project; and Nathan Bogle, an attractive boy from Leah and Natalie's secondary school called Brayton. Nathan flees from Kilburn in the penultimate part as he turns out to be complicit in Felix's murder. Natalie unwittingly accompanies him in the walk of "crossing" across NW as she herself seeks emancipation from her carefully fabricated life of socioeconomic superiority through her choice of profession as a barrister and an advantageous marriage. The once best friends, Leah and Natalie, despite their diverged life paths due to their pursuit of different careers, incompatible lifestyles and husbands with different backgrounds, come together in the last part; yet, both being dissatisfied with their private lives for different reasons, they fail to share secrets, empathize, and truly connect with each other. Leah conceives without her husband's knowledge with the pills stolen from Natalie's bathroom; Natalie seeks sexual adventures with couples unknown to her by using a fake e-mail address KeishaNW@gmail.com, which in fact reveals her true identity. When her infidelity is found out by her husband, she leaves home and traverses the streets of her area, momentarily thinking of suicide and eventually making her way to Leah's house. In this encounter, the one thing that seems to reconnect them is their search of justice for Felix by calling the police as Natalie is suspicious that Nathan has been involved in the murder. NW's locals' concerns are less collective than personal even if they share certain common aspirations and problems. All of the protagonists in the novel struggle for economic welfare and a respectable life and home.

These renegotiated notions of communication and identity in the novel bring to the fore the individual rather than the group although this may seem contradictory to the idea of cosmopolitanism. However, as Shaw rightly puts it, "[t]he localised focus of *NW* demonstrates that although cosmopolitanism is a global-cultural theory, it is intrinsic to ordinary encounters. [… It] concentrates on individual ethics, rather than the actions of collective groups" (2017, p. 98). Implicated in this idea is the acceptance of an individual's primacy over, and relative independence from, an ethnically or racially demarcated group in the endeavor to grasp cosmopolitanism as it is experienced on a daily basis. The emphasis is on the individuals', rather than the groups', cosmopolitan problems. In other words, the vernacular cosmopolitan novel focuses on the individualistic predicaments of the characters which are predominantly posed by economic forces and class divides, contrastingly deemphasizing the problems raised out of belonging to a particular group while not totally ignoring their persistence in a multi-ethnic and multi-racial community. David Hollinger proclaims, as summed up by Vertovec and Cohen, that "cosmopolitanism makes a decisive break with the celebration of 'communities of descent' in favour of individual choice and multiple affiliations", and it "assumes complex, overlapping, changing and often highly individualistic choices of identity and belonging" (2002, p. 18). Cosmopolitans cannot be reductively defined in terms of bearing the characteristics of a particular group, be it racial or ethnic, and living happily in tolerance and interconnection with other groups; rather they make their own malleable choices in the construction of not only their identity but also their community. Smith's cosmopolitan world in *NW* foregrounds agents with their own individualistic choices rather than "communities of descent" that can be clustered into smaller units of belonging. To put it differently, it is characters themselves in *NW*, not their groupings, that inform their own subjectivity through self-fashioning. Each and every subject, thus, resists simple categorization, often clashes with her / his fellow cosmopolitans in terms of self-interests and priorities. Contrary to universalist and unifying ideals of cosmopolitanism, in vernacular cosmopolitanism everyday problems experienced by local people, especially ones pertaining to cultural communication and class become the focus of attention. *NW* is, thus, a narrative "about being local, about a turn away from [universalist] cosmopolitan versions of migrancy" (Procter 2003, p. 126). Differently from multiculturalism where living in diversity, notwithstanding its difficulties, is celebrated, cosmopolitanism is divorced from discourses of otherness and cultural abyss in favor of promoting ideas of ordinary and everyday difference. As Shaw maintains, "Smith's realistic approach to contemporary urban life similarly involves [Gilroy's idea of] conviviality without resorting to a naive or utopian perception of cultural relations" (2017, p. 68). This positions *NW* in contrast to *White Teeth*'s motto that hails the future as "perfect", as Shaw claims: "Rather, the novel imagines a future imperfect, as citizens negotiate a fragile day-to-day existence in an atmosphere of conflict, diversity and socioeconomic discord" (2017, p. 100). Everyday diversity characterizing the novel is premised on the idea of class divides rather than other forms of difference, which are nonetheless acknowledged to exist, yet accepted as ordinary.

Cultural Communication in Vernacular Cosmopolitanism

Cultural communication and the need to connect with the locals are at the root of *NW*, which "encompasses the author's perennial preoccupation with the ethics of connection, which is thematized through the friendship at the center of the novel, as well as the protagonists' irresistible entanglement with others, even total strangers, within the urban coordinates of the text" (López-Ropero 2016, p. 127). The novel entails an understanding of a community predicated on communication and connection: "*NW* suggests that Gilroy's convivial society is only possible with Forsterian, interpersonal connections" (van Amelsvoort 2018, p. 419). Yet, it must be also noted that the novel, despite gesturing toward "the Forsterian imperative – 'Only connect!'" as David Marcus (2013) puts it, is "far from any real human connection" (p. 67). *NW*, for this reason, can be said to engender an interrogating response to the notion of cosmopolitan communication, going beyond universalist conceptions of community in favor of "more local, more empowering connections", which nonetheless remain disputable (2013, p. 67). In the same vein, "*NW* is less optimistic about the efficacy of a harmonious relationship between disparate and often contesting positions; its residing model of societal connection being local networks of friends while at the macro level, the world remains 'cross hatched'" (Bentley 2018, p. 740).

The novel's engagement with non-elite forms of vernacular cosmopolitanism underpins the very convulsion of cooperation and connectivity within this parochial community. The main characters of the novel struggle to procure a better life outside the working-class council estate house, Caldwell, in which they spent their earlier years. Yet, despite retaining their ties to their rooted identities, they are both inside and outside this community with partial existence and limited mutuality. At the root of their failure to connect is the economic forces of neoliberal capitalism which inflicts human isolation and feelings of self-seeking. In vernacular cosmopolitanism, not only the privileged groups and individuals, but also the non-elite are accorded the name cosmopolitan. It is their local lives around which the narrative revolves rather than some elite cosmopolitans' experiences with broader scope for global mobilization. In this sense, these ordinary inhabitants of northwest London seem to respond to cosmopolitanism in their own particular ways as they are located, if not centralized, within a twenty-first-century globalized world of a metropolitan London. *NW* denounces narratives of London without reference to these working-class locals who share the city spaces and the problems posed by them certainly more deplorably. There is always a sense of "distance" in the concept of cosmopolitanism, as Tomlinson puts it, which refers to "the remoteness, in terms of cultural experience and perception, of global issues and cosmopolitan outlook from the everyday life world of ordinary people" (2002, p. 243). This distance is most visible in the parochial circumstances in which working-class cosmopolitans grapple with their own problems on a daily basis, which are unknown to the elite. The principle of "egalitarian individualism" which, according to Held, presupposes equal worth and dignity among the cosmopolitan agents (2010, p. 69) is contested in the novel, where it is acknowledged by Leah's husband and widely shared by others that "not everyone can be invited to the party. Not this century" (Smith 2013, p. 3) as the narrator asserts. This is because, as Binnie et al. aver, cosmopolitanism is "classed in multiple ways" (2006, p. 9), and certain classes remain unincorporated in such divisive communities. What follows from this is the manifestation that cosmopolitan communication in the local spaces of the novel departs from utopian ideals of equality and empathy.

As the four characters make a passage into adult life, their life choices operated by economic forces mold their cosmopolitan experiences as well as relationships. The first part, "visitation", is mostly focalized through Leah Hanwell during her pursuit of her daily communal work and mutuality in relationship with others. Expectations of cosmopolitans differ considerably both from each other and the configuration authorities foist upon them. The working-class cosmopolitans in *NW* fail to conform to Margaret Thatcher's definition of success for her citizens: "Anyone over the age of thirty catching a bus can consider himself a failure" (p. 45). Definitely evoking a conception of elite cosmopolitanism, this definition fails to acknowledge the non-elite of the city. This reference to class consciousness is reminisced by Leah as she and her mother take the bus to Kilburn tube. Leah's mother further remembers Thatcher's quote from the front page of *Mail*: "Today this is Brent. Tomorrow it could be Britain!" (Smith 2013, p. 45). This can be explicated in the following way: "The implication is clear. Brent, the borough in which Kilburn and Willesden Green are located, is somehow outside Britain, "elsewhere," and not part of the national or city narrative" (Slavin 2015, p. 100). It is this marginalization of the narrative's space that is challenged in the novel. This national memory inscribed in the city spaces of London makes Leah confront her own parochial cosmopolitan longings, those of "emerging into a more gentle universe, parallel to our own, where people are fully and intimately known to each other" (Smith 2013, p. 45). Leah seeks cosmopolitan communication and intimacy within the local working-class society she resides in. The sharp contrast between these two cosmopolitan conditions and ideals, one belonging to Thatcher and the other to Leah, is manifested as the contradistinction between elite and non-elite perceptions.

Leah appears to be the most vernacularly engaged cosmopolitan character in the novel, yet even she is unable to sustain local communication notwithstanding her empathetic approach to her fellow cosmopolitans. Bauman (1998) draws attention to the ephemerality of today's communities primarily because "inner-community communication has no advantage over inter-communal exchange, if *both* are instantaneous" (p. 15). An example of inner-community or local communication takes place when Leah interacts with Shar, a local woman ringing Leah's doorbell to convey her invented story of an ill mother and obtain money to be able to fetch her to hospital, but in fact she is trying to find means to buy drugs. Leah gives her money, invites her, in and talks to her about several topics including their old friends from Brayton when it turns out that they have gone to the same local school. In keeping with her dream of a community where people are "intimately known to each other" (Smith 2013, p. 45), Leah brings up several "local" topics in an attempt to communicate with Shar, who in turn lacks a genuine interest. Shar can become involved at one point in the conversation, yet only temporarily, when Leah points with her finger at the house she was born in: "For a second, this *local* detail holds Shar's interest. Then she looks away, […] she is traumatized, or distracted" (p. 13; emphasis added). The omniscient narrator has a propensity toward the word "local", a concept which is brought to close attention throughout the novel. Despite the locality of the interaction, there is a long way to go for the attainment of connectivity.

Leah's occupation is aligned with her cosmopolitan sensibilities, too; she works "[f]or a good cause"; the charity group she works with "hand out money. From the lottery, to charities, non-profits – small local organizations in the community that need …" (p. 12). What follows from this incomplete sentence of Leah's is the narrator's comment that "[t]hey are not listening to their own conversation" (p. 12). The narrative is imbued with such narrative clues about how the mutual acts of speaking and listening often keep failing. Yet, Leah seeks minor signs of mutuality like "a look of neighbourly sympathy" by Shar (p. 12). Leah's yearning for connectivity with her local territory is made obvious by the narrator: "Leah is as faithful in her allegiance to this two-mile square of the city as other people are to their families, or their countries" (p. 6). Emphasis on the relation between locality and the need for attachment is evident in this narratorial comment. Shar also gives her credit for Leah's hospitality: "You the only one let me in. Rest of them wouldn't piss on you if you was on fire" (p. 13). Leah's attempts to stick to local allegiances characterize her as a vernacular cosmopolitan, reminiscent of Perowne's final transformation into one who believes in the unimaginable impact of even a tiny amount of goodness. Like the neurosurgeon, Leah begins with helping a disadvantaged local fellow in the conviction that communal good can only be guaranteed by small steps of intercourse.

The narrative wrestles with the idea of communication, be it either in a larger sense of cosmopolitan society or within an insular circle of a family. Unlike the Perownes, who exceptionally enact very successful interfamilial interaction, Leah's family fails to cooperate in many respects. Two discrepant non-elite citizens of NW, Leah and Michel, come together in matrimony despite their differences. Leah is white, born in the city, and more educated whereas Michel is black, country-born, and practicing his less learned occupation as a hairdresser; yet, these are "small" differences according to the narrator: "They were married before they noticed many small differences in background, aspiration, education, ambition. There is difference between the ambitions of the poor of the city and the poor of the country" (p. 23). In this comment, there is no mention of ethnic or racial difference at all, which is rendered ordinary in vernacular cosmopolitanism. Class consciousness, on the contrary, is evinced to be a forcing element of communal interactions. Their state of economic hardship is one thing that they have in common in spite of their differing response to this predicament. Michel longs for social upheaval, dreaming of quitting the poor lodging they inhabit, hence the identity they are obliged to assume accordingly. What Leah desires more, in contrast, is communicational satisfaction within her local circle, leading to a more cosmopolitan subjectivity. However, she too can be observed to be enmeshed in "us-against-them" discourses according to her husband (p. 90) because she is "a snob" although she complains that it is not her, but Natalie's snobbishness that puts a barrier between herself and her best friend. In fact, it is Natalie's upward transposition to middle class that separates the two school friends. Michel aspires to move "forward" like Natalie, and feels assured in the process that they actually make progress: "Things change! We're getting there, no?" (p. 24). Michel's progress-seeking mindset is a testament to the fact that working-class cosmopolitans possess their own particular needs and ambitions that are characterized by socioeconomic mobility. Communication as well as its failure are predominantly based on such socioeconomic relations.

Cultural communication and identity, implicated within each other, are underlying themes that are directly addressed by the narrative through its engagement with global economic realities. Unlike Leah, Michel emerges as a working-class cosmopolitan with ambitions of moving forward, separating himself from other people: "I'm always moving forward, thinking of the next thing. People back home, they don't get me at all. I'm too advanced for them. So when they try to contact me, I don't let this" (p. 29). Distancing himself from his countrymen, he also aspires to an identity which is premised on his individualistic choices rather than communal identifications. He looks forward to "going up the ladder", moving house to avoid the humiliation caused by the sign "*Brent Housing Partnership*" (p. 29) in front of his current house estate, thereby upgrading his status in the society. He articulates his wish to bring up a son somewhere else, to make him "live *proud*" (p. 29; emphasis in original). With the conviction that one can self-fashion one's identity through life choices, Michel longs for a different life from his current one. Leah's self-construction does not comply with her husband's urge for rearing a child in a respectable dwelling. This is evident in "Leah's compulsive termination of her subsequent pregnancies, in itself revealing a wish for deferral of her identity's formation" (Carbajal 2016, p. 81). The couple cannot form a communal "we" as their sense of self does not comply with each other. Furthermore, experiencing identical economic problems does not arouse senses of empathy or tolerance in the neighborhood. Michel looks down on the Jamaicans neighboring their estate, chiding them for not having "curtains" (Smith 2013, p. 30). Indeed, it is his need to distance himself from an attachment to such poverty-stricken fellow citizens, and from an identity constructed relatedly.

"We need attachments", Hall (2002) asserts, "but each person can have a variety, a multiplicity of these at their command. They need to stand outside them, to reflect on them and to dispense with them when they are no longer necessary" (p. 27). Hall's contentions on cultural identity reflect Natalie's willingness to opt out of her former attachments.

Natalie Blake, like others, desires to pursue her own aspirations, most of which she has partly fulfilled. Despite her analogous background with Leah due to sharing the same school and neighborhood, Natalie now leads a middle-class life as a barrister in the commercial sector with her banker husband, a life that can be regarded as accomplishment and socioeconomic ascendancy. What sets them thus apart is indeed their discrepant positioning in response to globalization; as part of "some multi-national company", Natalie is reluctant to listen to "Leah's self-righteous, ill-informed lectures about the evils of globalization" (Smith 2013, p. 271). Glad to be invited to a party in Natalie's Victorian house with fine decoration, Michel aspires to such a lifestyle that embodies his own desires. His attempts at conversing with Natalie's friends is embarrassing for Leah, who is more aware of the artificiality of this communication and Natalie's inattentive attitude, noticing her tapping her finger on the table and looking at the sky as she speaks; thus, Leah finds it "humiliating being the cause of so much abject boredom in [her] oldest friend" as well as being "reduced to bringing up these old names and faces in an attempt to engage her" (p. 64). Leah fails to engage Natalie, who now comes to represent the cosmopolitan elite with an indifferent attitude toward her fellow locals. This keeps disillusioning her old friend Leah, who comes to see her as a "bourgeois existence" (p. 68). Class difference informs the relationship between Leah and Natalie. This lack in empathy and tolerance dominates the connection between old close friends, and hinders the sustenance of inner-communal cosmopolitan communication. This is because northwest London, the novel's only setting, functions "as a microcosm for the kaleidoscopic transnationalism of the twenty-first century, interrogating the difficulties in practicing the cosmopolitan ideals of empathy, tolerance and belonging" (Shaw 2017, p. 70). As claimed here, the novel goes beyond such a universalist understanding of cosmopolitanism, paving the way to engage with the particularist forms of the concept in contemporary London.

Vernacular cosmopolitanism is more attentive to the particular sufferings of local people than universalist discourses of the concept. It shows what exactly it means to be a citizen of a twenty-first-century cosmopolis; seemingly, the world is a whole; nevertheless, as local cosmopolitans, people are alone in the face of problems accelerated by globalism. Felix Cooper, another vernacular cosmopolitan, is introduced in the section titled "guest". With similar aspirations of social climbing to Michel's, he, nonetheless, ends up in a tragic death, one briefly referred to at the time of the TV news in the previous section. Felix is alone, too, even when he tries to promote cosmopolitan cooperation on the underground, asking the two colored young men to let the white pregnant woman take the seat occupied by them. Despite appreciating Felix's humanistic attitude, other passengers do no more than give mere escapist looks of approval as he is being bullied by the two young men:

> No one looked – or they looked so quickly their glances were detectable. Felix felt a great wave of approval, smothering and unwanted, directed towards him, and just as surely, contempt and disgust enveloping the two men and separating them, from Felix, from the rest of the carriage, from humanity. (Smith 2013, p. 168)

This resonates with Tim Butler's assertion that a middle-class Londoner "values the presence of others [...] but chooses not to interact with them" (2003, p. 2484). Felix attains instantaneous interaction, though a silent one, with the community, which posits him in a cosmopolitan state of mind. This momentary and insidious cooperation comes at the expense of his life, though; the two men follow him into the Kilburn Station, where they rob him and stab him to death. His end sweeps all the temporary optimism about the emergence of communication and cooperation in the novel.

It must be accentuated once more that "Smith's depiction of the crafting of the self, of processes of subject-formation and self-transformation [...] are central to this novel" (López-Ropero 2016, p. 126). Like other characters, Felix also seeks self-advancement through changing the way to earn his living by quitting drug-dealing and replacing his xenophobic and middle-aged girlfriend with a socially and professionally successful one called Grace. As an ex-drug addict and seller, he now yearns for transformation and mobility in his life, giving up "dwelling" in his previous affiliations. He now looks forward to moving ahead: "People can spend their whole lives just *dwelling*. [...] I done that. Now it's time for the next level. I'm moving up in the game and I'm ready for it" (Smith 2013, p. 158). His rejection of stability can be observed in his shifting choices of relating to others. In other words, choices of affiliations indeed represent the attempt to define his sense of self. Felix breaks up with his ex-girlfriend Annie, an aged, white, alcoholic woman in favor of a financially independent, strong young woman in her twenties. Grace's promoted position at work allows her to interact with people on a daily basis whereas Annie avoids cosmopolitan encounter in entirety. Indeed, she is disturbed by multiculturalism, loathing different nationalities, such as the Norwegian sub-agent who is sent by her landlord to make her contribute to the costs in the apartment block as well as the neighboring happily-married couple of Japanese and French origins. She never leaves home in the fear of interpersonal communication: "she was afraid of what might happen between her and the other people" (p. 147). Her defiance for openness toward others distances Felix from Annie because he is well-aware that only with Grace can he move further.

The conflict between different groups is a matter of a socio-cultural gap and "a set of insurmountable cultural differences" rather than a racist white/black dichotomy: "Rather than being based on supposed biological differences, 'racism without race' adopts a culturalist logic" (van Amelsvoort 2018, p. 428). The confrontation between working-class cosmopolitans and elite ones is the main conflict in many local settings throughout London, which makes it "impossible to speak of coexistence" (2018, p. 428). Felix's meeting with Tom Mercer, a young white man who is selling his old car, exemplifies such cultural conflicts and prejudices as Tom assumes the other man's identity stereotypically as a drug-seller as Felix also complains that he has an invisible tattoo on his forehead: "PLEASE ASK ME FOR WEED" (Smith 2013, p. 132). Another difference is that Tom is globally minded contrary to Felix's localism; his occupation is "more about the integration of luxury brands into your everyday consciousness" (p. 123) while Felix works at a local specialist garage in Kilburn. In other words, Tom serves, and benefits from globalization, promotes worldwide luxury merchandise, hence the global flow of capital. Felix, on the other hand, with restricted means to earn his living, is not only a victim of globalization but also of a society where cosmopolitan ethics fail to sustain.

Vernacular cosmopolitanism that has something to do with class-based pursuits and aspirations, thus, designates less a global transposition of elites than a glocalized and socio-culturally unfixed positioning of non-elite cosmopolitans who, in Hall's words, "'live a global life' by *necessity*" (cited in Werbner 2008, p. 18; emphasis in original). This necessity, in turn, engenders a community in which individuals' economic problems outgrow their cosmopolitan feelings of empathy, tolerance, and communication. To put it briefly, the novel is characterized by vernacular cosmopolitanism with its direct engagement with material as well as emotional needs and concerns of non-elite cosmopolitans, departing from discourses of universalism embodied in notions of tolerance for difference and cooperation.

NARRATIVE GLOCALITY: COSMOPOLITAN SPACES IN *NW*

Glocality is a concept closely associated with the idea of space, and requires a spatial approach. Just as *Saturday*'s spatial focus, the title of *NW*, a postcode referring to the northwest of London, makes it obvious that it is space itself that is foregrounded, and viewed as constitutive of community as well as identity, in the novel. The novel's treatment of space complies with what Binnie et al. suggest: we need to "investigate how cosmopolitanism is formed and reformed in particular locales and everyday spaces" (2006, p. 12) precisely because "it is through spaces of (in particular) the city that we need to generate an understanding of how [the] key issues of class, commodification and the everyday intersect with, produce and reveal the attitudes and practices of cosmopolitanism" (2006, p. 13). In this sense, the engagement with everyday city spaces emerges as a narrative strategy in the cosmopolitan novel to understand such central issues as class and commodification which loom over the contemporary concept of vernacular cosmopolitanism.

The concept of glocality represents space as globally shaped and vernacularly specified, hence oriented toward, and premised on, the global and the local simultaneously. The narrative of the local opens up to the global, embarking on the characters' immediately lived experiences and moving up to the glocal perception as the narrative proceeds. In *NW*, the glocal space, northwest London, is reconfigured by globalization impacting on the very parochial lives of locals. Cosmopolitanism is closely affiliated with the concept of globality, which in turn invites contemporary citizens to participate in an endless act of consumerism. The commodification of culture as everything else is discernible in the portrayal of the city spaces in *NW*. A narratorial journey throughout this local area of London is relayed in the form of photographic images, providing a vision of locality dominated by transnational media and banks, citizens of discrepant ethnic backgrounds as well as commodification and consumerism. The first vision is a vernacularized picture of cultural specificities with the "[s]weet stink of the hookah, couscous, kebab, exhaust fumes of a bus deadlock" (Smith 2013, p. 40). Following a momentary image of these ordinary flavors of the city comes another cosmopolitan picture, that of the media: "Polish paper, Turkish paper, Arabic, Irish, French, Russian, Spanish, *News of the World*" (p. 40). Banks from diverse nations are also rendered an everyday part of the cosmopolitan atmosphere: "Bank of Iraq, Bank of Egypt, Bank of Libya" (p. 40). Everybody and everything transnational exist side by side in the city, and they are engaged in acts of consumption. The narrative makes references to a bulk of merchandise, such as "a battery pack, a lighter pack, a perfume pack, sunglasses, three for a fiver, a life-size porcelain tiger, gold taps" (p. 40), which represent London as a consumption space. The commodification of the English language and culture is also portrayed as the narrator passes by ads, such as "learn English" (p. 40) and "English as a second language" (p. 41) alongside other purchasable goods and services. This local vision of vernacular cosmopolitan life has nothing in common with the global debates in the media: "Bearing no relation to the debates in the papers, in Parliament" (p. 40). It is, thus, made clear that the universalist orientation of cosmopolitan thinking fails to take into consideration the more parochial and everyday cosmopolitanism of local territories of the cosmopolis. Yet, it is through narrative glocality that the local experiences in which vernacular cosmopolitans are far from embracing universal ideals are made visible. By drawing on Žižek's idea of "the parallax Real", Nick Hubble and Philip Tew (2016) argue that the depiction of London in this section is suggestive of

> the very liminality of London along these parallax gaps of economy, finance, past, future, home, workplace, country and city, and by doing so, radically refocuses the media images that have come to dominate representations of London in order to reveal glimpses of another London, which remains resistant to appropriation. (p. 8)

NW's London can, in this vein, be regarded as the "Real" London with its very realities confronted on a daily basis.

NW renders space vernacularly specified with the employment of narrative glocality in London. Like the widening focal lenses in *Saturday*, the narrator goes on to look at the distant situations which are not available to the protagonist otherwise. This narrative strategy also works in par with what Schoene calls "an elaborate compositeness", which is a way of viewing the world through a Nancean kaleidoscope, thereby constantly creating a composite picture of the world (2010, p. 98). This also mimics the filmic techniques of shifting angles of vision as the camera alternates among various scenes. In contradistinction to the local northwest London, the narrator discerns another composite picture of the world, zooming her unseen camera in. If you turn to the eastern part of the metropole and dream of the life there, in a private clinic, you can see through the lenses of the omniscient narrator the "united" cosmopolitans, yet more privileged ones: "[t]he Arabs, the Israelis, the Russians, the Americans" (Smith 2013, p. 41). Their aspirations are quite different from the non-elite cosmopolitans of the west: "If we pay enough, if we squint, Kilburn need not exist" (p. 41). Here is presented a contrasting idea which marks a subtle hint at the self-interest of the elite cosmopolitans. This short reference to elite cosmopolitanism that exists elsewhere in the city is set against the realities of non-elite versions of cosmopolitanism that predominates northwest London, where you can face unfavorable scenes like the school where the headmaster is stabbed, shops that can unlock your (stolen) phone as well as ones that offer you help with a "hundred and one ways to take cover" (p. 40), and where such illegalities are revealed as ordinary. In this sense, universalist cosmopolitanism does not pay enough attention to the particular experiences of less privileged cosmopolitans like those that inhabit the glocal spaces. "An integral part of the globalizing processes" as Bauman (1998) puts it, "is progressive spatial segregation, separation and exclusion. […] A particular cause for worry is the progressive breakdown in communication between the increasingly global and extraterritorial elites and the ever more 'localized' rest" (p. 3). The locale of northwest London is, thus, the focus of narrative glocality in the novel's attempt to manifest such "globalizing processes".

In Smith's work, there is a confluence between the global and the local, a status which informs the novel's glocality, the status of interpenetration of the two concepts in the narrative space. The employment of narrative glocality in the novel bears some affinities with *Saturday* in that in both novels, perspectives provided by the protagonists or the narrators broaden in order to make it possible to incorporate many viewpoints other than theirs. Even while we see things through the lens of Leah, for example, the narrator introduces, through free indirect discourse, other opinions which transcend those of the focalizing character. Hence, in *NW*, the narrative focus of attention is glocal due to the modernist-like wandering consciousness and more global political engagement. In this roaming narrative activity, multifarious and often conflicting visions and perspectives are equally and subsequently shared by the narrator. Another parallelism between the two novels lies in their stylistic propensity toward modernist narrative techniques, chief among them is stream of consciousness. *Saturday*'s a-day-in-life narrative evokes associations with Woolf's *Mrs Dalloway* while Smith's *NW* has undertones of another modernist masterpiece, Joyce's *Ulysses*, especially the part called "Aeolus". Yet, the miscellaneous representation of London in both postmillennial novels outplays that of their modernist precursors through their employment of narrative glocality. "In the face of catastrophe", Knepper argues, "the modernist quest for a new aesthetics responding to war, revolution, terror and global economic crisis seems highly relevant once more" (2014, p. 111). However, this renewed form of modernist experimentalism responds to global threats more forcefully. McEwan's protagonist dives deep into others' minds and perspectives with his aspiration to know everything about them. On the contrary, the lives of Smith's characters are imbued with their insurmountable secrets, a tenet that attests to the assertion that in *NW* "the emphasis is on the withholding of information while foregrounding experimental modes of writing" (Wells 2014, p. 98). This divergence accounts for their different forms of narrative glocality. *NW*'s narrator adds a new technique which becomes more effective in dealing with antitheses existing within cosmopolitan diversity: the reiterative use of a keyword. Certain cosmopolitan catchwords, like "everybody", "empathy", and "local", are employed by the narrator in repetition to the effect that the reader's attention is drawn to them while their meanings are, beyond surface level, put into dispute.

Narrative glocality begins with the specific and moves towards the general. The short one-and-a-half-page part depicting the streets Leah passes through is shown with the constantly shifting scenes of narrative glocality in which the narrator reprises one of the catchwords of cosmopolitan thought in order to challenge its underlying meanings. Notwithstanding the prevalence of difference, homogenization among the citizens of the metropole is embodied in the recurring word "everybody", a narratorial sign that emerges reiteratively in this depiction of cosmopolitanism; it recurs many times as a pattern to emphasize the common propensity among the cosmopolites toward acts of consumption: "Everybody loves fags. Everybody;" "Everybody loves fried chicken. Everybody;" "Everybody loves sandals. Everybody;" "Everybody loves the Grand National. Everybody" (Smith 2013, p. 40). The representation of the cosmopolitan city resonates with what Binnie et al. calls "the production of cosmopolitan space": "Contemporary urban governance is focusing upon the production of commodified spaces of alterity and difference which, [...] potentially result in a homogenisation and domestication of difference" (2006, p. 18). It is also difference itself that is commodified, and the consumption of everything by "everybody" culminates in the sameness of consumers' habits as well as the uniformity of consumption spaces. In this sense, this cosmopolitan "everybody" is less a universal community of shared values than a mass of random city dwellers who come together merely in their economic cravings and consumptive activities.

Narrative glocality also shows that city spaces are in sharp contrast to each other, which manifests the discrepancy between the territories inhabited by the elite and non-elite cosmopolitans. Even though the protagonists are positioned within non-elite cosmopolitan territories, like Willesden, Kilburn, and Caldwell Estate, the passing comment by the narrator indicates that elsewhere there exist more advantageous versions of cosmopolitanism lived in corporational offices of London: "Elsewhere in London, offices are open plan/floor to ceiling glass/sites of synergy/wireless/gleaming. There persists a belief in the importance of a ping-pong table" (Smith 2013, p. 31). Leah's office is the stark opposite of such elite spaces, rather fitting the latter definition: "Here is not there. Here offices are boxy cramped Victorian damp. Five people share them, the carpet is threadbare, the hole-punch will never be found" (p. 31). This non-profit organization office is also a local cosmopolitan area where diversity is made ordinary: it is shared by middle-aged women of color from St Kitts, Trinidad, Barbados, Grenada, Jamaica, India, and Pakistan. Leah is the only white woman there, and this fact (that she is white) is pointed out by the narrator, not the contrary; being black is not marginalized here. In fact, in the novel, "race is not the crucial factor, nor is it ever truly the point. Indeed, in *NW*, Smith deliberately only describes the race of the white character, subverting the way that race is normally portrayed in fiction" (Gerzina 2017, p. 49). Therefore, it is Leah herself—the white, university graduate, young woman—who is rendered a part of the diversified culture while blackness is not hailed, or emphasized as an integral element of describing characters.

There exist differing positions in response to the idealist cosmopolitanism, and this is explored in relation to the reiterating catchword "empathy". The word "empathy" recurs in this section that relates Leah's charity work: What is "essential for the smooth running here" is, in the words of the team leader, "relatability", "empathy", and "a personal connection" (Smith 2013, p. 32). These cosmopolitan words evoking senses of personal responsibility for the good of the community are under close examination in the narrative. From the perspective of Leah's coordinator, "[t]his work requires empathy and so attracts women, for women are the empathic sex" (p. 31). Yet the shifting perspective between this opinion of the talkative team leader and Leah's notion of empathy can be discernible in the narrative clues of actual moments when empathy disappears even in such a small group of colleagues. This ironic distance can be perceived in the discourse of the narrator, who shows the dangers of such gender stereotypes, pointing at the women in the office to make fun of Leah's cross-racial marriage, to accuse her of stealing one of their men, thus refusing to ensure local tolerance and understanding despite their assumed role in the society as the guarantor of empathy Leah laments that feelings of empathy cease to make sense even in this smallest unit of the society. The narrating voice further investigates inequalities that predicate not only Leah but also many women like her:

> Question: what happened to her classmates, those keen young graduates, most of them men? Bankers, lawyers. Meanwhile Leah, a state-school wild card, with no Latin, no Greek, no maths, no foreign language, did badly – by the standards of the day – and now sits on a replacement chair borrowed six years ago from the break room, just flooded with empathy. (p. 32)

The recurrence of the word "empathy" is a narrative strategy of interrogation. The narrator seems to challenge the idea of cosmopolitan ideals like empathy in the overwhelming existence of inequalities as Leah experiences first-hand. By doing so, the narrator also delves into another significant problem of the metropolis: education. Leah lacks career opportunities compared to her male counterparts; even with a university degree she cannot find a proper job in a proper office. In keeping with this, in reflections of her school days and her major, philosophy, she questions the meaning of her life and her education: "[W]hat was the purpose of preparing for a life never intended for her?" (p. 33). During the meeting in her office, Leah writes on a piece of paper in capital letters "I AM SO FULL OF EMPATHY" and "doodles passionately around it" (p. 33). Her passion is also indicative of the novel's attitude toward this disputed word: even though its significance is highlighted on several occasions, it is also encapsulated in a doodled box, suspected and opened up to interrogation. The narrator explores such common problems of cosmopolitan communities through these techniques of narrative glocality and the use of repetitive keywords.

The narrator passes from a local scene to a general conception through narrative glocality with the employment of shifting camera technique once more. While Leah and Michel purchase croissants from a local shop near Willesden Lane, the angle widens and presents an opinion in relation to a greater local problem. Leah's old school is a glocal space, the ironic mention of which by the narrator points at certain local problems such as lack of good educational opportunities for the working-class inhabitants of the area:

> Real croissants may be purchased from the organic market, on a Sunday, in the playground of Leah's old school. Today is Tuesday. From her new neighbours Leah has learnt that Quinton Primary is a good enough place to buy a croissant but not a good enough place to send your children. (p. 20)

As in the example of Leah's lack of equal educational opportunities, the local school where only croissants, not education, deserve praise becomes focal under the narrator's camera lenses. In cosmopolitan London, such places exist as many other problematic corners throughout the city. This picture of London fails to embrace Held's optimistic view of cosmopolitanism reflecting "the multiplicity of issues, questions, processes and problems that affect and bind people together" (2002, p. 57). Rather than connecting people, these cosmopolitan problems function as a hindrance for communal cooperation and communication.

The glocal spaces in the novel are characterized by the state of being "[u]ngentrified, ungentrifiable" (p. 48), which remain outside "the gentrifying neighbourhood", in Binnie et al.'s words, which is "[t]he inner city, where gentrified and cosmopolitan identity formations can be made and displayed, is constructed through an othering of the suburb" (2006, p. 15). This is because the novel "maps new relations to locality through a special aesthetics that registers the anxious dynamics of a globalizing neighbourhood" (Knepper 2014, p. 112). Kilburn's vision from the window of the carriage where Leah and her mother travel proves this kind of "othering": "Boom and bust never come here. Here bust is permanent" (Smith 2013, p. 48). Kilburn and Willesden stand out within the rest of the city by resisting change, progress, advancement, and gentrification. Here, the whole area is seen to have been constructed in 1880s altogether, and meant to represent "an optimistic vision" (p. 48); however, this optimism is contrasted with its current state. Despite being in sharp contrast to the city spaces in *Saturday*'s more gentrified areas of London, Smith's narrator, just as McEwan's, rebuts a too optimistic vision of the city by desisting to celebrate the idea of advancement by assuming a well-informed outlook.

The narrator also draws attention to the way in which the NW area is referred to in British literature, notably in that of the nineteenth century:

> A great hill straddles NW, rising in Hampstead, West Hampstead, Kilburn, Willesden, Brondesbury, Cricklewood. It is no stranger to the world of letters. The Woman in White walks up one side to meet the highwayman Jack Sheppard on the other. Sometimes Dickens himself comes this far west and north for a pint or to bury someone. [...] Once this was all farm and field, with country villas nodding at each other along the ridge of this hill. Train stations have replaced them, at half-mile intervals. (p. 55)

The scenery has changed since then, yet there is a sense of "othering" prevailing since the time of Dickens; marginal characters find their way into the area to cover their acts of illegality. Different from this earlier picture of the area, this stereotypical description becomes ordinary in the contemporary world of *NW*, where Smith's characters are somehow involved in crime; they steal money to afford drugs, are accused of murder, and even one of the protagonists is killed by his fellow citizens. Nonetheless, in this version of NW, such crimes are part of the everyday life of the cosmopolis, neither marginalized nor concealed. Everything happens out in the open; it is already part of everyday conversation: they talk about the gang of Ridley Avenue in Natalie's home party. Slavin, in reference to Smith's Willesden, contends that "[t]here are simply a multiplicity of voices at work, many of which are absent from the singular, neatly ordered myths of the pretty English village or prosperous London neighbourhood" (2015, p. 99). The change of English scenery in this twenty-first-century novel contrasting its classical-realist counterparts is reflected through narrative glocality.

Garvey House is another local site that is portrayed in the book *GARVEY HOUSE: A Photographic Portrait*, which is sent to Felix's father Lloyd by his girlfriend Grace as a gift. As can be evinced by the title itself, in the book, scenes and lives from the estate house appear to return in a way to claim their right to speak for themselves. Even though the publication of this book makes it globally available, the very locality on its pages brings the duality between the local and the global to the fore once more. As Felix tries to tear the cover of the gift, he catches a glimpse of his siblings from the old photo frame on television displaying them as children in Garvey House, reminding him of the very locality the family had experienced first-hand in the area, which is hard to be contained in the narrow vision provided by the book's pages. Felix sees the high price paid for the book at the back cover, and wonders if he will ever be paid for providing the story in the book: "Twenty-nine quid! For a book! And when would he get paid for it? Never" (Smith 2013, p. 107). It is certain that neither his family nor the locals are paid for this local story, which is commodified and made readable globally, yet can only be truly understood with a view to the particular experiences of the locals, like Felix and his siblings as children. The book's assured tone, its claims to "photographic" objectivity is contrasted by Lloyd's protests against its universality. Felix reads along: "This is a photographic account of a fascinating period in London's history. A mix of squat, half-way house and commune, Garvey House welcomed vulnerable young adults from the edges of" (p. 107), and his reading gets interrupted at this point by the frustrated Lloyd: "Don't read me shit I already know. I don't need the man dem telling me what I already know. Who was there, me or he?" (p. 107). He reclaims his local history, taking over the act of telling local anecdotes concerning the parochially lived lives of his fellow citizens: "I knew all of them!" (p. 108). As a reaction to the picture story, Lloyd adds some local flavor to the details in the book as photographs stir his first-hand memories, to which he thinks he can attach more meaning than the book's detached author. In an attempt to reclaim his local cosmopolitanism, he does not want it subsumed under more universal accounts of cosmopolitan citizenship.

This time, Lloyd directs his anger at his next-door neighbor, Phil Barnes, a white Englishman, who he thinks is a "fool" to talk about "The struggle!" because it is Lloyd himself that "*seen* the struggle", not his neighbor with his three-bedroom flat (p. 109; emphasis in original). From Lloyd's perspective, Barnes is not eligible to talk on behalf of the working-class cosmopolitans like Lloyd. However, in conversation with Felix, Barnes seems to be concerned with global as well as local problems. He still wears a CND badge on his waistcoat, showing his former engagement with Campaign for Nuclear Disarmament. Similarly, he also seems to be paying attention to more local matters such as the one concerning the discrimination against the "youths" in the neighborhood, against "our working-class lads" (p. 114), or "the community's kids" who the police ask after (p. 115). He posits himself along with his working-class neighbors and their children, becoming a part of this us-against-them dichotomy: "Save their big houses on the park from our kids!" (p. 115). This disagreement over who is included in and excluded from this "us" community evinces the instability of localism. Just like Lloyd, he blames his contemporaries for being unpolitical, for being only interested in having fun, hence far from being a good cosmopolitan. He asserts that "if you are interested in ideas and all that, ideas and philosophies of the past – it's very hard to find someone round here to really talk to" (p. 115). In an attempt to revoke his sense of cosmopolitanism, he declares that he "believe[s] in the people" (p. 117). Yet, his cosmopolitanism differs from Lloyd's in that each adopts a vernacularized version with diverse perspectives, unable to come to terms with each other.

Still, another glocal space is the café located outside Kilburn, where Natalie, her husband, and their couple-friends have a Sunday brunch, and contribute to the cosmopolitanism there by their local color: "They were all four of them providing a service for the rest of the people in the café, simply by being there. They were the 'local vibrancy' to which the estate agents referred" (p. 255). Like Perowne, they are exposed to the global by the media; conventionally everyone comes to brunch with their newspapers, and "[o]n the table lay a huge pile of newspaper" (p. 254). Opening a window to the global domain during a private gathering, they step out of their locally oriented mindset only momentarily: "They were all agreed that the war should not be happening. They were all against war" (p. 254). Reminiscent of Perowne's partial engagement with the impending war, this concern about the war is not long-lasting on the part of the group, remarked on there and then, only to be forgotten a few minutes later. All of a sudden, they return to their "private realm": "Only the private realm existed now. Work and home. Marriage and children. Now they only wanted to return to their own flats and live the real life of domestic conversation and television and baths and lunch and dinner" (p. 255). Their remote engagement is a testament to local cosmopolitans' opening a space for responding to the global world, but also their inability to sustain this interest due to the overwhelming impact of more immediate—both global and local—problems upon themselves. In keeping with this, the narrator states, these local characters "needn't concern themselves much with politics. They simply were political facts, in their very persons" (p. 256). Therefore, they inhabit both an awareness of the global matters and a first-hand experience of what it means to be a local: "Global consciousness. Local consciousness. Consciousness" (p. 255). This reiterative reference to the word "consciousness" functions, as in the case of previous repetitive keywords, as a way of drawing attention to, interrogating the meaning of, and by so doing creating an ironic distance in dealing with, this catchword.

Cosmopolitan Outlook of Identity

The question of identity has always been a central preoccupation in Smith's work; however, it can be claimed that her fourth novel, *NW*, lends itself to a new identity politics, diverging from her earlier celebratory account of flexible modes of agency, confirming Marcus's contention that "Smith was once more hopeful, believing in the liberating freedom of self-definition: finding solace, even empowerment, within the contradictions of twenty-first century identity". In *NW*, she seems to give the message that "[a] flexible, contingent sense of identity is no longer enough" (2013, p. 71). This disjunction in her approach to identity politics, as will be detailed below, can be explored with a view to the ways in which the novel embodies Ulrich Beck's idea of "cosmopolitan outlook" in *The Cosmopolitan Vision* (2006) and simultaneously contests the idea of freedom and flexible models of identity-making in that this outlook is "[a]n everyday, historically alert, reflexive awareness of ambivalences in a milieu of blurring differentiations and cultural contradictions. It reveals not just the 'anguish' but also the possibility of shaping one's life and social relations under conditions of cultural mixture. It is simultaneously a sceptical, disillusioned, self-critical outlook" (p. 3).

Beck's notion of "cosmopolitan outlook" occupies a central position in the section titled "host" which relates the identity-formation processes of Natalie Blake. Having asked "[w]hat do we mean, then, by the 'cosmopolitan outlook'?", Beck responds, "Global sense, a sense of boundarylessness" (2006, p. 3). The structure of this section formally reinforces this idea of "boundarylessness" by going beyond the previous sections' predominantly modernist inclinations and constructing a set of numbered and titled sub-sections or vignettes which differ in length and content reflecting Natalie's self-thoughts as well as self-formation since childhood. The "cosmopolitan outlook" has implications of self-fashioning and individual choice-making processes of identity formation on the part of postmillennial cosmopolitans. The line Leah hears on the radio at the onset of the novel echoes Natalie's self-definition: "I am the sole author of the dictionary that defines me" (Smith 2013, p. 3). The novel's structure resonates with this thematic preoccupation because the employment of such a stylistic device among many other forms of inventiveness in the novel evinces its emphasis on the theme of choice-making. This also serves another function: "Generic expectations are challenged by Smith's deployment of different text types to suit her purposes" (López-Ropero 2016, p. 132). As stated before, cosmopolitan writers feel free in their stylistic preferences so as to foreground thematic concerns. It is this section dealing with the most self-fashioned character, Natalie, that has typically sustained stylistic boundarylessness. Only when she unites with Frank, can she rise to the status of "a host", being "[n]o longer an accidental guest at the table – as she had always understood herself to be – but a host, with other hosts" (Smith 2013, p. 220), echoing the idea presented at the outset that "not everyone [is] invited to the party" (p. 3). Being a host now, she guarantees her place at the party.

Beck's conception of "cosmopolitan outlook" reverberates in the identification processes in which Natalie is involved. Out of Caldwell estates in northwest London, Keisha Blake, having transformed into Natalie De Angelis, emerges as the most ambitious, success-oriented young Black woman, and unlike many others, she really attains most of her life-goals, ending up in a profitable professional life, admirable marriage with a "perfect" husband, and a comfortable, highly sociable lifestyle. It is in fact through her choices that her identity-formation is attained; her transformation is a successful result of "a number of carefully monitored choices regarding education, career, partners, home ownership and even naming" (López-Ropero 2016, p. 130). It is true that "her process of self-invention" begins with her adopting a "less ethnic sounding" new name during her university education and choosing an "affluent and cosmopolitan Frank De Angelis" as a marital partner, as well as "devoting her career to defending the interests of corporations", an occupation devoted to the global rather than her local community (2016, p. 130). Throughout this pursuit for success, she adopts "a sense of boundarylessness" (2006, p. 4), in Beck's words, moving well beyond her restrictive surroundings in Kilburn. Her determined choices gradually transport her into her desired self-identification without knowing of any limitations: "If she climbed the boundary wall of Caldwell she was compelled to walk the entire wall, no matter the obstructions in her path" (Smith 2013, p. 180). This is exactly what she does on this hard journey because she is well-aware that "as working-class female pupils they were often anxious to get it right" (p. 234) with limited options given to them. However, she also faces the disillusionment of this transformative process even from the outset. She always keeps "wondering whether she herself had any personality at all or was in truth only the accumulation and reflection of all the things she had read in books or seen on television" (p. 187). This concern with self-knowing prevails throughout, intriguing her several times. She is also bothered, even as a child, by the gap between her "essential" and perceived self: "In the child's mind a breach now appeared: between what she believed she knew of herself, *essentially*, and her essence as others seemed to understand it" (pp. 180–181). She comes to the recognition, later in life, of "Ms Blake having no self to be", a self-thought on her part, but expressed by the omniscient narrator (p. 211). In fact, the narrator continuously reveals Natalie's worries about making sense of her own idea of self in the course of time in the form of interior monologue in the vignette titled "110. Personality parenthesis": "But for the sake of a thought experiment: what was Natalie Blake's personality constructed around?" (p. 233). Her ponderings reflect, in Beck's terminology, "self-critical outlook" (2006, p. 3). She keeps self-questioning her decisions in the making of her cosmopolitan identity.

Another aspect of the cosmopolitan outlook is "the possibility of shaping one's life and social relations under conditions of cultural mixture" (Beck 2006, p. 3). In *NW*, culture cannot be defined simplistically in terms of ethnicity and nationality; there are a number of factors that inform the decisions about cultural belonging. Class, undoubtedly, constitutes one of the most important elements of community culture, culminating, to a great extent, in mobility across diverse socio-cultural segments of the cosmopolitan society. Social relations are, thus, shaped by not only cultural but also class mixture, as in the case of Natalie Blake, who establishes her affiliations beyond her childhood friends and poor family members. Her situation also echoes Brah's theory of *diaspora space*, "where multiple subject positions are juxtaposed, contested, proclaimed or disavowed" and which is "the point at which boundaries of inclusion and exclusion, of belonging and otherness, of 'us' and 'them', are contested" (1996, pp. 208–209). Natalie's multiple social positioning as well as her vacillation between the status of the excluding and that of the excluded also marks the mutability of her indeterminate subject position.

Natalie's self-fashioning is in keeping with Beck's idea of "the logic of inclusive differentiation" to designate the rendering of contemporary forms of subjectivity (2006, p. 4). Natalie's self-change occurs within a couple of years when she is set apart from her old best friend, Leah, who represents everything to do with Caldwell and promises no improvement. Like Felix, her change of lover is in par with her yearning for social elevation; coupling with a self-confident Frank De Angelis in lieu of an economically and socially disadvantaged Rodney Banks. At first look, Frank appears as if "he was born on a yacht somewhere in the Caribbean and raised by Ralph Lauren" (p. 207). Like Natalie, her partner has also changed his original name Francesco De Angelis into a cosmopolitan name, "[u]niversally known as 'Frank'" (p. 208). Being Frank's "doppelgänger" (p. 212) as related by the narrator, indeed representing Natalie's own desires, she finds a reflection of her idealized "cosmopolitan outlook" in Frank and the life pledged by him. The narrator, sneaking into Natalie's mind, describes their relationship contrary to the mainstream conception that "[f]emale individual seeks male individual for loving relationship" (p. 230). Specifying her choice of a husband in terms of social and economic benefits, the narrator gives her character away as a self-important and classed-minded individual, yet referring to her as an impersonal "person": "Low-status person with intellectual capital but no surplus wealth seeks high-status person of substantial surplus wealth for enjoyment of mutual advantages, including longer life expectancy, better nutrition, fewer working hours and earlier retirement, among other benefits" (p. 230). The mention of a marriage in business terms as if listing a job's benefits is a testament to the novel's overall attention to class consciousness. Through this economically advantageous marriage, she takes another important step toward engrossing the boundaries of Caldwell, which in turn has implications for the construction of who she is eventually becoming. In the same vein, she values "a world governed by the principles of friendship" (p. 215) precisely because "[y]ou *choose* your friends, you don't choose your family" (p. 216; emphasis in original). Her conception of friendship is aligned with her idea of cosmopolitanism, in which it is acceptable to be ethnically diverse, but having socially and financially beneficial professions is the main requirement in this atomic community:

(I will be a lawyer and you will be a doctor and he will be a teacher and she will be a banker and we will be artists and they will be soldiers, and I will be the first black woman and you will be the first Arab and she will be the first Chinese and everyone will be friends, everyone will understand each other.) (p. 216)

This reference to community attests to the ironic distance between Natalie's idea of cosmopolitanism and that of the implied author. This parenthetical statement comes as a revelation of Natalie's viewpoint, which is tailored by her particular needs in a society where relationships, rather than biology, define subjectivity in significant ways. Her imagined community is composed of elite cosmopolitans, among which she situates herself comfortably.

Beck's idea that "[o]ne constructs a model of one's identity by dipping freely into the Lego set of globally available identities and building a progressively inclusive self-image" (2006, p. 4) resonates with Natalie's process of self-formation, which is inaugurated with a name-change that signifies her transformation from a locally enclosed Keisha Blake to a globally available Natalie De Angelis. Initially, she identifies herself with Jane Eyre in the belief that they share many commonalities in the face of being looked down on by others and emerging in their later lives as revenge-takers who deserve final happiness. Like her idealized self-image, Jane, her strengths can be characterized by "cleverness", "will-to-power", and "a sign of a superior personality" (Smith 2013, p. 185). Likewise, in the "Discourse Founders" costume party thrown by one of her friends, she turns up as Angela Davis, an American political activist of gender, race, and class issues, known for her book *Women, Race and Class*. Despite costume-dressing as a powerful social-equity advocate, Natalie herself is far from paying attention to community welfare, merely pursuing her own self-interests. Unable to get enough satisfaction from any of these identifications, Natalie is always "crazy busy with self-invention" (p. 212). It is through one's profession that one has the potential to thrive as Natalie thinks that "life [is] a problem that could be solved by means of professionalization" (p. 205).

Natalie's "quasi-cosmopolitan, but simultaneously provincial, identity" (2006, p. 4), to describe her in Beck's words, indicates an interplay between global and local forms of cosmopolitanism. In the vignette titled "Revisit", fed up with the daily commuting time to work, Natalie begins to live in a house near Caldwell, and as soon as she moves here, a sense of community calls forth. The narrative of this section introduces a repetitive pattern beginning each time with "People": "People were ill;" "People died;" "People were shameful;" "People were unseen;" "People were not people but merely an effect of language", and so on (Smith 2013, p. 251). Only in the locality of a place like Willesden do people become familiar and their life stories matter. They cease to be namelessly called "people" just as the dialog in this part specifies who these people really are; for instance, the statement "People were ill" is followed by its exemplification where the referent is Mrs Iqbal (a local woman, probably the one in *White Teeth*). It can be argued that these kinds of details show that in vernacular cosmopolitanism, local problems press so urgently that broader, yet more abstract, conceptions of cosmopolitanism do not predominate in this area, in which particular problems overweigh seemingly more important issues of the world. Back in Willesden, Natalie faces her "provincial" identity, becoming enthralled in the parochial rather than the universal.

This concept of self, on the other hand, has a "central characteristic [which] is its rejection of traditional relations of responsibility" (Beck 2006, p. 4). Natalie avoids full engagement with her former community and its people; they remain "people" for her rather than individuals with names. She also keeps a safe distance between Caldwell and her own house as the narrator acknowledges "[t]he money was for the distance the house put between you and Caldwell" (Smith 2013, p. 255). The insightful narrator also makes it apparent that Natalie makes charitable contributions to her family as well as her ancestry in the Caribbean islands not because of her innate goodness or sense of responsibility but out of "self-interest": "these good deeds were, in fact, a further, veiled, example of self-interest, representing only the assuaging of conscience" (p. 258). However, "[h]er perceived role as a new cosmopolitan subject, reintegrated into her transnational community with rediscovered humanist values, is […] questionable" (Shaw 2017, p. 92).

Beck's notion of the "cosmopolitan outlook" may seem to simultaneously promote and interrogate the possibility of boundarylessness with the implication that one is free to choose any "Lego set of globally available identities" (2006, p. 4), which presupposes the necessity, and in fact the possibility, of individualistic choices and self-determination. However, as the ending of *NW* demonstrates, such celebratory understanding of freedom must be approached cautiously. Beaumont's contention is, then, agreeable: "Smith persistently undermines the false promises of freedom that Natalie's social mobility represents by emphasising her alienation from her family, friends and herself" (2015, p. 199). In fact, Natalie's failure in identity formation contests affirmative senses of neoliberal human freedom as well as cosmopolitan concepts of communication and collectivity. The seemingly successful cosmopolitan, Natalie Blake, is in fact self-aware of the artificiality and inauthenticity of her self-constructed cosmopolitan agency: "Daughter drag. Sister drag. Mother drag. Wife drag. Court drag. Rich drag. Poor drag. British drag. Jamaican drag. Each required a different wardrobe" (Smith 2013, p. 282). All these globally available identities are no more than mere drag performances for Natalie. Her admired relationship with her husband is marked as another performance which, in reality, lacks a genuine tie, as the narrator observes through Leah's eyes in the August party and renders the couple nameless, hence selfless, stereotypes: "She sees the husband look at the wife, and the wife look at the husband. She sees no smile, no nod, no wave, no recognition, no communication, nothing at all" (p. 95). Disenchanted by her carefully configured identifications, Natalie seeks other satisfaction in threesome intercourses with unfamiliar people, and flees home when her husband discovers her secret e-mail messages. In the end, Natalie finds herself stripped of the tight control of time and space, embarking into an unknown journey heading "nowhere" (p. 300). The relative stability and certainty of her life and aspirations now disappear, replaced by a slippery act of "walking": "Walking was what she did now, walking was what she was. She was nothing more or less than the phenomenon of walking. She had no name, no biography, no characteristics. They had all fled into paradox" (p. 304). Name-changing does not bestow her a desired subjectivity; on the contrary, she is left with no name or nothing to cling to in her life. Perhaps, this sense of nothingness brings about her final emancipation from her former attachments as well as her fabricated sense of self. In this sense, it is through traversing the streets of her local area, not through a stabilized life of socioeconomic advantages, that she steps toward self-discovery. This mobilization can be necessary for "women of African and Caribbean diaspora [to] perpetually reinvent themselves and in order to do so, social mobility or small geographical displacements are vital. That's what Natalie achieves at the end of *NW*" (Siccardi 2020, p. 224). Individualistically choosing one's identifications independently from any group affiliations amounts to a deferral of fixity, hence an act of mobility. Although Natalie makes for "nowhere", "she also looks to the city as a place in which to strengthen a sense of self despite its polymorphous, almost paradoxical shape" (Carbajal 2016, p. 85). In the end, it is conspicuous that "the object mourned by the novel itself – the emancipatory promise of complex subcultural identities – is submerged, ineffable and beyond reach" (Beaumont 2015, p. 206). Natalie's cosmopolitan outlook for self can only be actualized as soon as she steps toward an unfixed, indefinable realm of city-roaming, hence a real sense of boundarylessness.

Toward Political Hyper-awareness: Economic Dimensions of Vernacular Cosmopolitanism

Political hyper-awareness refers to a direct engagement with ideology and contemporary politics by the cosmopolitan narrator by assuming a hyper-aware stance toward the multifaceted dimensions of global connections as well as the veiled ideology of neoliberal capitalism within cosmopolitan thinking. This new term resonates with Marcus's (2013) argument about Smith's transition from the "hysterical realism" of her debut novel, *White Teeth*, to the "post-hysterics" in her "fiction of austerity", in *NW*. Not only do the tones of these two London-based novels differ, but they also engage with the globalizing forces of contemporary life in different ways. *NW* invents new devices in order to deal with twenty-first-century conflicts. It must, then, be noted that "the very process and conditions of ongoing globalization call for new forms of writing, whether as a quest for new forms of mimesis or a more radical and experimental effort to enact change" (Knepper and Deckard 2016, p. 9). For Marcus, "despite lacking in stylistic austerity", replete with formal experiments, the novel displays "a catalogue of economic austerity: a work of socio-psychological genius that registers the psychic and material shocks of those left behind in Northwest London" (pp. 69–70). In the same vein, Tew (2014) contends that:

> [T]he experimental aspects of the novel are there to reinforce the always potentially inchoate qualities, the traumatologies of our lives, always subject to immense waves of acts of terror, criminality, death, debt, desperation, fear, poverty, suicide, unemployment, violence, wars and so forth that can be created by appalling events and the very economic systems that underpin our daily exchanges.

Such "traumatologies" of contemporary living can be embedded in new formal tenets of the novel in ways in which the novel has a hyper-aware stance toward the impact of globalization on contemporary society.

Globalization is widely defined as the compression of the world into a whole that brings people, goods, ideas, and information together regardless of their distinctness. Yet, this borderlessness of the globe benefits some cosmopolitans rather than the others. Corporations that operate transnationally usually hold the power to control the global flow of capital and production. "Cosmopolitanism" Calhoun asserts, "flourishes in the top management of multinational corporations" (2002, p. 106). On the other hand, local cosmopolitans who lead a life of economic hardships become the victims in this process of global capitalism. As Tomlinson argues, "localities become increasingly penetrated by globalizing forces" (2002, p. 252). According to Shaw's contention about *NW*, "[t]he narrative encapsulates how positive social relations and attachments begin at the most parochial level; lived experience in a contemporary urban cityscape is increasingly informed and shaped by more global processes of movement in general" (2017, pp. 98–99).

The omniscient narrator of *NW* can be said to be politically hyperaware, demonstrating this inevitable exposure of locals to the global. The narrator does so with a strident comment on the everyday life of Willesden's local cosmopolitans. For the narrator with a cosmopolitan mindset, Leah and Michel are assumedly bad cosmopolitans involved with a parochial vision of existence, ignoring broader global concerns. They seem indifferent to the replacement of the local grocer by a chain supermarket, and its exploitation of human labor as well as the environment, and the global exploitation of the land of less advantageous countries for agriculture by benefiting the chain traders rather than those countries themselves. The narratorial comment depicts Leah and Michel as non-ideal cosmopolitans:

> On the way back from the chain supermarket where they shop, though it closed down the local grocer and pays slave wages, with new bags though they should take old bags, leaving with broccoli from Kenya and tomatoes from Chile and unfair coffee and sugary crap and the wrong newspaper.
> They are not good people. They do not even have the integrity to be the sort of people who don't worry about being good people. (Smith 2013, p. 82)

The concept of cosmopolitanism in its universalist versions is often debated in relation to ethics. Universalism in terms of being a citizen of the world requires adopting certain universal ethics and values. The meaning of ethics is reconfigured in the couple's everyday practices since in a universalist sense, being ethical has something to do with being elite as the narrator claims that "[t]hey do not purchase ethical things because they can't afford them" (p. 82). One is compelled, then, to ask whether ethics is something purchasable or a commodity merely available to the wealthy elites. This statement brings up the idea of the misconception of the ethical within universalist cosmopolitanism, which is made explicit by the narrator's overt engagement with the idea of ethics. The protagonists' cosmopolitanism, obviously, is not in this vein; rather they are vernacular cosmopolitans who are compelled to cope with their particular and insular impediments, and with limited means of living, they fail to conform to the normative understanding of an ethical existence forged by mainstream thinking. The narrator seems to undermine, through hyper-awareness, the senses wrongly attached to the concept of cosmopolitanism and ethics in universalist philosophy.

Political hyper-awareness on the part of the narrator is demonstrated in her attentiveness to the invisible barrier between elite and non-elite cosmopolitans. The contrast between discrepant forms of cosmopolitanisms is rendered visible in the dinner party that brings Leah and Michel together with Natalie's elite friends, a gathering, as asserted by the narrator, to which the couple is "invited to provide something like local colour" and where they feel out of concord (p. 87). "Multiculturalism and ethnic diversity" as Schoene puts it, "serve as mere exotic wallpaper to the self-fashioning of middle-class identities, whose quality of life and sense of self are appealingly enhanced by being able to 'feel cosmopolitan' due to the apparent, yet far from actively neighbourly, proximity of 'others'" (2010, p. 5). Natalie's middle-class friends attest to this idea. Too shy to converse with the barristers and bankers in the party, Leah and Michel let their anecdotes be related by Natalie, yet in her own version, only "nodding to confirm points of facts, names, times, places" (Smith 2013, p. 87). These local stories about them are "[o]ffered to the table for general dissection" by the participants, and for "local colour" as stated by the narrator before (p. 87). They also lay the foundation for a comparison between their vernacular cosmopolitanism and a more universal version idealized by the gentle folk of the party. The transition from their local, thus supposedly less significant, stories to those of others with more universal concerns seems sharp. Others tell their anecdotes "with more panache, linking them to matters of the wider culture, debates in the newspapers" (p. 88). Unlike these elite cosmopolitans, Leah and Michel are devoid of stories that can relate to world matters that occupy the commonplace agenda of others.

The dinner table emerges as a glocal space where the global concerns and world matters seem the central preoccupation of elite cosmopolitans. Natalie's dinner table surrounded with cultivated people is reminiscent of Perowne's kitchen table where he discusses global issues with his son. The inseparability of the local from the global is discernible in the conversation in Natalie's table, too, as Leah listens to others talk about her future child's educational opportunities:

> But Leah, someone is saying, but Leah, in the end, at the end of the day, don't you just want to give your individual child the very best opportunities you can give them individually? Pass the green beans with shaved almonds. Define best. Pass the lemon tart. Whatever brings a child the greatest possibility of success. Pass the berries. Define success. Pass the crème fraîche. (p. 89)

Like the scene in *Saturday* as Perowne simultaneously cooks and listens to the global news, ordinary dinner dialogs here are also intertwined with more serious topics like education. In the same vein, this table is also concerned with global threats, like the ones that constitute the "the early-twenty-first-century menu, the specials of the day" (2005, p. 34) in McEwan's novel: "Water shortage. Food wars. Strain A (H_5N_1). Manhattan slips into the sea. England freezes. Iran presses the button. A tornado blows through Kensal Rise. There must be something attractive about the idea of apocalypse" (Smith 2013, p. 89). Like the characters of *Saturday*, they are relieved to handle such matters from a distance, from the comfort of their dinner table. Yet, the narrator seems to subtly criticize these elite cosmopolitans' partial engagement and their inadequate solutions. All the guests agree about "the evils of technology, what a disaster, especially for teenagers, yet most people have their phones laid next to their dinner plates" (p. 88). As made clear by the hyper-aware narrator, the inconsistencies between their thoughts and acts flourish. The narrator lays bare in an exacerbated tone the discrepancy between what they say and how they actually act. Most of the conversation at the table is shown by the narrator to be nothing more than a cliché: "Everyone says the same things in the same way. Conversations tinged with terror" (p. 89). Moreover, they complain about their generational difference with their mostly immigrant parents of Jamaican, Indian, Irish, and Chinese descent in pursuing the old customs like inviting their elders to live with them as the aged and infirm parents fail to sustain their living on their own. Rather than adopting the traditional view, they find other solutions: "Technology is offered as a substitute for that impossible request. Stair lifts. Pacemakers. Hip replacements. Dialysis machines" (p. 88). These problems that are discussed by Natalie's financially advantageous guests can only be solved through capital means. It is made evident once more that ethnic, national, racial, and religious differences are viewed ordinary while class plays a significantly determining role in this cosmopolitan society.

In this version of cosmopolitanism, contradictions prevail; cosmopolitan ideals of tolerance, understanding, and openness remain irrelevant to the desires of the elite cosmopolitans whose social solutions fail to include everyone in the community, rather they are involved in acts of segregation, eliminating the unwanted in the society that becomes a menace for their potential for welfare and peace:

> Solutions are passed across the table, strategies. Private wards. Private cinemas. Christmas abroad. A restaurant with only five tables in it. Security systems. Fences. The carriage of a 4x4 that lets you sit alone above traffic. There is a perfect isolation out there somewhere, you can get it, although it doesn't come cheap. (p. 88)

Their yearning to transcend the community they live in is indeed a part of the class consciousness on their part. This vein of thinking is akin to the idea asserted by Binnie et al.: "The new middle and gentrifying classes are definable through their particular combination of economic and cultural capital that enables them to distinguish themselves from other classes" (2006, p. 14). It is through the hyper-aware narrator that this departure of the novel from universalist discourses of cosmopolitanism is revealed.

It is also manifest, with the employment of political hyper-awareness, that cosmopolitan solidarity cannot be attained in contemporary London, where groupings and divisions still predominate. The Caribbean carnival of Notting Hill, known as the August carnival in the novel, a public event that presupposes conviviality, is celebrated by Natalie's party group within the isolated interiors of one of their Italian friends, not in public. This private group, like *Saturday*'s Perowne, who refuses to join the peace-marchers in the streets, separates themselves from the rest of the community, watching the event from the privileged position of the window as the neurosurgeon did before. Leah and Michel are also invited to this privileged space "with 'an amazing carnival pad'" (Smith 2013, p. 93). They can see the event from this perfect spot, not desiring any active participation because it is safer here to stay distant from the local inhabitants of lower classes. It is also this private space where the guests hear the news story on TV announcing a local murder (that of Felix's) in their area just before the carnival day; the Italian host and the others remain callous to the news about the murder, turning off the television and putting on music instead, allowing the party to go on. This act of switching off the TV set in an uncaring attitude to the news stories is also reminiscent of Perowne's habitual disengagement from the world news that he happens to hear. The news report explicates the details about the victim:

> – The young man, named locally as Felix Cooper, was thirty-two years old. He grew up in the notorious Garvey House project in Holloway, but had moved with his family to this relatively quiet corner of Kilburn, in search of a better life. Yet it was here, in Kilburn, that he was accosted by two youths early Saturday evening, moments from his own front door. It is not known if the victim knew – (p. 94)

This event can only alert local cosmopolitans like Leah and Michel as they know their own susceptibility to such crime as inhabitants of Kilburn. Michel's immediate reaction is to offer to move house, confused with feelings of fear and hope for a better living elsewhere. Yet, the victim's similar aspirations for betterment in life culminate in his meaningless murder, as if to refute Michel's belief in the parallel advancement in home-changing and life status. This is because "class overdetermines immobilities, especially when tied to factors of race and ethnicity" (Arnett 2018, p. 6). This struggle mostly posed by the economic threat globalization brings about has serious social consequences as can be discerned in this murder instance. This resonates with the idea that at the center of "new wars" lies the immense influence of globalization, and that they "constitute a new distorted social formation" (Kaldor 2002, p. 274). The narrator is attentive to the ramifications of global inequalities that also have an impact on local individuals. What Smith presents as a response to such impacts of neoliberal capitalism is the idea of communication and empathy, which are also, nonetheless, engaged critically.

The end of the novel in the section called "visitation" returns to Leah's garden mirroring its very first part with the same name, a narrative structure that also parallels *Saturday*'s circular pattern with a beginning and end in the same location (in Perowne's bedroom). This denouement is also premised on the idea of local communication and empathy as the two main female characters' relationship with each other is mended in the end despite following a catastrophe in a similar way to *Saturday*'s final renegotiation of the notions of human interaction and goodness. Leah and Natalie, both dissatisfied with their life and marriage, are reunited in Leah's garden, immersing in solving the mysterious murder of Felix Cooper, and meanwhile revitalizing their disjointed friendship. Carbajal underscores:

> Smith's continued literary investment in private reconciliation between individuals over communal disquisitions, a technique that flouts communitarian identities and societal prescription. In this case, Felix Cooper's murder is the trigger of Leah and Natalie's rekindled friendship in a moment that prizes interpersonal communion and individual epiphany. (2016, p. 87)

Just as Perowne's initial problematic relationship with Baxter is placated in the end as he operates on his former assailant and saves his life, Smith's characters culminate in compromise, endorsing a sense of communication ignited within local circles and with small steps toward goodness. In fact, the suggestion is that connection within the cosmopolitan society is, and can only be, ensured through a small-scale communication of the locals: "The personal (re)connection that is central to *NW*'s narrative can become the basis of wider, more public connections" (van Amelsvoort 2018, p. 420).

It must be noted that *NW*'s response to the idea of communication, connection, and empathy is distinct from that of *Saturday* in that the former is characterized more by hyper-awareness by exposing the limited repercussions of human interactions which are inevitably informed by globalization's dehumanizing effects. "Rather than offering a counterbalance to the excesses of the free market, as promised", as Houser puts it, "empathy brings only alienation and even violence" (2017, p. 118). This is proven by Felix's act of empathizing with the pregnant woman on the underground by giving his place to her, and his culminating murder by the two black young men who feel insulted by Felix's behavior. Intercultural communication fails to bring conviviality in this scene. Unlike *Saturday*'s relatively happy ending with the protagonist managing to keep another character alive, however temporarily, *NW* ends in ultimate violence, ironically galvanized by a counterbalancing act of communication as one of the characters is stabbed to death, effacing hope for even the small portion of human interaction in cosmopolitan community. This is because NW's "estranged cosmopolitan world" is "tinged with instability and insecurity, where strangers are forced into non-intimate proximity" (Houser 2017, p. 124). Furthermore, disjunctions in McEwan and Smith's cosmopolitan novels are discernible in their protagonists' (and also narrators') claim to the capacity to transcend into others' perspectives. Perowne is willing, and somehow able, to see through people's minds even if they are total strangers to him. *NW*'s focalizing characters, on the other hand, have limited vision as they prove to fail in terms of mutuality and understanding even in the face of very intimate relationships. "*NW* highlights the contradictory forces that run through modern society, which idealizes the humanistic promise of fellow-feeling even as it thwarts or deeply distorts the imaginative movement of entering the perspective of another person" (Houser 2017, p. 145). This conclusion may be a testament to the claim that Smith holds "an interest in local places as sites for the struggle toward an unromanticized and, for that reason, potentially durable cosmopolitan vision" (James 2013, p. 205). It is vernacular cosmopolitanism, then, that is offered as a solution in the end. The meanings of feelings of empathy, cooperation, and friendship are reconstructed by the novel's engagement with vernacular cosmopolitanism. Its solution seems to suggest that if everyone does something—even a small amount of goodness—for everyone else, for those living within an immediate distance by feeling responsible, then everything may change, and minor solutions may pave the way for major ones.

Contemporary fiction's espousal of vernacular cosmopolitanism and its overt preoccupation with showing the ways in which it is epitomized in the rendering of narrative elements can be evinced in *NW*, where narrative spaces, cosmopolitan characters, identities, and the narrator yield together this contemporary understanding of cosmopolitanism. Central to this understanding is the predominance of class dimension and consciousness, which is in fact a key element while other differences in terms of race, ethnicity, and culture are considered an ordinary and everyday phenomenon. Narrative glocality in the novel, in this respect, functions as a sign of the irreversible impact of globalization upon very local territories, which are premised on economic and cultural capital/consumption. Moreover, the distinction between elite and non-elite cosmopolitans is made visible in such urban glocal spaces. Cosmopolitan identities, in the same vein, are informed by this classed structure of the community to which individuals lack allegiance in any form, be it ethnic, racial, ethical, or cultural. The idea of vernacular cosmopolitanism is thus embodied in *NW* through its politically hyper-aware stance.

REFERENCES

Arnett, James. 2018. Neoliberalism and false consciousness before and after Brexit in Zadie Smith's *NW*. *The Explicator* 76: 1–7. https://doi.org/10.1080/00144940.2017.1416329.

Bauman, Zygmunt. 1998. *Globalization: The human consequences*. Cambridge: Polity.

Beaumont, Alexander. 2015. *Contemporary British fiction and the cultural politics of disenfranchisement: Freedom and the city*. Basingstoke: Palgrave Macmillan.

Beck, Ulrich. 2006. *The cosmopolitan vision*, trans. Ciaran Cronin. Cambridge and Malden: Polity Press.

Bentley, Nick. 2018. Trailing postmodernism: David Mitchell's *Cloud Atlas*, Zadie Smith's *NW*, and the metamodern. *English Studies* 99: 723–743. https://doi.org/10.1080/0013838X.2018.1510611.

Binnie, Jon, Julian Holloway, and Steve Millington. 2006. Introduction: Grounding cosmopolitan urbanism: Approaches, practices and policies. In *Cosmopolitan urbanism*, ed. Jon Binnie, Julian Holloway, Steve Millington, and Craig Young, 1–34. London: Routledge.

Brah, Avtar. 1996. *Cartographies of diaspora: Contesting identities*. London: Routledge.

Butler, Tim. 2003. Living in the bubble: Gentrification and its 'others' in North London. *Urban Studies* 40: 2469–2486.

Calhoun, Craig. 2002. The class consciousness of frequent travellers: Towards a critique of actually existing cosmopolitanism. In *Conceiving cosmopolitanism: Theory, context, and practice*, ed. Steven Vertovec and Robin Cohen, 86–109. Oxford: Oxford University Press.

Carbajal, Alberto Fernández. 2016. On being queer and postcolonial: Reading Zadie Smith's *NW* through Virginia Woolf's *Mrs Dalloway*. *The Journal of Commonwealth Literature* 51: 76–91. https://doi.org/10.1177/0021989414554630.

Gerzina, Gretchen. 2017. Zadie Smith: The geographies of marriage. In *The contemporary British novel since 2000*, ed. James Acheson, 48–58. Edinburg: Edinburg University Press.

Hall, Stuart. 2002. Political belonging in a world of multiple identities. In *Conceiving cosmopolitanism: Theory, context, and practice*, ed. Steven Vertovec and Robin Cohen, 25–31. Oxford: Oxford University Press.

Held, David. 2002. Culture and political community: National, global, and cosmopolitan. In *Conceiving cosmopolitanism: Theory, context, and practice*, ed. Steven Vertovec and Robin Cohen, 48–58. Oxford: Oxford University Press.

Held, David. 2010. *Cosmopolitanism: Ideals and realities*. Cambridge: Polity Press.

Houser, Tammy Amiel. 2017. Zadie Smith's *NW*: Unsettling the promise of empathy. *Contemporary Literature* 58: 116–148.
Hubble, Nick, and Philip Tew. 2016. Introduction: Parallax London. In *London in contemporary British fiction: The city beyond the city*, ed. Nick Hubble and Philip Tew, 1–16. Bloomsbury Studies in the City. London: Bloomsbury.
James, David. 2013. Wounded realism. *Contemporary Literature* 54: 204–214. www.jstor.org/stable/43297914.
Kaldor, Mary. 2002. Cosmopolitanism and organized violence. In *Conceiving cosmopolitanism: Theory, context, and practice*, ed. Steven Vertovec and Robin Cohen, 268–278. Oxford: Oxford University Press.
Knepper, Wendy. 2014. Revisionary modernism and postmillennial experimentation in Zadie Smith's *NW*. In *Reading Zadie Smith*, ed. Philip Tew, 111–126. London: Bloomsbury Academic.
Knepper, Wendy, and Sharae Deckard. 2016. Towards a radical world literature: Experimental writing in a globalizing world. *Ariel: A Review of International English Literature* 47: 1–25. https://doi.org/10.1353/ari.2016.0018.
López-Ropero, Lourdes. 2016. Searching for a 'different kind of freedom': Postcoloniality and postfeminist subjecthood in Zadie Smith's 'NW'. *Atlantis* 38: 123–139. www.jstor.com/stable/26330848.
Marcus, David. 2013. Post-hysterics: Zadie Smith and the fiction of austerity. *Dissent* 60: 67–73. https://doi.org/10.1353/dss.2013.0035.
McEwan, Ian. 2005. *Saturday*. London: Vintage.
Procter, James. 2003. *Dwelling places: Postwar Black British writing*. Manchester and New York: Manchester University Press.
Schoene, Berthold. 2010. *The cosmopolitan novel*. Edinburgh: Edinburgh University Press.
Shaw, Kristian. 2017. *Cosmopolitanism in twenty-first century fiction*. Basingstoke: Palgrave Macmillan.
Siccardi, Julia. 2020. 'There is such a shelter in each other': Women looking for homes in Zadie Smith's *White Teeth*, *On Beauty* and *NW*. *African and Black Diaspora: An International Journal* 13: 215–226. https://doi.org/10.1080/17528631.2020.1750173.
Slavin, Molly. 2015. Nowhere and Northwest, Brent and Britain: Geographies of Elsewhere in Zadie Smith's 'NW'. *The Journal of the Midwest Modern Language Association* 48: 97–119. www.jstor.org/stable/43549873.
Smith, Zadie. 2013. *NW: London*. London: Penguin Books.
Tew, Philip. 2014. Will self and Zadie Smith's depictions of post-Thatcherite London: Imagining traumatic and traumatological space. *Études Britanniques Contemporaines* 47. http://ebc.revues.org/1886.
Tomlinson, John. 2002. Interests and identities in cosmopolitan politics. In *Conceiving cosmopolitanism: Theory, context, and practice*, ed. Steven Vertovec and Robin Cohen, 240–253. Oxford: Oxford University Press.

van Amelsvoort, Jesse. 2018. Between Forster and Gilroy: Race and (re)connection in Zadie Smith's *NW*. *Tulsa Studies in Women's Literature* 37: 419–434.

Vertovec, Steven, and Robin Cohen. 2002. Introduction: Conceiving cosmopolitanism. In *Conceiving cosmopolitanism: Theory, context, and practice*, ed. Steven Vertovec and Robin Cohen, 1–22. Oxford: Oxford University Press.

Werbner, Pnina. 2008. Introduction: Towards a new cosmopolitan anthropology. In *Anthropology and the new cosmopolitanism*, ed. Pnina Werbner, 1–29. New York: Berg.

Wells, Lynn. 2014. The right to a secret: Zadie Smith's NW. In *Reading Zadie Smith*, ed. Philip Tew, 97–110. London: Bloomsbury Academic.

CHAPTER 5

Cosmopolitan Identity and Narration in Salman Rushdie's *The Golden House*: The Move Toward Vernacular Cosmopolitanism

The responses to Salman Rushdie's novel, *The Golden House* (2017), vary. Rushdie's previous oeuvre has been predominantly received as a landmark and pinnacle of postmodern fiction, and accordingly one expects his twenty-first-century novel to put a new face on contemporary fiction. Although it is principally regarded as a narrative in the convention of realism, giving up the magic realism of his former fiction, its form is, rather than a return to classical realism, in fact in alignment with twenty-first-century concerns of representing the political and economic climate of the day. In the first place, the book's publisher promotes it as a "return to realism". In an interview in the eve of the publication of the novel, the author himself affirms his changing orientation in this recent work: "In the novel I have just finished, *The Golden House* (Rushdie 2017), there is essentially no fantasy in it. It's essentially a realist novel because that's what the story seemed to demand" (Guignery 2018, p. 272). Obviously, what his new story demands is a different and more direct engagement with the contemporary world's material realities, which have exacerbated after the 2008 financial breakdown.

Rushdie himself suggests that the realism in *The Golden House* is a form of engaged and straightforward writing: "I'm on the Technicolor end [...] It's realism, but it's kind of amped up, boosted", which enables him to get involved with the contemporary political and social landscape revisiting the form of Stendhal, Balzac, and Wharton (Tuttle 2017). Defining

© The Author(s), under exclusive license to Springer Nature Switzerland AG 2024
E. Toprak Sakız, *Culture and Economics in Contemporary Cosmopolitan Fiction*, https://doi.org/10.1007/978-3-031-44995-6_5

147

Rushdie's recent work as "operatic realism" by borrowing the term of *The Golden House*'s narrator who employs it to define his own art form, Hoydis claims that this new style is a culmination of the urge for reconstructing contemporary reality: "This politically and ethically oriented realism is infused with a kind of utopian potential, a search for alternative futures and other realities, counteracting a contemporary culture encouraging forgetfulness, fakery and apathy" (2019, p. 153) because the novel's "interest lies in political representation and ethics" (2019, pp. 156–157).

One must also notice, as this chapter will show, the changing attitude and critical tone of the author in the face of contemporary cosmopolitan encounters, a tone departing from his former celebratory standpoint regarding cultural, racial, and ethnic mixing-ups, which can often be found in his multicultural novels. Rushdie's postmillennial cosmopolitan world deems difference as an ordinary, everyday matter where discourses of discrete cultures and their happy amalgamation no longer sustain. Implicit in Rushdie's assertion that with the turn of the century "we live in an age which is defined by migration" (Guignery 2018, p. 271) is his more direct preoccupation with everyday diversity in a cosmopolitan center like New York. This chapter will suggest that *The Golden House* goes beyond Rushdie's former affirmative perspectives on multiculturalism, and successfully incorporates the distinctive features of postmillennial cosmopolitan fiction. The novel draws its main characters as universalist (elite) cosmopolitans with aspirations of uprootedness, and with a view to their exceptionally sumptuous and free worlds, displays a critical attitude toward universalist cosmopolitanism. This critique intensifies to the point of bringing this world to a destructive end, meanwhile demonstrating the impossibility of dispensing with local associations, and instead proclaiming vernacular cosmopolitanism as a true representative of twenty-first-century culture.

The Golden House revolves around the cosmopolitan character, Nero Golden, and his three sons, who decide to move to New York from an unnamed country (which is later revealed to be India), after his wife's death and the unfolding dark business events that the Goldens wish to leave behind once and for all. By the end of the novel, Nero's background comes out into the open as the old man is revealed to be formerly implicit in organized crime in Mumbai by laundering illegal money and assisting a fundamentalist terror attack on a bunch of monumental buildings of the city. Having recognized that his wife was also a victim of the assault during a tea party in the city's most famous hotel, the Taj Mahal Palace, Nero seeks salvation through a purgatory flight from his former life to a new beginning in New York, with which the family effortlessly correlates. Nero Golden's Spinozian philosophy of moral relativism, to which he himself articulates his adherence, subtly challenges universalism, in the conviction that man can be both good and evil. The interrogation of universal human goodness is epitomized in the character of Nero, whom one hesitates to judge as either good or evil. Another thread in the narrative is the Joker-Trump analogy, which is evoked by Gary "Green" Gwynplaine, the businessman in the real estate sector, who is the white-skinned, red-lipped mirror image of the notorious cartoon character Joker, and who has become triumphant in the presidential election of November 2016. While a number of cosmopolitan scenes from contemporary New York City constitute the bulk of the narrative, the ending brings the family and the country, the United States of Joker—both cosmopolitan on a small or broad scale—into a state of destruction, respectively by a fire and an election, which bring about their tragic end. Unlike the celebratory and universalist standpoints of Rushdie's twentieth-century novels *Midnight's Children* (1981) and *The Satanic Verses* (1988), this novel is an engagement with vernacular cosmopolitanism with its emphasis on hyper-aware representation, choice-making, and cosmopolitan identity as well as its insight into global matters and socioeconomic crises in the second decade of the twenty-first century.

Rushdie's cosmopolitan narrative manifests discrepant formations or particularist versions of cosmopolitanism. The main cosmopolitan space of the novel, the Golden house, houses a number of everyday cosmopolitans, ranging from the "elite" Goldens to working-class cosmopolitans of the estate, like its Italian-American house manager and its Hispanic handyman named Gonzalo, and Petya's Australian hypnotherapist, Murray Lett. The MacDougal–Sullivan Gardens, the focal setting of the narrative, is also typically cosmopolitan with the ordinary diversity of the inhabitants, including a Myanmaran UN diplomat U Lnu Fnu, an Argentine-American Mr Arribista, Sicilian aristocrats, Vito and Blanca Tagliabue, among others. "My imagined community", the narrator asserts, "was an international bunch" (Rushdie 2017, p. 32). Recalling Benedict Anderson's conception of "imagined communities", this statement also emphasizes that not only the notion of nation but also cosmopolitanism itself is imagined and defies a straightforward definition. In Vertovec and Cohen's terms, cosmopolitanism "transcends the seemingly exhausted nation-state model" (2002, p. 4), and one implication here is that cosmopolitanism, like nationalism, is far from being defined in a monolithic way. In the novel, the very concept of cosmopolitanism, like nationalism, is also manifested as imagined, especially in its universalist sense. Fictional cosmopolitan "worlds" in the novel are "imagined" as they can be seen "in different sizes and styles" (Robbins 1998, p. 2).

The Golden family's four men, the central characters of the novel, emerge as elite cosmopolitans, enacting a sense of universalist cosmopolitanism, cosmopolitanism from above. They live a life of luxury in Greenwich Village in the house that formerly belonged to a wealthy man called Murray, and is now called the Golden House, which is believed to hide some secrets within its borders. Having left their home country behind, they start a new life in New York, and shortly after their arrival, they are accepted as part of the well-off community consisting of New York's well-known artists, musicians, and businessmen. In fact, their positioning in American culture is seamless and unproblematic. It is through their universalist cosmopolitanism that Rushdie makes a commentary upon the contemporary world and politics with an ironic distance. In keeping with the concern in this novel, Rushdie interrogates the meaning and associations of "elite", one of the disputed words of the century: "I mean, how did university professors, journalists and writers become the elite? Meanwhile there's a government which has more billionaires in it than at any point in American history. It's an amazing reversal of meaning" (Tuttle 2017). Certainly, his novel revolves around one of these "elite" billionaires that represent universalist cosmopolitanism.

The cosmopolitan novel creates fictional worlds that are, in Vertovec and Cohen's words, "culturally anti-essentialist" (2002, p. 4). With the absence of a monolithic definition and straightforward delineation of diverse cultures, *The Golden House* bears the characteristics of cosmopolitanism owing to the employment of multiple cultural references as well as resistance to cultural stereotypes and denigration of the other. Cosmopolitan identities in the novel are separated from a condition of hybridity, inclining toward everyday difference since the categories of culture, race, and ethnicity are considered less relevant to the contemporary structures of the society than class. Stuart Hall's version of cosmopolitanism as "the ability to stand outside of having one's life written and scripted by any one community, whether that is a faith or tradition or religion or culture [...] and to draw selectively on a variety of discursive meanings" (2002, p. 26) is aligned with what lies behind the Goldens' decision to leave their place of birth, dissociating themselves from all forms of cultural, national, or religious ties. Nero Golden firmly believes that being American means a disconnection from roots, departure from place-boundedness, and instructs his sons not to reveal anything about their background: "Say we are from nowhere or anywhere or somewhere, we are make-believe people, frauds, reinventions, shapeshifters, which is to say, Americans" (Rushdie 2017, p. 8). As newly-arriving cosmopolitans in New York, the family is completely stripped of their erstwhile identity and affiliations. René, the narrator, acknowledges their first impression as cosmopolitans: "I looked at the Goldens and I saw cosmopolitans" (p. 38). For their neighbours living in the Gardens, theirs is "the most immediate fruit of exile, of uprooting" (p. 11) as they are skilful at veiling their identities and their secret history. Although they are not "conventionally 'white'", they have nothing in the house hinting at their origin and speak with a perfectly-accented Oxbridge English (p. 11). It is "their chameleon identities" that "[tell] us much about America itself", and their "invented American personae" that has been "unquestioningly accepted" by their fellow residents (p. 11). In fact, their cosmopolitan identities are endorsed as acceptable and ordinary as any other American citizen's: "They had excellent taste, excellent clothes, excellent English, and they were no more eccentric than, say, Bob Dylan, or any other sometime local resident. So the Goldens were accepted because they were acceptable. They were Americans now" (pp. 12–13). The narrator affirms that "they didn't seem so odd to us" (p. 12). This acceptance of difference applies not only to the state of the Goldens, but to all citizens who call themselves American. This complete departure from the rhetoric of otherness is visible in the novel's engagement with contemporary cosmopolitanism.

The Goldens emerge as an epitome of universalist cosmopolitanism, which distinguishes, despite its claims to commonness and plurality, between elite and non-elite cosmopolitans. Like the widespread view in *NW* that "not everyone can be invited to the party. Not this century" (Smith 2013, p. 3), the family hosts only a privileged group in their home parties. Likewise, the family's selected destination for their Christmas holiday, a private island in Miami, to which they fly with their "P.J." (private jet), is impenetrable: "[N]o outsiders were allowed to set foot on the charmed soil unless spoken for by residents" (Rushdie 2017, p. 80). Their greed for privacy contradicts with cosmopolitan feelings of sharing and cooperation. In the novel, however, cosmopolitanisms are multiple and various, and cannot be only defined by the Goldens' version. The feelings of sharing can be seen, by contrast, in Riya's version of local cosmopolitanism. Her urge for sharing her read books with other citizens of the city by leaving them randomly on a park bench is a testament to her imagination of local and complimentary goodness, which is "a gift from the city" (p. 103). Moreover, she is not alone in this kind of vernacular cosmopolitanism as she discovers others' books left in the park awaiting her, "the random gifts of unknown strangers", through which she is capable of "wandering through the discarded stories of the city" (p. 104). This worldview is overtly articulated by her in her conviction that "[t]hings are good which reduce the amount of global misery, or the quantity of injustice, or both" (p. 88). It must be noted, then, that the novel engages with various types of cosmopolitanisms which are departing from the Golden's universalist orientation, and emphasizing the particular, local, and parochial versions.

The cosmopolitan novel deemphasizes form, or designates stylistic and generic devices as a matter of choice in favor of subject-matter or content, which in turn comes to the fore in twenty-first-century fiction. In this sense, Rushdie's constantly changing employment and indeterminate choices of realist, modernist, or postmodernist devices in this novel are actually in par with his assertion that "it's the material that dictates the technique rather than the other way around" (Guignery 2018, p. 272). In fact, *choice* comes as a catchword in the novel in the creation of both cosmopolitan identities and formal features. The new art form of the twenty-first century, "mockumentary" (Rushdie 2017, p. 222) is a matter of choice. In other words, just like a cosmopolitan's identity, cosmopolitan fiction is composed of multiplicity and mutability of choices in the course of its creation. "*A golden story*", René muses, is for the Romans "a tall tale, a wild conceit. A lie" (p. 233). The missing parts in the Goldens' narrative are, therefore, open to reinvention, imagination, or "post-factualness" just as the genre of mockumentary presupposes. In this information age, post-factualness is accepted and praised by people who seek all forms of information even if they are perfectly aware that most of what they believe is true is actually not: "Post-factual is the mass market, information-age, troll-generated. It's what people want" (p. 222). No one is after the truth in this century, it is declared, because "*[t]rue* is such a twentieth-century concept" (p. 221). Post-factualness requires a sort of hyper-awareness, hence the freedom of choosing what to believe, on the part of contemporary cosmopolitans who are no longer involved in a naïve commitment to, and belief in, concepts like truth, universal meanings, and human goodness. Such universal concepts in cosmopolitan thought are abandoned in favor of vernacularism, which in turn takes into account different and even incompatible versions of cosmopolitanisms.

The Goldens' twenty-five-year-old neighbor, René Unterlinden, is the first-person narrator of the novel who gradually positions himself to the center of the narrative, which is originally supposed to relate the Goldens' story. Not only the characters but also the narrator creates his self-image and identity by means of his individualistic choices; like his characters he is self-named, acknowledging: "I forebear to say unto you plainly, my name's René. Call me René" (p. 24). Setting off as a movie script project about the Goldens in documentary fashion, the narrative also turns out to be a mixture of genres, a border-transgression, as the narrator himself asserts, leaning toward a state of *"genrequeer"* (p. 222). The narrator acknowledges his act of the violation of borders while writing the Goldens' story: "I crossed the line that divides the reporter from the participant" (p. 286) as he gradually meshes himself into the narrative he creates. The homodiegetic narrator does so by embedding his own choices into the narrative as well as centralizing himself as a character. René's narrative concerning primarily the man who is an embodiment of universalist cosmopolitanism, Nero Golden, culminates in his ultimate replacement of this protagonist by not only surviving a tragic end that all the other main characters fail to evade, but also supplanting their universalist values with vernacular ones. In the rest of the narrative, he becomes a key figure even at the heart of events. Yet, the narrator must be distinguished by the other cosmopolitans with a universalist outlook through his deepening attention to everyday cosmopolitanism around him as well as to local and parochial meanings of the conception.

Cosmopolitan Identity and Choice

Beck (2006) describes the identity-making of the "cosmopolitan outlook" as constructing "a model of one's identity by dipping freely into the Lego set of globally available identities and building a progressively inclusive self-image" (p. 4). In this respect, as Shaw (2016) maintains, "cosmopolitanism focuses on the identity of an individual, rather than that of a group (ethnic or otherwise)" (p. 171). Cosmopolitan identity[1] is a self-made process, characterized by one's disengagement from group affiliations and making individualistic choices, including even a crucial process of self-naming. The main characters of the narrative, the Goldens, are involved in this act of self-making with their life choices: "their relocation to New York was not an exile, not a flight, but a choice" (Rushdie 2017, p. 41). The father calls himself Nero Golden after the great emperor of Rome, and the three sons have also assumed Ancient Greek names—Petronius, Lucius Apuleius, and Dionysus—despite their Hindu origins; "[a]fter they made their choices their father used their chosen names for them always" (p. 41). Nero's sense of self-image is in line with an elite cosmopolitan with cultural as well as economic privileges; his comfort zone is "his true self" in which he is "the man of power, the financial titan, the quondam construction and steel magnate, head of his family, the colossus standing in the great courtyard of the golden house, the once and future king" (p. 90). Vasilisa Arsenyeva emerges as another character whose self-construction resembles that of the Goldens due to her life choices including her earlier arrival in America with aspirations of leaving her poverty-stricken life in Russia behind. Self-aware of her own processes of subjectivity making, she asserts: "I know my presence here is the fruit of my own labor" and "I leave the past behind and I am myself in this place" (p. 93).

Petronious (Petya) Golden, Nero Golden's oldest son, is depicted as "a twenty-first-century genius", despite his many social deficiencies, including his agoraphobia, high-functioning autism as well as his verbal outbreaks. Known to spend most of his time in his blue-lighted room playing video games, he is later understood to be the creator of very famous games, which earn him his fortune, "leaving the rest of us in his wake, floundering in a second-millennium world" (p. 208). His universal language is his mobile games that are enjoyed by people worldwide and rank the first in the most prestigious and profitable games list. Petya never fully recovers from his condition notwithstanding his frequent meetings with the hypnotherapist, Murray Lett. Especially after the woman he loves, Ubah Tuur, has been taken by his brother, Apuleius Golden, he suffers the pain of the couple's long-lasting love and loses his composure to the point of starting a fire in the gallery where both artists exhibit their works of art.

Lucius Apuleius Golden, preferring to be called Apu in short, is a self-made universalist cosmopolitan on account of his choices as well as his identification with America with an eager departure from his old country. As Held (2002) avers, "[c]ultural cosmopolitanism emphasizes the possible fluidity of individual identity" (p. 58). It is this cosmopolitan territory that renders possible for Apu to become who he desires to be.

That is why "Apu's greed for America was omnivorous" (Rushdie 2017, p 55). René gets astonished by his bond with America as Apu becomes sentimental with tears in his eyes while listening to René's account of the night when Barack Obama is elected president: "Could this relatively recent arrival in America already be so invested in his new country that an election result could make him cry?" (p. 56). Both Apu and René's "relief mingled with elation" (p. 56) at the election outcomes reflects their response, as cosmopolitans, to America's acceptance of difference. This election's relation with the idea of cosmopolitanism is attested in the narrator's account of the night when Obama is elected. *Cosmoflâneurs* like René wander around the city's most representative cosmopolitan buildings and places like Rockefeller Center and Union Square in crowds in sentiments of "optimism [...] flowing all around us" (p. 56). This presidential change also evokes unifying senses among the community and is celebrated by opposing political groups at the election night party "jointly" organized by "a well-known doyenne of Upper East Side society, a Republican" and "a distinctly downtown Democrat film producer" (p. 56).

Apu is portrayed as a "gluttonous agoraphile" (p. 59) who traverses the streets of New York and embraces them, just as a *flâneur* does, by wandering "voraciously through the city, embracing it all like a young Whitman, the undergrounds, the clubs, the power stations, the prisons, the subcultures, the catastrophes, the flaming comets, the gamblers, the dying factories, the dancing queens" (p. 58). Aligned with the definition of a *flâneur*, he lives the life of an artist, mostly involved in abstract and conceptual ideas, yet is not discharged from class divisions that characterize the cosmopolitan life in the city. His art studio at Union Square eventually becomes a cosmopolitan hub where he draws "portraits of *le tout* New York, the elite ladies" (p. 58), and his paintings of these privileged customers are exhibited in his solo show titled "*The Privilege of Owning Yourself*", a name suggesting the freedom of choice in the delineation of identities. He is a cosmopolitan in his clothing as well: "[h]is clothing embraced all the fashions of the planet", including the Arab dishdasha, the African dashiki, the South Indian veshti, the bright shirts of Latin America, the English three-piece tweed suit, or a Scotch kilt (Rushdie 2017, p. 59). Apu's status is in alignment with Mikhail Epstein's definition of transculturalism as "the freedom from one's culture" as well as "freedom from any of [the willingly assumed cultures]" (2009, p. 330).

Despite embracing diversity, Apu is also "a sort of genius of compartmentalization" keeping "different groups of friends in sealed-off boxes" (p. 59) as many elite cosmopolitans do owing to their class consciousness. Cosmopolitanism, in Hollinger's words, "is more oriented to the individual, and expects individuals to be simultaneously and importantly affiliated with a number of groups, including civic and religious communities, as well as with communities of descent" (2002, p. 231), which is reminiscent of Apu's version of cosmopolitanism with multiple, yet only superficial, attachments.

Dionysus, the third and illegitimate son of Nero Golden, bears the characteristics of a self-fashioning cosmopolitan identity in terms of his choices concerning who he wants to be. To start with, he chooses the mythological name, Dionysus, and even reduces it to a "near-anonymous single-letter nickname, 'D'" (Rushdie 2017, p. 67). Gender identity is made a matter of choice, and young D opts to create an image of this god in himself precisely because "Dionysus the god was always an outsider, a god of resurrection and arrival, 'the god that comes'. He was also androgynous, 'man-womanish'. That this was the pseudonym the youngest child of Nero Golden chose for himself in the classical-renaming game reveals that he knew something about himself before he knew it" (p. 66). D is "a Dorian Gray type [...] bordering on the effeminate" (p. 70). Only when he arrives in cosmopolitan New York can he completely become entitled to make a free choice for his gender identity. He seems at first glance "in exile from [himself]" to his girlfriend Riya when they first meet as she can detect in him "a man's alienation from his own identity" (p. 73). She pointedly questions his aspiration back at home to take the place of his step-mother: "What part of you wanted to be her, the mother, the housewife, with the household keys, in charge of domestic duties?" (p. 102). It is his supporter and girlfriend Riya, who is a museum manager and a lesbian, that provides him with a set of gender-defining vocabulary: "*MTF* was male to female, *FTM* was vice versa [...], *gender fluid*, *bigender*, *agender*, *trans* with an asterisk: *trans**, the difference between *woman* and *female*, *gender nonconforming*, *genderqueer*, *nonbinary*, and from Native American culture, *two spirit*" (p. 76). These are like the lego-set of identities, in Beck's words, from which he can assume the most suitable ones for himself. D's "*imminent transformation*" (p. 98; emphasis in original) actualizes as a result of his identity crisis when he is bestowed with numberless possibilities.

Riya is an insightful character that can read the clues and perceive the significance of the past in D's confusion about his gender identity, insisting that he is bound to transform, and it is only here that he can carry out this transformation because "there, where you came from, you weren't free to be who you need to be, to become who you need to become" (p. 101). With a typical camera flashback returning to the time when Michael Jackson performs in Bombay and D sees, for the first time as a twelve-year-old boy, a giant "hijra" cross-dressed as the admired singer walking around the cars, and this sight creates in him mixed feelings of disgust, incredulity, and fascination (p. 107), it is made clear that this past event lies at the root of D's ultimate transformation. Riya supports his choice—whatever it may be—by making references to, and reading aloud from a book about, beliefs in India's history about cross-gender identity: "According to the poet-saints of Shaivism, Shiva is *Ammai-Appar*, Mother and Father combined. It is said of Brahma that he created humankind by converting himself into two persons: the first male, Manu Svayambhuva, and the first female, Satarupa. India has always understood androgyny, the man in the woman's body, the woman in the man's" (pp. 107–108). Moreover, Riya goes on reading about those hijras who "usually take those new identities to new places, where new families form around them and take them in" (p. 108), which echoes D's choice of abandoning his life in the Golden house and moving into Riya's flat in Chinatown.

Aminatta Forna sees at the heart of the novel a contemporary identity crisis: "The notion of identity as overlapping and many-layered as something with which large sections of white America are grappling, in a nationwide identity crisis" (2017). Rushdie's preoccupation with cosmopolitan identity has something to do with his addressing himself as "a big-city writer" because he believes that "Nowadays the city has become almost a parable of the way in which the world is now, partly because of mass migration as people who live in cities very often come from somewhere else" (Guignery 2018, p. 270), and this way, diversity is regarded as an ordinary aspect of identity. In keeping with this understanding, Beck's "cosmopolitan outlook" (2006, p. 4) must be taken as a definitive term for the identity-making processes of Rushdie's characters. American identity is composed of a "cosmopolitan outlook", problematizing the nation-bounded and culturally essentialist delineation of identity. One can encounter all sorts of names in an American phonebook:

People in America were called all sorts of things –throughout the phonebooks, in the days when there were phonebooks, nomenclatural exoticism ruled. Huckleberry! Dimmesdale! Ichabod! Ahab! Fenimore! Portnoy! Drudge! [...] Americans also constantly decided what they wanted to be called and who they wanted to be, shedding their Gatz origins to become shirt-owning Gatsbys and pursue dreams called Daisy or perhaps simply America. (Rushdie 2017, p. 12)

This "nomenclatural exoticism" dates back to the time of phonebooks, and is nothing new, yet rather than being exotic, the assortment of names is a characteristics of America, a country which is cosmopolitan just from scratch as the narrator puts it:

many of us, as immigrants –or our parents or our grandparents –had chosen to leave our past behind just as the Goldens were now choosing, encouraging our children to speak English, not the old language from the old country: to speak, dress, act, *be* American. (p. 12)

It is their everyday life, activities, and connections that characterize them as cosmopolitans; despite their discrepancies, they share a common local space, if not shared purposes or aspirations. This is the American version of Gilroy's (2004) portrayal of cosmopolitanism in Britain and elsewhere, which is "the process of cohabitation and interaction that have made multiculture an ordinary feature of social life in Britain's urban areas and in postcolonial cities elsewhere" (p. xi). However, despite advocating the everydayness of difference, the novel does not agree with Gilroy's idea that such communities are "convivial" and "planetary" (2004, p. xi). The community here is far from this condition, and is rather characterized by everyday problems created by street violence and murders as voiced by many characters.

Another feature of cosmopolitans in America is their "secret identity", that is their refusal to be identified with their past affiliations in terms of nations, countries, ethnicities, or specific groups. The narrator, thus, inquiries rhetorically: "do we not celebrate everyday, do we not *honor*, the idea of the Secret Identity?" (Rushdie 2017, p. 21). The answer partly lies in the assumption that American identities are bound to be unknown because it is this unknowingness of roots that makes them cosmopolitans. Vasilisa, Nero's young wife, conspicuously does away with the past: "The past is a broken cardboard suitcase full of photographs of things I no longer wish to see" (p. 93). She longs to "keep the suitcase closed"

(p. 93) just as the Golden men do. Likewise, the Goldens are claimed to tell "stories about themselves, stories in which essential information about origins was either omitted or falsified" (p. 71). Nero Golden has "cloaked himself in benami anonymity" and "formed habits of secrecy long before he arrived among us" in New York, particularly in terms of his illegal business dealings (p. 119). It is, however, impossible to entirely dispense with origins, keep the secret, and aspire to universalist cosmopolitanism without any local affiliations. Well-aware of this, the narrator seeks insight in order to reveal their secrets by evaluating their "tells" like card players' unwitting gestures to unfold their hands (p. 71). By reading these clues, the narrator gradually manages to trace their past by finding out about Nero's illegal business affairs and the family's flight from India.

Rushdie's cosmopolitan identities are in alignment with Vertovec and Cohen's definition of cosmopolitanism as "capable of representing variously complex repertoires of allegiance, identity and interest" (2002, p. 4). Rejecting to pin down identity on group dynamics, the novel renders individuals independent of allegiances to any racial, ethnic, or cultural community, and considers them the main constituents of contemporary cosmopolitan society. As Shaw maintains, "cosmopolitanism explores heterogeneous forms of belonging both individually and culturally" (2016, p. 171). However, this freedom of choice must be separated from the aspiration to detach oneself altogether from one's roots, which the novel regards as a dream. The narrator relates this dream of the Goldens to free themselves from the "historical", the rooted:

> They would wipe the slate clean, take on new identities, cross the world and be other than what they were. They would escape from the historical into the personal, and in the New World the personal would be all they sought and all they expected, to be detached and individual and alone, each of them to make his own agreement with the everyday, outside history, outside time, in private. (Rushdie 2017, p. 20)

All these states of contemporary identity inclined toward the "personal", "detached", "individual", and "private" (p. 20) hint at the fallacious aspirations of universalist cosmopolitanism in territories, in what is referred to as "the New World" (p. 20). In this world, individuals are bound to "move beyond memory and roots and language and race into the land of the self-made self, which is another way of saying, America" (p. 20). The novel views such universalist tendencies and detachments from local identifications as a project of American cosmopolitanism. This universalism is, however, contradicted by the ghost stories of an old lady named Mrs. Stone, who lives on the Gardens and visits René after his parents' death and tells him about a ghost she saw on MacDougal Alley, a black boy walking on his knees, a vision explained by her in rational terms: "The street level of the alley had risen over time and he was walking on the old ground level and I could only *see* him down to his knees" (p. 154; emphasis in original). In fact, she is not the only one who is capable of seeing ghosts of dead people; René is exposed to many others' stories like this, and he even witnesses firsthand Nero's talking to the apparitions of his two former wives and apologizing for causing them to die. All these supernatural stories, which are nevertheless very realistically handled in the narrative, are a testament to the indispensability of the history that keeps haunting the citizens who wish to escape their past.

In the novel, the idea of choice does not mean a total detachment from local affiliations, rather it is a possibility of multiple subjectivities. To put it differently, cosmopolitans can both be free in their choices and at the same time rooted. This is actually in keeping with the idea of vernacular cosmopolitanism, a conception which marks the underlying message of the novel. Identity, in this world of limitless choices, is defined in terms of choosing; it is about metamorphosis, about constant transformation: "Transition is like translation. You're moving across from one language into another" (p. 116). However, getting rid of history in this process is not acceptable. It is this paradox of cosmopolitan thought that is brought to close attention in the novel through an emphasis on the conception of identity. In this "new world" in which Riya invites D to participate, there are various identity museums: a museum for Native Americans, the Italian American museum, the Polish American Museum, museums for the Jews, and most importantly, the MoI—the Museum of Identity, one which displays this idea of the fluidity of identity by manifesting it as "the mighty new force in the world, already as powerful as any theology or ideology, cultural identity and religious identity and nation and tribe and sect and family, it was a rapidly growing multidisciplinary field" (p. 75). This is congruent with Kaldor's (2002) idea that at the center of the "new wars" lies the immense influence of globalization, and that "these wars are fought in the name of identity" (p. 273). In the same vein,

> at the heart of the Identity Museum was the question of the identity of the self, starting with the biological self and moving far beyond that. Gender

identity, splitting as never before in human history, spawning whole new vocabularies that tried to grasp the new mutabilities. (Rushdie 2017, p. 75)

It is this new world of cosmopolitanism that makes it possible to talk of identity (national, gender, or any other forms) in terms of many "new mutabilities" (p. 75). The gender zones in these museums evince that gender fluidity has been a timeless and universal phenomenon, existing in many cultures from east to west. Although gender identity is seen to be mutable even in ancient times as observed in the great statues of gods and goddesses, this diversity is now made an accepted—and displayable—part of everyday life in cosmopolitanism. This can be seen as a topic of everyday conversation for D and his two female friends while they are sipping their cocktails: the two women suggest that D can be transgender, transsexual, transvestite, or cross-dresser; rather than "he", thus, D can assume other pronouns, such as *ze*, *ey*, *hir*, *xe*, *hen*, *ve*, *ne*, *per*, *thon*, or *Mx*. (p. 115), by concluding that "[s]exual identity is not a given. It's a *choice*" (p. 116; emphasis added). Just like other dimensions of identity, gender is a part of the choosing process, of free associations, by which cosmopolitan identities are shaped. However, the novel seems to say that much freedom can sometimes be dangerous as the self-destruction of D proves in the end. Getting lost in the plethora of choices and in a state of uprootedness, D cannot survive identity crisis, the disease of the contemporary age.

All in all, cosmopolitan identity is a matter of choice, composed by a set of self-fashioning processes rather than attachment to any sort of allegiances, viewing identity as a culmination of cosmopolitanism and normalization of discrepancies. Yet, the idea of choice must be approached cautiously so as not to take it as a total detachment from local affiliations altogether, rather than as a possibility of limitless mutabilities. Vernacular cosmopolitanism, then, also emphasizes the impossibility of erasing the historical, local, and vernacular in the delineation of identity. This type of cosmopolitan identity chimes harmoniously with the new worldview of cosmopolitanism. As Schoene (2010) sums up,

> To call oneself a cosmopolitan involves not so much excising one's local affiliations, or rounding off one's personal repertory of identities with a final outer finish, as opening oneself up to a radical unlearning of all definitive modes of identification. It involves stepping out of narrow, self-incarcerating traditions of belonging. (p. 21)

This is where the Goldens go wrong by striving to dispense with local and vernacular identifications in order to call themselves cosmopolitans. Not only the desire to cede their roots, but also the aspiration to finalize their identity formation as if it was an end in itself bring about the destruction of all family members, as will be elaborated in the rest of the chapter.

COSMOPOLITAN NARRATION: COMPOSITENESS, NARRATIVE IMMEDIACY, AND POLITICAL HYPER-AWARENESS

The cosmopolitan narration is a site of multiple, and often clashing, viewpoints. To illustrate, New York's representation and embrace of cosmopolitanism, as one of the leading cosmopolitan centers in the world, are both emphasized and interrogated. The narrator first brings up a *The New York Times* report indicating an annual twenty-five percent decrease in murder rates in New York. However, René challenges this account later in his monologue of rage after his parents' accidental death, which reflects the voice of the whole city suffering from the everyday murders of citizens, a condition far from the assumptions of this optimistic news report. René expresses in this speech "the anger of the unjustly dead, the young men shot for walking in a stairwell while black, the young child shot for playing with a plastic gun in a playground while black, all the daily black death of America, screaming out that they deserved to live" (Rushdie 2017, p. 150). The homeless orator, Kinski, appears every now and then in the narrative, voicing similar concerns to ones articulated by René and drawing attention to the overpopulation of guns in America, and the subsequent "decimation and eventually the conquest of the human race [by] [t]hree hundred million living guns in America, equal in number to the human population, and trying to create a little *lebensraum* by disposing of significant quantities of human beings" (p. 178). The cosmopolitan narration, thus, incorporates various and opposing views altogether as René's inclusive manner demonstrates:

> I could feel, too, the fury of white America at having to put up with a black man in a white house, and the frothing hatred of the homophobes, and the injured wrath of their targets, the blue-collar anger of everyone who had been Fannie Mae'd and Freddie Mac'd by the housing calamity, all the discontent of a furiously divided country, everyone believing they were right, their cause was just, their pain was unique, attention must be

paid, attention must finally be paid to them and only them, and I began to wonder if we were moral beings at all or simply savages who defined their private bigotries as necessary ethics, as the only ways to be. (pp. 150–151)

All these visions juxtaposed in his fierce soliloquy are ultimately a critique of universalist cosmopolitanism and its most defining term, universal ethics. Cosmopolitanism in its mainstream sense has connotations of universalism and an understanding of humanity sharing common values and ethics. This type of cosmopolitanism is most conspicuously upheld by René's Belgian parents, the Unterlindens, who hold strong convictions regarding the "moral instinct" of "the human animal" as well as the conceptions of "right" and "wrong" that are presumed to be naturally distinguishable by all humanity (p. 151). René's parents keep expressing an inner optimism regarding human ethics and morals in keeping with their strong commitment to and belief in "[d]e best word in the world" which is "[s]ynderesis", or "[d]e supposed innate ability of de human mind to realize de basic principles of ethics and morals [...] signifying de innate principle in de moral consciousness of every man, which directs him to good and restrains him from evil" (p. 152). His own outlook contradicts these basic assumptions of universalist cosmopolitan thinking. After his parents are killed by a car crash, this idealism embodied by their naïve commitment to this kind of universalism proves wrong, at least for René, who concludes that "they were wrong. The human race was savage, not moral" (p. 152). He discusses the word *goodness*, and its being emptied of meaning as a universal value, like many other "poisoned words" ("spirituality", "final solution", and "freedom") (p. 7). Contrary to the cosmopolitan utopias, the hyper-aware narrator is resentful that "[w]e are so divided, so hostile to one another" (p. 7).

Stylistically, Schoene's term "compositeness" (2010, p. 14), which characterizes the cosmopolitan novel, is discernible in the narrative form of *The Golden House*, where the cosmopolitan representation displays simultaneously multifarious and incompatible pictures. This type of composite representation is similar to contemporary cinema's montage and perspective-shifting effects as it brings together a limitless number of alternative and incongruous scenes together, assembling orderless lines of plot and characterization within a single narrative (Schoene 2010, p. 14). The novel's narration's affiliation with cinematic creation is structurally reinforced by the narrator's specific aim of writing a script for his first movie that will be named "The Golden House". Rushdie asserts the advantage of using a cinematic technique in his novel as it "freed up a lot of things about the form of the book, and being able to use movie references as reference points, and I liked all that. And there's a kind of montage, a cross-cutting between scenes" (Tuttle 2017). An overt cinema analogy and the use of its jargon prevail in the narrative, especially in the scene where Nero's three sons and Riya discuss at the beach in Miami the consequences of his commencing relationship with a young Russian gymnast and golden-digger, Vasilisa: "it's now a movie"; "Wide screen, black and white"; "the camera watches them in extreme close-ups until they speak, but cuts to wide shots when we hear their voices" (Rushdie 2017, p. 85); "Circling, tight shot, around and around them" (p. 86); "Water on the camera lens. Fade to white" (p. 88). The narrative organization of *The Golden House* also complies with the definition of compositeness as one cannot fail to recognize the cinematic shifting of focus on different characters and worlds as the chapters proceed. This fictional tool, for Schoene, displays "a momentarily composite picture of the world" in an analogy to a kaleidoscope (2010, p. 27). On the very first page of the novel, a kaleidoscopic image of the world is visible when the narrator creates quick pictures of the global problems, such as economic crisis and terrorism:

> On the day of the new president's inauguration, when we worried that he might be murdered as he walked [...] among the cheering crowds, and when so many of us were close to economic ruin in the aftermath of the bursting of the mortgage bubble, and when Isis was still an Egyptian mother-goddess, an uncrowned seventy-something king from a faraway country arrived in New York City with his three motherless sons to take possession of the palace of his exile, behaving as if nothing was wrong with the country or the world or his own story. (Rushdie 2017, p. 3)

In this passage, through the narrator's "[y]ielding to fruitful interpermeation only intermittently" (Schoene 2010, p. 14), one can have an overlook into the world with a quick but knowing eye while also viewing the alteration of focus on various and incompatible scenes in this specific moment of the cosmopolitan city. This composite picture makes the Goldens' relatively less consequential arrival scene simultaneous and equivalent with events of paramount significance for the country. The seemingly unrelated events—the election of Obama in 2012 and the arrival of Nero Golden with his sons to the country—are given together in this opening scene with the use of the camera shift technique. References to the mortgage crisis as well as religious terrorism are also made in this representation of the contemporary state of the world. This kaleidoscopic image is also prone to change and re-representation with the possibility of the narrator's choices.

In Schoene's words, the picture of the cosmopolitan world, like a child's kaleidoscope, is composed only momentarily before it is collapsed and reproduced in another possibly perfect representation (2010, p. 27). Due to his mental condition of Asperger syndrome and his multiple sensory stimuli, Petya, the oldest son of Nero Golden, is capable of seeing "the kaleidoscopic blaze of images", at times departing from reality and ending in his frequent floods of chatter and stream-of-consciousness monologues reflecting "the adversarial fragmentation of American culture and [making] it a part of his personal damage" (Rushdie 2017, p. 202). Petya's verbal explosions illustrate the kaleidoscopic representation of the world:

> Obamacare, terrible!, Maryland shooting, don't politicize it!, minimum-wage rise, scandalous!, same-sex marriage, unnatural!, religious objections to serving LGBT people in Arizona, in Mississippi, freedom!, police shootings, self-defense!, Donald Sterling, free speech!, shootings on university campus in Seattle shootings in Vegas shootings in Oregon high school, guns don't kill people!, arm the teachers!, the Constitution!, freedom!, ISIS beheading, Jihadi John, disgusting!, we have no plan!, take them all out!, we have no *plan*!, oh, and Ebola! Ebola! Ebola! (p. 202)

Despite being instantaneous and undetailed, Petya's references to contemporary issues and his rage in the form of overflowing soliloquys exemplify cosmopolitan fiction's engagement with global matters by creating a composite, if only a momentary and arbitrary, picture of the world. This versatile imagery is rich in contemporary references, ranging from political to religious, from everyday murders to homophobia, to the fatal virus epidemic. The rapidly shifting images within the same scene are also representative of the constantly renewing problems of the world.

The two terms proposed in Chapter 2 as essential formal characteristics of contemporary cosmopolitan fiction, narrative immediacy, and political hyper-awareness, can be substantiated in *The Golden House*. Drawing on Walkowitz's terms referring to modernist experimental styles, these two terms emerge as innovative ways of grappling with contemporary world crises. That is particularly because they encapsulate and exemplify what Knepper and Deckard call "forms of experimental writing that mediate the challenges associated with the quest for alternatives to the hegemonic global order, beginning with the question of creative expression as an object and agent of social transformation" (2016, p. 13). In this line of thought, these concepts that can be employed to analyze Rushdie's cosmopolitan novel emphasize the engaged role attached to literature, which in fact aligns them with Nealon's call for literary "intensification" (rather than "fragmentation") informing a post-postmodernist reading shaped primarily by socioeconomic realities (2012, p. 150). Similarly, post-postmodernist literature is, for McLaughlin, "inspired by a desire to reconnect language to the social sphere or, to put it another way, to reenergize literature's social mission, its ability to intervene in the social world, to have an impact on actual people and the actual social institutions in which they live their lives" (2004, p. 55). Both of these concepts are, then, characterized by responsibility and engagedness.

The first term, narrative immediacy refers to the directness of response, often in the form of prompt and critical listings, to contemporary events with an immediate and direct narrative engagement with today's world. The narrator's directness of criticism is palpable in his reaction to the resultant social segregation that has become more conspicuous in the aftermath of 9/11 events; "after the planes hit the buildings", the narrator asserts the necessity to be careful "not to blame the innocent for the crimes of the guilty" (Rushdie 2017, p. 38). His argument is made more forceful with his visions of what it means to be an immigrant in post-9/11 New York: "God Bless America" stickers on the partition screens of taxis and "Don't Blame Me I'm Hindu T-shirts" worn by young men of colour (p. 38). Direct narrative engagement with the contemporary world may appear like a journalistic reporting of the day's events, often in headlines, a technique which is also resorted to in the novel: "Spring, the last of the ice gone from the Hudson, and happy sails breaking out across the weekend water. Drought in California, Oscars for *Birdman*, but no superheroes available in Gotham" (p. 220). Yet, cosmopolitan narrative does more than just reporting; it actually comments upon the political agenda of the day. "The Joker was on TV, announcing a run for president", René regrets, referring to the expected one and a half year ahead election of Gwynplaine. Considering the impending catastrophe in the future, René expresses his nostalgia for the present (when he is not yet the president), the days when gay marriage is legalized and a new ferry service to Cuba is inaugurated (p. 38). The narrator's immediate movements from contemporary politics to public news also illustrate the narrative immediacy of cosmopolitan fiction:

> A gunman shot a doctor in El Paso and then himself. A man shot his neighbors, a Muslim family in North Carolina, because of a parking dispute. [...] In Tyrone, Missouri, a gunman killed seven people and then made himself his eighth victim. Also in Missouri, a certain Jeffery L. Williams shot two policemen in front of the Ferguson city police headquarters. A police officer named Michael Slager shot and killed Walter Scott, an unarmed black man, in North Charleston, South Carolina. (p. 220)

It is in the form of narrative immediacy that this section provides a quick but insightful vision into the everyday life of cosmopolitans. By so doing, this part also draws attention to the terror of homicides in contemporary New York.

The depiction of Joker's America, "the United States of Joker" or "U.S.J" (p. 248), in terms of two bubbles takes shape as narrative immediacy. One bubble portrays it as a world of dystopia, as if it existed in "nineteen eighty-four" (p. 250): climate change and the end of the Arctic icecap are regarded as a new real estate opportunity, the murder of un-American citizens is seen lawfully acceptable, a wall must be built in order to prevent killers and rapists from America's neighboring country in the south, wars are obliged to happen to defeat the country's enemies, the financial failures of the country are perceived to be great business competence, nuclear weapons are okay to be executed, and so on. "In that bubble", the narrator goes on, "knowledge was ignorance, up was down, and the right person to hold the nuclear codes in his hand was the green-haired white-skinned red-slash-mouthed giggler" (p. 249). This brisk and sketchy depiction of the first bubble correlates it with the characteristics of universalist cosmopolitanism, where many environmental, economic, and political issues are ignored and a naïve optimism about the condition of the country and the world predominate while money's prominence is accepted. The political and economic failures of the new president, Joker, are taken lightheartedly by the citizens who support him; street murders, especially those of the colored, are tolerated; the governmental ownership of nuclear weapons is supported; and in brief, everything is turned upside down. The dystopian representation in this bubble is discerned by many as a utopian world, one which is not taken seriously, and is viewed only in positive terms:

> In that bubble, razor-tipped playing cards were funny, and lapel flowers that sprayed acid into people's faces were funny, and wishing you could have sex with your daughter was funny, and sarcasm was funny even when what was called sarcasm was not sarcastic, and lying was funny, and hatred was funny, and bigotry was funny, and bullying was funny, and the date was, or almost was, or might soon be, if the jokes worked out as they should, nineteen eighty-four. (pp. 249–250)

The reiterated word "funny", in the way Smith also uses repeated catchwords in *NW*, is employed critically to demonstrate the lack of insight and seriousness in the attitude of those who vote for the Joker president.

The other bubble, on the other hand, represents vernacular cosmopolitanism that exists in the city of New York, a counter world in which "a kind of reality still persevered" (p. 250). In this world, New Yorkers are more conscious about the political, economic, and environmental issues and more cautious against imposters like Joker. They, too, laugh at Joker, not with approval, but out of knowingness of his dishonesty. These bubbles reflect "the great battle between deranged fantasy and grey reality" as well as the contrast between Joker's world of "a lurid graphic novel" and Kantian "*la chose en soi*, the possibly unknowable but probably existing thing in itself, the world as it was independently of what was said about it or how it was seen, the *Ding an sich*" (p. 250). The implication here is that the world with its very realities and real problems exists independently of the utopian perception of those in the first bubble, and thus, it is necessary to assume a more perceptive and inclusive vision about it. By making use of the technique of narrative immediacy, this passage provides a summary of the political climate in the country before the election of November, and in fact, comments on it effectively even with an immediate and expeditious picture.

René acts as a hyper-aware narrator throughout the narrative, articulating his concerns about the condition of the world, the country, and the Golden family, representing several viewpoints, and at least unearthing his own self-fallacies in the course of the narrative. Self-knowingly, René asserts: "I am aware that by drifting into the third person and alleging the failure of my will I am making a bid to be exempted from moral judgment" (pp. 180–181). His commentary on universal ethics is far from being utopian with his acceptance of human weaknesses like his own, unlike that of his academic parents, who represent another—over-optimistic—version of universalist cosmopolitanism, and believe that "'right' and 'wrong' were ideas that came naturally to the human animal, that these concepts were born in us, not made" (p. 151). As a repudiation of this idea and an act of betrayal, René fails to spurn Vasilisa's secret plan to entice René to impregnate her because Nero is biologically incapable of being a father. Meanwhile, she convinces her husband to the contrary with a fake doctor report. Alongside many other people and events in the story, the narrator himself is under the scrutiny of his own hyper-aware lenses: "I am further aware that 'he couldn't help it' is not a strong defense. Allow me this at least: that I am self-aware" (p. 181). He is further capable of getting out of his physical body and look at himself from above, rendering the scene where he is going to make love to Vasilisa for this task as if it was a film shot with references to a number of similar scenes from famous movies. Initially fascinated by the exceptional beauty of Vasilisa, René imagines her as "one of the goddesses of the screen" (p. 181), but he soon changes his perspective, "reminding [himself] of the powerful feminist critiques of New Wave cinema, Laura Mulvey's 'male gaze' theory in which she proposed that audiences were obliged to see these films from the point of view of the heterosexual male, with women reduced to the status of objects" (p. 182). He even comments "[o]n the subject of [his] self-awareness" and his weaknesses, "the treacheries of [his] true nature", which "are sometimes obscure to [him]", acknowledging that he is "obliged to face directly who [he] actually was" (p. 182) as "her co-conspirator, as morally compromised as she was" (p. 183). It is not only himself, but also the world in general suffering from this moral deficiency, as the narrator perceives: "When I looked at the world beyond myself I saw my own moral weakness reflected in it" (p. 188).

Political hyper-awareness corresponds to a direct engagement with ideology and contemporary politics without recourse to a naïve approach to, and acceptance of, cosmopolitan universalism. Hoydis asserts that "[t]he intention to represent contemporary conditions 'realistically' and with more urgency is clear in Rushdie" (2019, p. 156). This realist propensity in the author's recent novel can be expounded through its preference for directness: "[N]otable in contemporary writing is a stylistic shift away from (but by no means a discarding of) linguistic and formal experimentation, self-referentiality and irony to more straightforwardly realist representations" (Hoydis 2019, p. 155). In keeping with his political hyper-awareness, the narrator makes references to, and comments upon, a number of political events and protests that come as a reaction to them. Having given up his initial momentary optimism after the election results of 2012, René foretells the disappointment that will be caused by the same president whose triumph resonates with the cheers of the crowd. The same group of protestors consisting of mostly young white college students gather once more in the streets eight years after the election to show their desire "to rip that system up and throw it away" (Rushdie 2017, p. 57). René's attitude toward these people is reminiscent of Perowne's reactions against the war protestors in *Saturday*; aware that the crowd is irresolute in their cause, both express their criticism by viewing "that kind of grand gesture" on the part of the protestors as "an expression of the same spoiled luxuriousness that its proponents claimed to hate" (p. 57). René further claims that "when such gestures were made they invariably led to something worse than what had been discarded" (p. 57). Perowne is also less concerned with the global reason that brings the crowd together than its environmental effect, hence the local consequences of the demonstrations on his closer surroundings. Like Perowne's, René's attitude is "different [from the rest], more cautious, gradualist, and, in the eyes of the generation following [him], [a] contemptible point on the (political) spectrum" (p. 57). Although both of them are condemned by others for their detachment, they display hyper-awareness through their inclusive visions and aspirations of insight into others' minds in the form of narrative glocality.

Not only the public movements but also their limitations are under the critical examination of the narrator. Another dissenting act is the famous New Yorkian gallerist, Frankie Sottovoce's notorious protest of the war in Vietnam by spray-painting the letters NLF on a Claude Monet painting at the Museum of Modern Art (p. 60). Like other protestors, Sottovoce loses his idealism over time. Despite being "boastful about his radical-left activist younger self" (p. 60), Sottovoce now hosts many elite New Yorkers in his gallery, giving up his idealist activism after having "a distinguished career" (p. 60). This short reference to the life of the famous gallerist is a testament to a hyper-aware comment on the part of the narrator.

Revolts in various forms populate the pages of the novel in its depiction of everyday life in New York, yet they are also presented critically through the hyper-aware lenses of the narrator. Most protests are cosmopolitan in nature, like the people gathering in the Financial District, protesting the banks, and expressing themselves in the costumes of an international band of historical characters like Goethe, G.K. Chesterton, Ghandi, and Henry Ford during these demonstrations. To the disapproval of his family, Apu Golden joins the dissenting crowd in the streets to enrich his art as an artist and draw scenes from the event. He is only fond of "the visual and also literary aspects of the event", finding some of the co-protestors as "you-cross-the-road-to-avoid-contact-with-them types" (p. 139). Nevertheless, this "carnivalesque character of the crowd" is appealing for Apu, especially the marchers costumed as dead celebrities walking among the crowd. Yet, rather than having such fun, René's attention is drawn to such spelling mistakes on the placards as the one regarding Ghandi's name, which is misspelled as "Gandhi", and the fact that nobody cares about correct spelling and correct information in general any longer in this age of post-truth: "[N]obody can spell anymore, spelling is so boozhwa" (p. 139). Impressed by the placards quoting these dead people, Apu recognizes that the quote by Ghandi ("First they ignore you, then they blah blah blah, then you win".) does not actually belong to the Indian politician, but he does not care about this mistake in the mainstream conviction that "nobody knows anything, [...] knowing things is boozhwa too" (p. 140), in line with the conception of post-factualness. In contrast, René favors a cardboard "motivated primarily by hunger" declamating an anonymous thinker scolding financial inequality: "One day the poor will have nothing left to eat except the rich" and another one conveying the same message in sum in the words "Eat a banker" (p. 140). Yet, it turns out that this thinker-protestor wearing "an Anonymous mask, the moustachioed smiling white-faced Guy Fawkes face", which is the one popularized in the film *V for Vendetta*, is not actually familiar with the reference the mask he is wearing makes, concerning "the Gunpowder Plot" and "the fifth of November" (p. 140). This is the point where the narrator, René, gets critical about the protestors in the way Perowne in *Saturday* questions the crowd's sincerity in their cause, asserting that "[s]uch was this would-be revolution" (p. 140). The permeating yet meaningless elatedness among the protesters in New York as in London is noted by both Perowne and René. Perowne finds this "general cheerfulness" of the people "baffling", and refuses to join them outright (McEwan 2005, p. 61); René, unlike Perowne, joins the crowd but at the same time acknowledges that it is not because of his genuine interest that he goes there but "because [Apu's] giggling enthusiasm was infectious", and thus, accompanies him, becoming an involuntary participant of this naïve happiness (Rushdie 2017, pp. 139–140).

Providing various pictures from the local spaces of the city, the narrative unfolds in a way to comply with Schoene's (2010) assertion about cosmopolitan community:

> Contemporary cosmopolitanism projects a community that bears rupturing and indeed thrives on recurrent reassemblage – a community that will always tear as well as mend untidily, avoiding clear-cut contours or perfect patterns. This community has no *telos* except its own continuation, which remains resolutely finite and of this world. (p. 21)

As discernible in the assemblage of revolting groups, American community is malleable in distinct ways and shapes. This is tantamount to claiming that *The Golden House*, as a cosmopolitan novel, sets itself apart from a universalist outlook. Schoene's definition of cosmopolitan fiction draws heavily on Jean-Luc Nancy's theory (1991) of "inoperative community", which corresponds, in Nancy's words, to a "community without essence" and "a bond that forms ties without attachments, or even less fusion […] a bond that unbinds by binding" (qtd in Schoene 2010, p. 22). The fictional name given to America, "United States of Joker", signifies such an "inoperative community" which is without a *telos*, an essence, and thus, bound to rupture ultimately. Protesters residing in New York City act in "in-operation" because, as Schoene puts it, "inoperative community *is* properly communal, and it also does 'work' in the sense of bringing about political results. What it militates against is ideological organisation and teleology, as well as any other form of 'management'" (2010, p. 23). Apu's disconnection from Occupy protesters in Zuccotti Park stems from this lack of teleology and "management", from "his frustration at their leaderless anarchic rudderlessness" as well as their interest in "the posture than the results" (Rushdie 2017, p. 226).

The Golden House's cosmopolitan detachment from universalism can be observed in the treatment of contemporary events and matters with the employment of compositeness, narrative immediacy, and political hyper-awareness, devices that are highly definitive of the postmillennial cosmopolitan novel.

Considerations About the Economic Dimensions of Cosmopolitanism

As a vernacular cosmopolitan novel, *The Golden House* is concerned with considerations of neoliberal capitalism and economic implications of globalism, which have intensified after the 2008 financial crisis. In *The Golden House*, in alignment with the urge to respond to neoliberal capitalism, global and local cosmopolitan spaces are reflected as mutually permeable and indistinguishable. The ambiguous distinction between the global and the local is reflected in the novel in the portrayal of spaces. "Modern localities", as Tomlinson puts it, "integrate local and distant (global) cultural experiences within the same phenomenological space" (2002, p. 253). In spatial terms, with the gradual departure from "the local" and an orientation toward "the global", or vice versa, the division between the two territories is problematized, precisely because, as Held puts it, "the effects of distant events can be highly significant elsewhere and even the most local developments can come to have enormous global consequences" (2010, p. 29), especially in economic terms.

The novel displays an awareness of neoliberal capitalism which proves to be prevalent in contemporary cosmopolitan spaces. Certain approaches to cosmopolitanism regard it as a disguise or cover for new forms of Americanization. Cosmopolitanism, for Brennan, is in fact "a veiled Americanism" (2001, p. 682), and Calhoun suggests that "it needs to disentangle itself from neo-liberal capitalism" (2002, p. 106). *The Golden House*, as a contemporary cosmopolitan novel, assumes a cautious positioning, rejecting to delete ideology and cover up this new "Americanism" under the title "cosmopolitanism". It adopts an overtly critical stance toward the complicity between capitalism and universalist cosmopolitanism. Despite the demolition of first- and third-world dichotomy, the novel pays attention to power inequalities that have emerged in a renewed form and veiled version. Nero Golden is well aware of capitalist ventures beneath the idea of Americanism: "If America wants to be what America is capable of being, what she dreams of being, she needs to turn away from God and toward the dollar bill. The business of America is business" (Rushdie 2017, pp. 52–53). In fact, Nero Golden himself is a powerful capitalist just like the country he identifies with and opts to spend the rest of his life in. Back in India, he has been in a wide range of businesses as the indefinite source of his fortune: construction, real estate, yarn trading, shipping, venture capitalism, film production, and steel, to list some of them (p. 118). Yet René's investigations also reveal his illegal involvement in "the notorious 2G Spectrum scam", a scandalous selling of cellphone frequency licenses at extremely low prices to favored multinational telecommunications corporations by the government, which ranks second in *Time* magazine's "Top Ten Abuses of Power list", following "the Watergate affair" (p. 119). Nero Golden's top-down cosmopolitanism is a testament to Calhoun's definition of cosmopolitanism as a "project of capitalism" flourishing "in the top management of multinational corporations" (2002, p. 106). The very name Nero Golden assumes for himself resonates with his capitalist mindset recalling the monetary value of gold: "[T]he word GOLDEN, a golden word, colored gold, in brightly illuminated gold neon, and all in capital letters of gold, began to be seen on hard-hat sites around town, and out of town also" (Rushdie 2017, p. 143). The value reflected by the name equals the prestige the protagonist gains as soon as he arrives in the metropole: "[T]he name's owner began to be spoken of as a new power player in that most closed of elites, the small number of families and corporations who controlled the building of this golden city, New York" (p. 143). This reference to the prevailing power of multinational corporations and Americanism in contemporary cosmopolitanism testifies to the novel's vernacular consciousness.

Calhoun contends that contemporary engagement with cosmopolitanism simultaneously reflects "the challenge of an increasingly global capitalism" (2002, p. 102). The global mobility of people, goods, information, and capital, several examples of which we see in the novel, shows the extent to which globalization becomes an everyday phenomenon, an accepted part of daily conversation. In the chapter titled "Regarding The Family: An Interrogation", the narrator converses with an unknown speaker concerning Nero Golden's allegedly illegal business affairs, mostly in cooperation with a band of notorious international mafia leaders who are known worldwide with the nicknames "Chicken Little, Little Archie, Crazy Fred and Fat Frankie" (Rushdie 2017, p. 144). In another instance, during his visit to Nero's house for a warning speech, Mastan, the retired police officer from India talks of the constantly growing Indian community living in America composed of businessmen in different sectors: recyclers of plastic bottles, new technology geniuses, acclaimed actors, campaigning attorneys as well as important politicians. This community also includes rapidly growing families, gangs, from the mother country living in America now, "*gharaney*", or "households", or a popular name for them nowadays, "*companies*" (p. 350). They have a growing "interest in globalization, in shared activities" (p. 350) consisting of assisting political as well as financial affairs back at home. Beck cautions against the danger of confusing "global citizenship" with "global capitalists" consisting of a global managerial class and the bourgeois that is capable of acting freely within a transnational framework (2010, p. 228). The novel demonstrates this collaboration between globalization and capitalism in line with the concerns of the cosmopolitan novel after 2008.

Calhoun's contention that "[c]apitalist cosmopolitans have indeed traversed the globe, from early modern merchants to today's World Bank officials and venture capitalists" (2002, p. 103) as well as Beck's (2010) "global capitalists" can be observed in the cosmopolitan community depicted in *The Golden House*. Echoing the dinner table conversations concerning the harms of mobile phones in Natalie's house in *NW*, one of the guests at Nero Golden's wedding reception in the Golden house, Andy Drescher, a capitalist-minded New York icon, talks of "his celebrated complaints", a list of things and people to complain about, which contains machinery, particularly smartphones. Likewise, in the fashion of Natalie's well-off friends who find solutions to distance themselves from the poor of the city in their 4 × 4 SUV cars, Andy boasts of his plan to purchase "a ten-million-dollar apartment" as well as being "a transbillionaire" (Rushdie 2017, p. 122). Examples of capitalist cosmopolitans abound. René's girlfriend, Suchitra Roy, condemns her parents for being "global capitalists" in Beck's terms (2010, p. 228). Having listed a variety of communist parties of India, all "Marxist-Leninist" at the core, but assuming about fifteen different party names, Suchitra tells René about how her Indian parents, "two intrepid capitalistically inclined entrepreneur types" (p. 158), have moved to America to escape the predominantly leftist politics of the country, become economically successful in a range of businesses upon their arrival, and consequently are befriended with the exclusive members of "the political institutions of the Hindu right [...] being fruitful and multiplying on fertile American soil" (p. 159). In another conversation, U Lnu Fnu, the Myanmaran UN diplomat who welcomes René after he decides to leave the Golden house, talks about his former tenant, an airline pilot who has flown a wide range of cargo and people from mercenaries into Iraq to two hundred million dollars' worth of Venezuelan currency which is printed in Britain and loaded at the Heathrow without any security measures, yet regarded in Caracas as a huge military operation (p. 211). It is the mobilization not only of people but also of money, legally or illegally, that attest to the prevalence of globalization, and the resultant capitalism in contemporary cosmopolitan centers.

Universalist cosmopolitanism cannot be separated from the considerations of economic inequalities and class divides. In keeping with this, the narrator asserts that "[i]f you owed the bank a buck you were a deadbeat with an overdraft. If you owed a billion you were rich and the bank was working with you" (p. 163). Having heard of rumors about Nero's businesses' awaiting bankruptcy, René recalls, in reference to Nero's aspirations of conquering New York City, a kind of impossible utopia from Calvino's book, in which he is actually an inhabitant of only an imaginary, invisible city called Octavia "a spiderweb city hanging in a great net over an abyss between two mountains" (p. 164). The implication in this analogy is that utopianism and the universalist cosmopolitanism represented by not only Nero himself but also New York City exist in an abyss, a net, which will not last forever, and will soon give way to other understandings of contemporary cosmopolitanism. The narrator also accuses the deceived protagonist of lack of insight or the failure to look down, which will culminate in his "calamitous ending" (p. 164). Nero's association with the idea of universalist cosmopolitanism is made clear when René thinks that the old man refers to "pan-globalism" when he says, "One world. When they let us in, I'll be the first in the door", to recognize his mistake immediately and understand that Nero is actually referring to his plan to rent offices in One World Trade Center, the reconstructed buildings of twin towers after the 9/11 attacks. The reason for Nero's plan to move to "One World" is twofold; first, he desires to give up his current tenancy in Gary "Green" Gwynplaine's, a.k.a Joker's, business center because he dislikes this presidential candidate and supports his rival, and secondly, he hopes to deal for new offices at the top of the new tower at very low prices as a clever business endeavor on his part. He is, however, disappointed at Romney's defeat and Joker's triumph in the 2016 presidential elections.

THE VERNACULAR ENDING

The Golden House opens space for the representation of many local versions of cosmopolitanism with a view to the vernacular. The elite district which is called MacDougal–Sullivan Gardens is portrayed in stark contrast to the broader outside world: "the Gardens [...] was the enchanted, fearless space in which we lived and raised our children, a place of happy retreat from the disenchanted, fearful world beyond its borders" (p. 9); yet the rest of the narrative problematizes this distinction as the private space becomes as much fearful as the world outside of it, causing those "borders" to get blurred. The tranquility of the Gardens set against the chaotic outside city is hazarded as the inhabitants of this local area witness the one-after-another death of the Golden sons, and the eventual surrender of the house and its inmates to the blazes. For Rushdie himself, this is "a private tragicomedy inset inside a larger public tragicomedy", which reflects the more general condition: "The reason the Gardens as a setting was so helpful is that it makes that physical: there's this physically enclosed space, like a little theater, in which the characters can act out their lives. But it's also a secluded space. And around that secluded space there is the larger tragicomedy of America" (Tuttle 2017). The correlation between the family and the country becomes manifest in the end.

The fatal end of all of the Golden men may represent the destruction of the universalist understanding of cosmopolitanism and the serious consequences of extracting the self from locality and the desire for detachment from one's past. The implied author's fierce critique of universalist cosmopolitanism becomes more visible by the end of the novel. The reason for each of these deaths is inevitably connected to what takes place in the outside world as well as their inescapable past, "the slow fatal resurrection of the past" (Rushdie 2017, p. 285) and Nero's "far-away yesterdays that shone more clearly than last week" (p. 318). René is well-aware of the invasion of the past in his narration, of all the "ghosts and death angels [...] like a ticketless crowd bursting through the gates at a big game" (p. 287). René further cautions against the Goldens' biggest fallacy, the desire to rid themselves of history, even at the outset: "They wanted to step away from the responsibilities of history and be free. But history is the court before which all men, even emperors and princes, finally must stand" (p. 53). By implication, the self-named emperor, Nero Golden, and his prince sons, with ancient gods' names, are in the end relegated to this position of accounting for their past, ironically having to renounce their unbridled freedom. René's girlfriend Suchitra, another character representing vernacular cosmopolitanism, and also known for her departure from her parents' capitalist orientations, reproaches the Goldens for their lack of local associations, for "denying their race": "These deracinated rich people rejecting their history and culture and name. Getting away with it because of the accident of skin color which allows them to pass" (p. 184). She further anticipates their end although she speaks in a metaphorical sense: "[T]o pretend [your land] doesn't exist, that you never existed there, that it's nothing to you and you're nothing to it, that makes me feel they're agreeing to be, in a way, dead. It's like they are living their afterlife while they are still alive" (p. 184). It is this unboundedness, in fact, that brings about their destructive end. Apu and his girlfriend are murdered by Nero Golden's enemies during their visit to his former city, Mumbai, so as to get rid of the ghosts of old days that chase him to his new life, which are portrayed in his detailed Manhattan cityscape, an image of the "empty city populated only by translucent figures" (p. 228), "the ghosts of the lost past, haunting him" all from his home country (p. 230). It is his conviction that they "just ripped [themselves] away" from their old life without conciliation that propels him back to India for "a journey backwards" (p. 231). Eventually, the family needs to confront the end predicted by Apu: "I think a dark force out of the past would fly across the world and probably destroy us all" (p. 232). His death at home becomes a testament to the inevitability of escaping the past as well as dividing the local from the global. Petya also decides to confront his past "phantoms", "a ghost or a memory", in a self-transforming walk, his "great saunter" along a thirty-two-mile route around Manhattan Island to recover him from his agoraphobia as well as other past fears (p. 205). Nero's oldest son, however, eventually becomes a victim of a street attack during Halloween parades, unable to protect himself from imminent terror, ironically instigated by Kinski, the homeless orator, who has chidden street terror in his former speeches. Unlike his brothers, the youngest Golden son, D, chooses the Gardens for self-shooting as a result of his identity crisis that originated back in his childhood years when he saw the Michael Jackson-costumed hijra on the streets of Mumbai. Eventually, the fire in the Golden house has implications of taking revenge on Nero Golden's former business affairs back in India, causing Nero and Vasilisa's downfall. It is the impossibility to distinguish the global from the local, the historical from the present that rules the affairs and inescapable deaths of the Goldens.

The Golden house is symbolic in many respects as suggested by Walonen:

> [O]n a symbolic level the house that Nero Golden inaugurates represents the capitalist dream of reaching the pinnacle of wealth and power, the

version of it for the era of neoliberal globalization that involves leaving one's roots behind and becoming part of the transnational, post-national plutocratic capitalist elite based in such global city "command centers" of global economy as Manhattan, London, and Tokyo and flitting freewheelingly between these and other global cultural, leisure, and economic centres. (2020, p. 258)

The house embodied by Nero Golden himself is also depicted in a way to emphasize the analogy between him and America. They are both mighty, ruling, capitalist, yet unable to avoid destruction on a symbolic level. Continuously weakening both mentally and physically, Nero is now more dependent on others. Toward the end, he becomes willing to listen to non-elite cosmopolitans, including the street speaker Kinski, who is invited to the Golden house and allowed to preach on the evils of guns. Likewise, Nero needs the friendship of a prostitute called Mlle. Loulou, whom he visits occasionally to listen to her philosophizing, rather than have sexual adventures, on several topics, similar to Kinski's, like street violence. The country Nero is associated with also undergoes a radical change through the impending effect of elections: "The world outside the haunted house had begun to feel like a lie. Outside the house it was the Joker's world, the world of what reality had begun to mean in America, which was to say, a kind of radical untruth: phoniness, garishness, bigotry, vulgarity, violence, paranoia" (Rushdie 2017, p. 284).

In the closing pages, Nero Golden is destroyed by fire in the Golden house, and symbolically the country is put on fire when the Joker president is elected in November 2016. The fate of the family and the country is similar: "And the demented Joker out there, swinging from the Empire State Building with his greedy eye on the White House [...] Tragedy or chance? And were there escape routes for the family and the country, or was it wiser to sit back and accept one's fate?" (p. 276). Both cosmopolitan territories, the Golden house and America, face a failure of their universalist outlook—the international staff of the house begin to desert the house one by one following the handyman Gonzalo's departure and Vasilisa's remarks about "the unreliability of Mexicans" (p. 368) while on a larger scale, the American government remains unwilling to accept Mexican immigrants on account of their unreliability and the problems they will supposedly bring to the country alongside. In a similar vein, the burning of the Golden house signifies more than a fire for the narrator, who views it as the burning of all civilization:

Civilization itself seemed to be burning in the fire, my hopes, the hopes of women, our hopes for our planet, and for peace. I thought of all those thinkers burned at the stake, all those who stood up against the forces and orthodoxies of their time, and I felt myself and my whole disenfranchised kind bound now by strong chains and engulfed by the awful blaze, the West itself on fire, Rome burning, the barbarians not at the gates but within, our own barbarians, […] rising like savage children to burn the world that made them, claiming to save it even as they set it ablaze. (p. 374)

The house's burning, as an epitome of Western civilization and thinking, represents the collapse of over-optimistic approaches within universalist cosmopolitanism, and in this sense, the narrator gradually quits his initial lamenting tone regarding the fire, and gains a final recognition. This apocalyptic portrayal of the destruction of the house turns out to be a comment on the futility of the attempt to divide the global from the local, and an interrogation of cosmopolitan universalism which is implicated in the family's refusal of their local associations. It becomes certain that the past is inescapable, as epitomized by the huge gunnysack of dirty laundry full of Indian clothing left at the Golden house's door a few days before the fire as a reminder of the old days when they called Nero "*dhobi*", meaning the laundryman (p. 377). The final lesson drawn by René is that such an enclosed local place like the Gardens can be susceptible to demolition as much as the outside world surrounding it: "That there was no safe place, that the monster was always at the gates, and a little of the monster was within us too, […] no matter how lucky we were in life or money or family or talent or love, at the end of the road the fire was burning, and it would consume us all" (p. 374). René's musings have resonances of Bauman's assertion that "[c]ontemporary fears, the typically 'urban fears', […] focus on the 'enemy inside'" (1998, pp. 47–48). The fire stops being the foremost symbol of civilization's progress in this contemporary picture, instead becoming its very eradicator. What is at stake here is the foundations upon which the notion of universalism is built.

In the end, the only survivors are the representatives of vernacular cosmopolitanism, René, Suchitra, and the new generation Golden baby, Vespa. In a moment of recognition, René, together with Suchitra, understand that "the world was neither meaningless nor absurd, that in fact it had profound meaning and form, but that form and meaning had been hidden from us until now, concealed in the hieroglyphs and esoterica of power, because it was in the interests of the masters of the world to hide meaning from all but the illuminated" (Rushdie 2017, p. 162). Perhaps "the illuminated" corresponds to the hyper-aware cosmopolitans who have an insight into the covered dangers within the conception of the universalist understanding of cosmopolitanism, and thus, favor certain vernacular feelings, including love in its most local and purest sense. René concludes that "it was up to the two of us to save the planet and that the force that would save the planet was love" (p. 162). This vernacular sensation that is inspired by human feelings in its purest sense without recourse to naïve optimism is love that must connect people in a locality first.

Another survivor of the final tragedy and a local cosmopolitan, Riya, reconsiders her long-held beliefs in identity politics, regretting that they actually have failed to prevent her lover, D Golden's death, and instead embraces a new set of ideas concerning love: "[L]ove is stronger than gender, stronger than definitions, stronger than the self. [...] Identity – specifically, gender identity theory – is a narrowing of humanity, and love shows us how broad we can be. To honor my dead lover I reject the politics of identity and embrace the politics of love" (p. 298). Convinced that it is the compulsion to identify with a specific gender identity—despite the multiplicity and freedom of choice—that brought about the demise of D, Riya contends that he could only have been saved through love. This orientation toward love recalls Rushdie's own testimony in an interview concerning *The Golden House* and the theme of love: "Certainly I've increasingly found in my writing that love becomes the dominant value" (Tuttle 2017).

René in the end retreats from the universal "macro garbage" completely, deciding to return to vernacular cosmopolitanism altogether, to "hold on to life [...], its dailiness and strength" (Rushdie 2017, p. 359). At this point, he invites Joker and his stories "to take a back seat and let real people drive the bus" (p. 359). It is the "little lives" and real stories of those local cosmopolitans that must be understood now as everything else gets even less comprehensible in this world of ambiguities. He manages to complete his golden tale, yet attains only partial satisfaction with the conviction that "without love it was all ashes" (p. 362). In the course of his deprivation in terms of love in the absence of Suchitra after he reveals that he is the real father of Vasilisa's baby, he holds on to the idea of love even more, and wishes "for love to conquer all" (p. 364).

Upon his reconciliation with his lover, he thus gets even more preoccupied with the emotion, expressing his belief in the power of love not as a universalist ideal, but as a human feeling ensuring cooperation only on the level of a couple's relationship:

> [W]e needed to come together and set love and beauty and solidarity and friendship against the monstrous forces that faced us. Humanity was the only answer to the cartoon [of Joker]. I had no plan except love. [...] [F]or now there was only holding each other tightly and passing strength to each other, body to body, mouth to mouth, spirit to spirit, me to you. There was only the holding of hands and slowly learning not to be afraid of the dark. (p. 365)

This final revelation on the part of the narrator, who can now be regarded as the new central character, summarizes the gradual passage in the novel from universalism to the vernacular understanding of cosmopolitanism. The only obstacle to his happiness is removed when he is entitled to be the legal parent of his four-year-old son Vespa, and Suchitra accepts a life with him and the child. In the final paragraph where he announces that "there are the three of us, Little Vespa, Suchitra and myself", their faces get continuously raddled as the camera spins around them, and they become a whole: "There is only the whirling movement of life" (p. 380). Their entanglement in love represented in this final move of the camera lens making them a whole, a unified entity is, far from being utopian, the type of actual and local cooperation which is attainable and sought for by vernacular cosmopolitans.

NOTE

1. The more general terms "cosmopolitan identity" or "cosmopolitan outlook" are exempt from the distinction between universalist and vernacular cosmopolitanism, so these terms are not used with these defining adjectives "universalist" and "vernacular". Regardless of this distinction, identity can be defined by cosmopolitan outlook. Rushdie's characters—those in both universalist and vernacular camps—assume cosmopolitan outlook as a prerequisite, as do the ones in *NW*, but are also defined as universalist or vernacular for different reasons, mostly in relation to their positioning as elite or

non-elite cosmopolitans. Therefore, these terms are also apt to delineate American identity in general, which can of course refer to both the universalists and the vernaculars.

REFERENCES

Bauman, Zygmunt. 1998. *Globalization: The human consequences*. Cambridge: Polity.

Beck, Ulrich. 2006. *The Cosmopolitan Vision*, trans. Ciaran Cronin. Cambridge and Malden: Polity Press.

Beck, Ulrich. 2010. The cosmopolitan manifesto. In *The cosmopolitanism reader*, ed. David Held and Garrett Wallace Brown, 217–228. Cambridge: Polity Press.

Brennan, Timothy. 2001. Cosmo-Theory. *The South Atlantic Quarterly* 100: 659–691.

Calhoun, Craig. 2002. The class consciousness of frequent travellers: Towards a critique of actually existing cosmopolitanism. In *Conceiving cosmopolitanism: Theory, context, and practice*, ed. Steven Vertovec and Robin Cohen, 86–109. Oxford: Oxford UP.

Epstein, Mikhail. 2009. Transculture: A broad way between globalism and multiculturalism. *American Journal of Economics and Sociology* 68: 327–352. www.jstor.org/stable/27739771

Forna, Aminatta. 2017. *The Golden House* by Salman Rushdie review: A parable of modern America. *The Guardian*. www.theguardian.com/books/2017/sep/16/the-golden-house-salman-rushdie-review. Accessed 12 August 2020.

Gilroy, Paul. 2004. *After empire: Melancholia or convivial culture*. London and New York: Routledge.

Guignery, Vanessa. 2018. Salman Rushdie in conversation. *Journal of Postcolonial Writing* 54: 268–283. https://doi.org/10.1080/17449855.2017.1380070.

Hall, Stuart. 2002. Political belonging in a world of multiple identities. In *Conceiving cosmopolitanism: Theory, context, and practice*, ed. Steven Vertovec and Robin Cohen, 25–31. Oxford: Oxford UP.

Held, David. 2002. Culture and political community: National, global, and cosmopolitan. In *Conceiving cosmopolitanism: Theory, context, and practice*, ed. Steven Vertovec and Robin Cohen, 48–58. Oxford: Oxford UP.

Held, David. 2010. *Cosmopolitanism: Ideals and realities*. Cambridge: Polity Press.

Hollinger, David A. 2002. Not universalists, not pluralists: The new cosmopolitans find their own way. In *Conceiving cosmopolitanism: Theory, context, and practice*, ed. Steven Vertovec and Robin Cohen, 227–239. Oxford: Oxford UP.

Hoydis, Julia. 2019. Realism for the post-truth era: Politics and storytelling in recent fiction and autobiography by Salman Rushdie. *European Journal of English Studies* 23: 152–171. https://doi.org/10.1080/13825577.2019.1640422.

Kaldor, Mary. 2002. Cosmopolitanism and organized violence. In *Conceiving cosmopolitanism: Theory, context, and practice*, ed. Steven Vertovec and Robin Cohen, 268–278. Oxford: Oxford UP.

Knepper, Wendy, and Sharae Deckard. 2016. Towards a radical world literature: Experimental writing in a globalizing world. *ariel: A Review of International English Literature* 47(1–2): 1–25. https://doi.org/10.1353/ari.2016.0018

McEwan, Ian. 2005. *Saturday*. London: Vintage.

McLaughlin, Robert L. 2004. Post-postmodern discontent: Contemporary fiction and the social world. *Symplokē* 12: 53–68.

Nancy, Jean-Luc. 1991 [1986]. *The inoperative community*. Trans. P. Connor, L. Garbus, M. Holland and S. Sawhney. Minneapolis: University of Minnesota Press.

Nealon, Jeffrey T. 2012. *Post-postmodernism or, the cultural logic of just-in-time capitalism*. Stanford: Stanford UP.

Robbins, Bruce. 1998. Actually existing cosmopolitanism. In *Cosmopolitics: Thinking and feeling beyond the nation*, ed. Pheng Cheah and Bruce Robbins, 1–19. Minneapolis: University of Minnesota Press.

Rushdie, Salman. 2017. *The Golden House*. New York: Random House.

Shaw, Kristian. 2016. Teaching contemporary cosmopolitanism. In *Teaching 21st century genres*, ed. Katy Shaw, 167–185. Basingstoke: Palgrave Macmillan.

Schoene, Berthold. 2010. *The cosmopolitan novel*. Edinburgh: Edinburgh UP.

Smith, Zadie. 2013. *NW: London*. London: Penguin Books.

Tomlinson, John. 2002. Interests and identities in cosmopolitan politics. In *Conceiving cosmopolitanism: Theory, context, and practice*, ed. Steven Vertovec and Robin Cohen, 240–253. Oxford: Oxford UP.

Tuttle, Kate. 2017. Salman Rushdie on the opulent realism of his new novel, 'The Golden House'. *Los Angeles Times*. https://www.latimes.com/books/jacketcopy/la-ca-jc-salman-rushdie-20170914-story.html. Accessed 2 June 2021.

Vertovec, Steven, and Robin Cohen. 2002. Introduction: Conceiving cosmopolitanism. In *Conceiving cosmopolitanism: Theory, context, and practice*, ed. Steven Vertovec and Robin Cohen, 1–22. Oxford: Oxford UP.

Walonen, Michael K. 2020. Debunking the myth of the entrepreneur through narrative in the contemporary South Asian novel. *Interventions: International Journal of Postcolonial Studies* 22 (2): 246–260.

CHAPTER 6

Posthuman Cosmopolitanism and Post-COVID-19 Sensitivities in Kazuo Ishiguro's *Klara and The Sun*

Cosmopolitanism, due to its vernacular aspect, can exist in all-encompassing modes, involving the global and the local, the elite and the non-elite, human and the posthuman/nonhuman. Vernacular cosmopolitanism is more sensitive to the particularities of the cosmopolitan experience in everyday life. As discussed throughout this book, twenty-first-century cosmopolitan novels have a propensity toward representing inclusively a wide range of cosmopolitans. Humanoid robots and nonhuman living beings take their place in the spectrum of discrepant cosmopolitans in postmillennial fiction with the growing recognition that we share the same universe, this "one-world", with them, and they are indisputably a part of our contemporary life. The themes of posthuman ethics are central to the alternate cosmopolitanism portrayed in the world of the novel. Having robots and nonhumans in our cosmopolitan culture leads to two-way debates regarding posthuman ethics. The first interrogates the ethical demands put on the Anthropocene concerning the centralization of the human and neglect of other living beings on Earth. On the other hand, questions are also raised as to the degree robots can learn to act ethically during their participation in human life.

The argument of this chapter is that Ishiguro's nod at vernacular cosmopolitanism is discernible in the portrayal of his protagonist, the artificial friend Klara, as a true representative of, and a catalyst for, a cosmopolitan society in which affect and affection can help us by alleviating human sufferings triggered by a contemporary life ruled by social distance and inequality. Cosmopolitan impetus that we can witness in Klara's day to day activities attests to Kendall et al.'s assertion below regarding the observable nature of cosmopolitan sentiments:

> As part of the expression of cosmopolitan sentiments within spheres of everyday life, we suggest that there should be identifiable carriers of the cosmopolitan – humans and non-humans alike – which act as symbolic containers of cultural difference, and which we can track and map, talk and listen to, observe and interpret. These are mobile, portable symbolic tokens of cosmopolitan sentiments, interacted with and observed by social actors and social scientists alike in everyday settings. (2009, p. 10)

Klara's distinguishable diurnal activities, most notably her very material interaction with the Sun, function on a symbolic level as a token of cosmopolitanism. Just as she traces the city and people's observable actions in order to make sense of their various emotions, we as readers can, in the same vein, interpret her day-to-day mobilities and exchanges against the backdrop of a set of cosmopolitan sensitivities.

Revolving around a speculative future where children are "lifted", genetically enhanced for the prospects of a better adult life, Ishiguro's eighth novel, *Klara and The Sun* (2021), centralizes the concerns of bio-genetic engineering, ecological crisis, and posthuman ethics. The protagonist and the narrator, Klara, is an artificial friend (AF), who is assigned to accompany one of those privileged "lifted" children, Josie. Unlike Josie, her best friend and intended future partner, Rick, is one of the "unlifted" children, who are raised in socioeconomically less advantaged families, and whose chances for a university education are decreased. It is also solely the families of the lifted that can afford an AF, a humanoid robot that would befriend their lonely children. Loneliness emerges as another significant theme, one which comes to the fore in the aftermath of the pandemic as it becomes acute by reason of practices of lockdown and online education. As part of the post-pandemic sensitivities of the novel, human health, which is also at stake in the face of interventions to nature—both human nature and the natural world, receives attention. Josie is ailing, just like her late sister, Sal, as a side effect of the process of lifting. Her condition is not only instigated by her genetic modification, but implicitly it is also worsened due to the disturbance of the Sun by

Pollution raised by the Cootings Machine. In this sense, the implication at the heart of the novel is that the well-being of the human is dependent on that of the environment. Klara is keen to see this connection unlike Josie's mother, Chrissie, who plans to find solace in the artificial child to be made from Klara and a "portrait" identical to Josie should she losses her younger daughter, too, as a result of her genetic programming. Klara, despite having the capacity to be a near perfect substitute for Josie, goes for an alternative solution by making an agreement with the Sun to recover Josie in return for her service to destroy the Cootings Machine.

Contemporary cosmopolitan fiction is concerned with a wide range of global matters, involving not only cultural and socioeconomical but also ecological and environmental ones. Climate change, loss of biodiversity, pollution, overconsumption of the earth's resources and energy sources are frequently covered explicitly in cosmopolitan novels. *Klara and The Sun* can be viewed as a new type of cosmopolitan novel in this respect, too. Central to the problems on both global and personal levels in the novel is the Cootings Machine, whose dark and intense smoke produces "Pollution" and prevents the Sun from offering his nourishment to the world. The Cootings Machine threatens not only AFs whose sole life energy can be received from the Sun, but also human health and ecological well-being.

Notwithstanding the apparent dystopia lying beneath it, the novel is a typical world in which the themes of vernacular cosmopolitanism become discernible. Set against the realities of a universalist version of cosmopolitanism which is defined by Jessie's and other lifted children's elite families, vernacular cosmopolitanism is represented by Klara herself, if not robots' world in general. Contrasting two versions of cosmopolitanism—universalist and vernacular, elite and non-elite, the novel shows that these alternative worlds may have diverse orientations and mark at totally different ends for human living on earth.

The novel offers an alternate solution in engagement with eco-health problem, which has much to do with the definition of vernacular cosmopolitanism in this book, one which is quite different from the universalist-idealist senses of the concept. Vernacular cosmopolitanism takes into account a very wide range of human and nonhuman entities that are affected by global events like the COVID-19 pandemic as well as the alterations to ecosystems. In addition, it engages with inequalities that arouse from such global risks and their disproportionate influence on socioeconomically varied communities and individuals. The noxious impacts of global problems can be alleviated, as Ishiguro's robot protagonist Klara shows us, through vernacular cosmopolitanism, through an emotive and proactive engagement with the local and the nearest first.

The novel's glimpse at vernacular cosmopolitanism offered as alternative to the universalist one is more hopeful than the version in *The Golden House*, where top-down cosmopolitanism and its dire consequences are manifested, yet vernacular solidarity and feelings are retrieved only in the very end. Ishiguro, on the other hand, presents his idea of cosmopolitanism through the theme of the possibility of AI outweighing humans in many cosmopolitan aspects, moral and empathetic faculties. He does so by portraying a humanoid robot endowed with insight and intuition to understand the other, as more human than humans. Klara the AF sets a model for her real human counterparts for interacting with others in her attempt to fully comprehend and make sense of their emotions and motivations. At the outset of the novel, while being exhibited in the AF store, Klara has "never been *outside*" (Ishiguro 2021, p. 66, emphasis in original), not even locally, yet she has a unique global understanding of feelings, which warrants greater openness to the other and necessary means to take her own part in the cosmopolitan world. Even if she finds certain human feelings hard to grasp in the beginning, she learns them and their implications as she keeps observing, and in this sense, "Klara's learning makes her more human" (Ajeesh and Rukmini 2022). Through Klara, we learn to be cosmopolitans in that, as Patell puts it, "speculative fiction asks us to adopt a cosmopolitan perspective in which we confront otherness and thereby learn more about ourselves" (2015, p. 88).

Josie and other lifted children's "interaction meetings" are, on the other hand, far from ensuring a real communication among the members of this micro community of the privileged, let alone one with the unprivileged and unlifted children like Rick. Although Josie hates these meetings, she is bound to attend them as her mother rationalizes that "[t]his crowd happens to be your peer group. And when you get to college, you'll have to deal with all kinds" (Ishiguro 2021, p. 73). This statement reveals the assumption that their future community at college will, in the majority, consist of lifted children like Josie, and dealing with such a community will not always be very easy. The paradox lies in the way these lifted children are raised, and educated online in isolation at home devoid of a genuine peer contact, and brought into artificial societies in scheduled meetings to assuage their loneliness. Both escaping from community and simultaneously producing a synthetic one containing only the elite are far from being genuine ways of engaging with a cosmopolitan society and opening to the world. Not seeing the other lifted children as her real friends, Josie invites Rick to the gathering even though he is, unlike them, neither rich nor lifted. All the children treat him as an Other, someone quite different from them, and keep asking him absurd questions as if he was an alien, which make him furious. Upon an argument between Rick and one of the lifted boys, the latter's mother cannot help commenting that "[y]ou shouldn't be here at all" (p. 91). This remark as well as their attitude toward Rick attest to that this created community of the privileged is not able to be inclusive or promote cosmopolitanism. Rick's presence implicitly arouses anxiety; "[w]hat's important", asserts one of the mothers, "is that this next generation learn how to be comfortable with every sort of person" (p. 78). This tension about cultural difference is far from defining a cosmopolitan attitude.

The homodiegetic narrator of *Klara and The Sun*, like the other cosmopolitan narrators in the previous chapters, is inclusive and representative of diverse cosmopolitan sentiments. Third-person narrators can easily roam through different minds and distant locations, which makes them more comprehensive. Yet, Klara's focalization also proves to be capable of such global mobility and penetration into others' emotive worlds through her keen observations and interpretations. Her willingness to engage with the other and the world as well as her active participation in world-making in her belief that alternate—and better—worlds are possible are her distinctive features. In this sense, Klara can be categorized as a vernacular cosmopolitan character and narrator. The novel is replete with diverse cosmopolitan themes, also including emerging sensitivities in the aftermath of the COVID-19 pandemic. These aspects of the cosmopolitan novel—posthuman cosmopolitanism, the *cosmoflâneur* and post-COVID-19 sensitivities—are elaborated in the sub-sections of this chapter.

POSTHUMAN COSMOPOLITANISM: DO ANDROIDS DREAM OF BEING COSMOPOLITAN?

With the humanoid robots becoming important actors in our contemporary life, cosmopolitanism comes to connote broader inclusiveness, and interaction with, and openness toward, not only local and global fellow humans but also the nonhuman other in every sense of the word—be it androids or other living existences in the ecological system. Focusing on the necessary coexistence of animals in cityscapes and conceptualizing this type of cosmopolitanism as "species-diversity", Narayanan and Bindumadhav (2019) call for a "'posthuman cosmopolitanism' that can radically expand cosmopolitanism to include *all life*" (p. 408, emphasis in original). Other similar views see animals as integral to cosmopolitan living, approaching to posthuman cosmopolitanism as "a critical account of cosmopolitan belongingness to detail how our being on earth is also a 'being-with' animal others" (Leep 2018, p. 47). Haraway celebrates, in the figure of the cyborg, human's interaction with both animals and machines: "A cyborg world might be about lived social and bodily realities in which people are not afraid of their joint kinship with animals and machines, not afraid of permanently partial identities and contradictory standpoints" (1990, p. 154). In this part, I will suggest the need for inclusiveness of the nonhuman, encompassing not only all species on the planet but also humanoid robots in the spectrum of posthuman cosmopolitans. Coexistence of AFs like Klara offers, as Ishiguro's narrative suggests, new possibilities for boosting both human and nonhuman capacity to address social and ecological problems in the world. In this sense, Klara can be observed to display certain cosmopolitan characteristics.

Braidotti (2016) views posthuman ethics as "a grounded form of accountability, based on a sense of collectivity and relationality, which results in a renewed claim to community and belonging by singular subjects" (p. 26). Klara is characterized by all these tenets of posthuman ethics on account of her desire to connect to both human and nonhuman living on earth. She is also the one who recognizes the interconnectivity between these agents. Braidotti (2013) states that:

> A posthuman ethics for a non-unitary subject proposes an enlarged sense of inter-connection between self and others, including the non-human or 'earth' others, by removing the obstacle of self-centred individualism. [...C]ontemporary bio-genetic capitalism generates a global form of reactive mutual inter-dependence of all living organisms, including non-humans. This sort of unity tends to be of the negative kind, as a shared form of vulnerability, that is to say a global sense of inter-connection between the human and the non-human environment in the face of common threats. The posthuman recomposition of human interaction that I propose is not the same as the reactive bond of vulnerability, but is an affirmative bond that locates the subject in the flow of relations with multiple others. (pp. 49–50)

The reactive interdependence of all species is, according to Braidotti, a result of bio-genetic capitalism, and thus implies that all these living organisms become more vulnerable to global ecological threats. Ishiguro's dystopian world also makes such vulnerabilities visible by materializing both the threat (Pollution) and the threatened (humans and nonhumans). The other form of interconnection between the human and the nonhuman is, on the other hand, affirmative in the sense that the recognition of their interdependence may benefit all living organisms on Earth. This idea echoes the novel's celebratory rendering of posthuman cosmopolitanism, which is envisioned in Klara's interactions with this world of multiplicity.

The novel's interrogation into the status of robots as ethical beings in fact raises questions as to what it means to be human, and how ethical we are as human beings compared to our more idealized versions. The coexistence of humanoid robots in our everyday life is undeniable; they are no longer a part of a fictional dystopia, but "a cultural other" that exists in our everyday reality (Kim and Kim 2013). The nonhuman also helps define the future human "being": "Being is being-with, living-with strangers and foreigners, including the foreigners within – be it within a cell or a nation or, to end on a more cosmopolitical note – our planet" (Rossini 2017, p. 165). Being an integral element of posthuman cosmopolitanism, robots like Klara may lay bare our fallibilities: "The novel's world is set up to provide an uncanny distance from our own, making us prone to pass judgments on the characters' moral faults that we later come to recognize are also our own" (Mejia and Nikolaidis 2022, p. 304). The novel also draws a picture of the world in the future while simultaneously reminding us of our own responsibility in the construction of this future: "[S]cience fiction provides envisioned futures that assist humans not just foresee what could happen and how humankind is responsible for making morally altering reality decisions" (Ajeesh and Rukmini 2022).

Humanity's failures to create a healthy and interconnected society become more manifest in the human characters' stark contrast to Klara's cosmopolitan attitudes. This insight into humanity itself also sheds light upon an understanding of a cosmopolitan community. In fact, Klara challenges the robot stereotype in a way in which what we learn from her and through her eyes is the deepest layers of human nature and emotions. Klara is a different kind of robot altogether: "By departing from the conventional and antiquated view of AI as a cold, emotionless machine,

Kazuo Ishiguro's *Klara and the Sun* forges a new route in the posthuman investigation of AI in SF" (Ajeesh and Rukmini 2022). The idea of robots having emotions is embodied in Klara, who exemplifies what Zhou (2021) calls "emotional thinking": "The emotional factor should be formally included in AI research, and emotional thinking should be proposed as an ideal type of human thinking" (p. 122). Ishiguro's protagonist capable of thinking emotionally enables us to understand the significance of human emotions, which are in fact necessary for the construction of a cosmopolitan culture. Zhou demonstrates the cognitive processes involved in emotional thinking:

> [T]he external manifestation of emotions in the organism provides the necessary information for others to empathize with us and understand our emotions and experiences. This feeling of empathy creates a sense of belonging and identity, often leading to a significant increase in the ability to engage in emotional thinking. (2021, p. 120)

These senses of empathy, belonging, and identity are elemental principles of a community, especially in terms of vernacular cosmopolitanism. Above-mentioned processes define Klara's acceptance and integration into her new community, with which she interacts through emotional thinking. This kind of thinking is, then, essential for both human and AI consciousness to form cosmopolitan societies.

Klara has the attributes of a cosmopolitan even from the outset, and proves the development of her cosmopolitan feelings as her story as an AF unfolds in her new home. Her openness to the world is manifest in her longing to see more of the outside even when she is confined within the interior of the store where AFs are sold. She not only observes the street attentively, but she also interprets people's behaviors and motives with insight to the amazement of Manager: "Klara, you're quite remarkable" (Ishiguro 2021, p. 11); "You never miss a thing" (p. 25). She is very good at seeing the world through others' eyes as well as being capable of empathy, especially toward those who suffer the most. "A child like that, with no AF, would surely be lonely", (p. 12) discerns Klara. Human loneliness is central to the novel and the protagonist's empathetic world. Klara perceives Josie's loneliness soon after she begins to live with them: "I understood then that if she failed to join the Mother for the quick coffee, there was the danger of loneliness creeping into her day, no matter what other events filled it" (pp. 58–9). Klara discovers how Chrissie's quick coffee sessions are needed by Josie as a temporary solution for her loneliness, and how her role as Josie's AF is important to alleviate her loneliness. However, what she discovers about loneliness perplexes her: "[W]hat was becoming clear to me was the extent to which humans, in their wish to escape loneliness, made maneuvers that were very complex and hard to fathom" (p. 127). This undesired feeling is in fact a result of the failure of the community to understand others and make meaningful connections with them. Klara's cosmopolitanism is offered as an antidote to this common problem of loneliness. In the novel, Klara can achieve this since she has loyalty both to local and global attachments, to the nearest people who suffer from loneliness and to the whole world that suffers from Pollution and from the disability to become a community. The novel "call[s] not for a wholesale change in how society is organised, but teases us into contemplating accepting a new attitude to others and the world" (Groes 2022, p. 1042). At this point, I will define this new attitude as cosmopolitanism, a form of world engagement that envisions a better society that values vernacular feelings such as local communication, cooperation, and empathy.

Klara values human feelings and communication even though she is aware of their complex nature. The division between loneliness and privacy is carefully drawn by Klara, who knows very well that people do not want to be lonely most of the time, yet their privacy should not also be violated. Considering this as a way of respecting privacy, she is always careful not to interfere in Josie's conversation with her mother and Rick. She also regards personal spaces as private and steps into them with caution; nevertheless, she remains close enough in case Josie feels lonely. The sense of loneliness is something to be discovered further for her because it involves, as she recognizes, multiple dimensions. She is astounded to find out that human beings may sometimes prefer loneliness for the sake of others, as does Rick's mother; she wishes to send her son to university even if she is going to be lonely: "Until recently, I didn't think that humans could choose loneliness. That there were sometimes forces more powerful than the wish to avoid loneliness" (Ishiguro 2021, p. 172). Rick's mother's is an unselfish way to engage with the other in which the other comes before herself; her desire for her son to have a better future at university outweighs her preoccupation with her own illness and loneliness. On the other hand, Josie's mother does have a different attitude toward loneliness when she thinks of her own situation—not that of Josie nor Klara, resorting to unethical ways of consoling herself in case of Josie's imminent demise; she wants Klara to substitute Josie by putting an end to her own self, and continuing to live in a physical form identical to Josie if the feared death occurs. Unable to face loneliness and the tragic consequences of her decision to lift Josie, Chrissie diverts from Rick's mother's selfless attitude. Moreover, Chrissie's attempt to wave off Klara's sense of identity, even if she seems to possess one, and her subjugation of the robot echo posthuman concerns about human appropriation of other species that are thought to serve human existence as their primary reason d'etre.

Another cosmopolitan feeling Klara values is kindness to others, which she sees a precondition in human communication. Some other feelings like a desire to harm others, on the other hand, are quite meaningless in Klara's well-intended world. She watches two taxi-drivers fighting each other for some unknown reason, but whatever justification that may lie beneath is not enough for Klara to understand the urge to harm one's fellows. She forces herself to make sense of the taxi drivers' behavior, but ends up in finding such rage totally ridiculous:

> I tried to feel in my own mind the anger the drivers had experienced. I tried to imagine me and Rosa getting so angry with each other we would start to fight like that, actually trying to damage each other's bodies. The idea seemed ridiculous, but I'd seen the taxi drivers, so I tried to find the beginnings of such a feeling in my mind. It was useless, though, and I'd always end up laughing at my own thoughts. (p. 22)

It is argued by some commentators that Klara is not programmed to understand complex human feelings to this extend, yet it must be noted that other very high-level feelings such as empathy, reasoning, and pity for others are definable in Klara's emotive world, feelings that characterize a vernacular cosmopolitan society where empathy replaces personal interest, sharing replaces greed. Ishiguro offers Klara's version of a cosmopolitan world as an alternative to ones which are defined by greater global connectedness and a resulting progress in digital technology and commerce, yet a lack in human proximity. Klara equates smiling with kindness: "Josie smiled at me, her face full of kindness" (p. 66). For Klara, smiling, not anger, characterizes human communication. Likewise, she desires sheer goodness in the world, from which she wants to banish adverse feelings. Even when she knows she needs to feel utter rage toward the Cootings Machine, she is unable to feel that way; she has various feelings, but anger: "I knew I should feel anger, but coming on it after the surprise about the store, I felt something almost like kindness towards the terrible machine" (pp. 214–5). In the same way, the furious bull that they encounter on the trip to Morgan's Falls represents adversity, "signals of anger and the wish to destroy" (p. 113). The world, according to her, must be a site of kindness, and everything else that fails to be kind must belong somewhere else:

> I felt something more, something stranger and deeper. At that moment it felt to me some great error had been made that the creature should be allowed to stand in the Sun's pattern at all, that this bull belonged somewhere deep in the ground far within the mud and darkness, and its presence on the grass could only have awful consequences. (p. 113)

The anger and the destructive impulse represented by the taxi drivers and the bull neither make any sense for Klara, nor fit into her perception of a cosmopolitan world. On their way back home, a group of sheep "filled with kindness – the exact opposite of the terrible bull" (p. 121) belong to this world to which kindness is the prerequisite to achieve stronger attachments to others.

Klara's preoccupation with Josie's problem from the start is a sign of her cosmopolitan sensibilities, which are attained by human characters like *Saturday*'s Perowne only in the end. The idea of vernacular cosmopolitanism which is defined by unambitious and "tiny" steps toward locally closer others marks the final message of McEwan's *Saturday*, but the same idea is dispersed throughout Ishiguro's novel with his cosmopolitan protagonist's altruistic attitude toward, and engagement with, others. Perowne needs to be transformed in the end to come to such recognition that the well-being of others around him, including his patients, is implemental to form a cosmopolitan society more than what can be achieved through abstract global attachments and ideals. Klara, as another caretaker figure, possesses this consciousness even at the outset, and desires to present her reassurance to Josie: "I wanted also to tell her that if there was anything difficult, anything frightening, to be faced in her house, we would do so together" (p. 29). She smoothly fits into her role as a comfort giver, a helpful companion. Josie, too, Josie's mother observes, is "definitely more mindful of others these days" (p. 122) after Klara's arrival at the house. Klara draws not only Josie's but also the reader's attention to others and the ways in which we engage with others' emotions, however complex these emotions may be: "Ishiguro's novel serves as a prism to sensitize readers to the spectrum of emotional complexities pertaining to human relationships in the rapidly changing posthuman world through the lenses of Klara" (Sahu and Karmakar 2022). In this sense, Klara's understanding of human emotions may sometimes be limited (Sahu and Karmakar 2022); however, her understanding of, and preoccupation with, the other is what distinguishes her from other human and nonhuman characters in the novel.

Insight and understanding are prerequisite characteristics that a cosmopolite needs in order to open her/himself to an attachment to the local and the global. Klara has these traits to some extend and wishes to improve her abilities to make sense of everything and everyone around her. Her thirst for knowing the world and interacting with the other is an attestation to her cosmopolitan sensibilities. With an aspiration to be a perfect companion for Josie, Klara observes her actions and interactions prudently. She knows the importance of observation, and reminds Rick of the opportunity the interaction meeting creates by making it possible for her to "observe Josie in many situations. And it was very interesting, for instance, to observe the different shapes the children made as they went from group to group" (Ishiguro 2021, p. 92). Viewing the interaction meeting as "a source of valuable new observations" (p. 95), Klara acknowledges the basic human need to be in a community, which provides one with a scope for multiple feelings, a state Klara herself is not devoid of, since she is an active participant of the cosmopolitan society. On the way to Morgan's Falls, Klara claims that she possesses many feelings by objecting to Chrissie's assertion that "[i]t must be nice sometimes to have no feelings. I envy you" (p. 111). What makes Klara even more engaged with others is her capacity to learn feelings: "The more I observe, the more feelings become available to me" (p. 111).

While others cannot see what is inside a human being, Klara can. Mr Capaldi believes that Klara will be able to "*become*" Josie (p. 232), continue her perfectly with the outer AF shell created as the exact copy of Josie, and as for her character traits, it is Klara's perfect observation skills that will fill this gap. Mr Capaldi does not believe in "something unreachable inside each of us" (p. 233), and tries to reassure Chrissie that: "There's nothing there. Nothing inside Josie that's beyond the Klaras of this world to continue" (p. 233). Klara thinks, on the other hand, that others' love for someone is the most important thing that makes her /

him unique; thus, it is impossible for her to fill Josie's place because of this missing element. Paul, Josie's father, interrogates about the uniqueness of the human heart: "Do you believe in the human heart? I don't mean simply the organ, obviously. I'm speaking in the poetic sense. The human hearth. Do you think there is such a thing? Something that makes each of us special and individual?" (p. 242). He, then, reveals his true feelings about human specialness and a conception of community:

> I hate Mr Capaldi because deep down I suspect he might be right. That what he claims is true. That science has now proved beyond doubt there's nothing so unique about my daughter, nothing there our modern tools can't excavate, copy, transfer. That people have been living with one another all this time, centuries, loving and hating each other, and all on a mistaken premise. (p. 249)

Human communities are based on a complex structure of relationships, involving both togetherness and battles. Paul's idea of a community lacks genuineness, which is far from principles of vernacular cosmopolitanism represented by a sense of community in Klara's mind. In the vernacular version, despite the complexity of feelings which exist within diverse realms, within Klara's visionary boxes, cosmopolitan understanding of empathy toward others may be a simple, yet effective solution to social problems. Klara tries her turn in this attempt to help recover Josie's health. Paul's sense of community, on the other hand, is predicated on a primitive human urge to come together for common benefits. Miss Helen's portrayal of this community from an outside point of view aligns it more with universalist cosmopolitanism: "[Y]ou did say you were all white people and all from the ranks of the former professional elites. You did say that. And you were having to arm yourselves quite extensively against other *types*" (p. 258). His parochial society is neither inclusive nor willing to engage with others outside its boundaries.

Posthuman cosmopolitanism in the novel, in line with the understanding of vernacular cosmopolitanism, resists universalist-idealist abstractions, and instead values human feelings, broad inclusiveness, and cosmopolitanism from below. Not only Klara's sense of empathy but also her sense of responsibility for the world's well-being through her actions of *cosmoflânerie* become testament to the novel's posthuman cosmopolitanism.

THE COSMOFLÂNEUR AS A CARRIER OF POSTHUMAN COSMOPOLITANISM

Klara is a figure of the *cosmoflâneur* in that her engagement with the world is beyond mere observation. Her genuine interest in others as well as the world distinguishes her from the *flâneur*, who is, as van Leeuwen explains, "essentially preoccupied with the practice of observing, with the role of passive spectator" (2019, p. 307). On the other hand, Klara is far from assuming a passive role; thus, she complies more with the definition of the *cosmoflâneur*. As detailed in Chapter 2, this book outlines three distinctive features of the *cosmoflâneur*: cosmopolitan outlook, consciousness, and activity. The first process involves the ability to observe the city through the lenses of the global and the local simultaneously. This cosmopolitan outlook is a defining feature of the cosmopolitan character or narrator's inclusive and wide-angle vision, which yields a picture of the world in swift, yet variable constellations. The second feature—cosmopolitan consciousness—requires a perception of urban life in terms of class consciousness and economic disproportions. While these two features of the *cosmoflâneur* are more or less achievable, it is the last process of *cosmoflânerie*—cosmopolitan activity—that is the hardest to attain as we see in the case of Perowne in Chapter 3. This process involves responding to the world with an urge to take an active role in its formation and preservation with a particular attentiveness to the world's economic and ecological problems. Klara, as this chapter attempts to show, proves to be a good model of the *cosmoflâneur*, going through all these three processes with a degree of success.

The *cosmoflâneur* is characterized by observation, perception, and enthusiasm in the sense that her openness to the world is in the first place through her keen eyes, which facilitates her virtual mobility. It is her ability to perceive others' deeper feelings and problems that marks the first step of being a *cosmoflâneur* on Klara's part. From the outset, Klara is good at observing the world both inside and outside the AF store, where she willingly seeks interaction with the other—both human and robot. Her vision of the world is in fact through a kaleidoscopic lens, which, as Groth describes, has "immersed the observer in a visual field that never allowed the eye to rest" (2007, p. 217). She continues to observe tirelessly as the previous section also makes clear. It is the feature of narrative glocality of the twenty-first-century cosmopolitan fiction, in the same vein, that makes plausible the kaleidoscopic, and hence alternating, visions of the world as perceived from Klara's lens.

Klara's focalization is broader than that of ordinary first-person characters, whose focal area is usually limited to their immediate environment. Klara, on the other hand, is able to transcend physical boundaries, especially in moments of crisis through a special way of seeing in a vision that becomes available in the form of multiple boxes. This is a natural way in which she views the world since being a robot perhaps allows her to have such an extraordinary ability of vision; nevertheless, being a cosmopolitan character and narrator also renders her open to, and representative of, various perspectives. At a critical moment in Mr Capaldi's house when the Mother reveals the plan to continue Josie through Klara, such a transcending vision occurs to Klara as she begins to see the Mother "partitioned into many boxes", each of which yields a distinct version of her so that Klara's perception of different feelings and motives is enrichened through this multifarious image. When these multiple boxes become visible to her, Klara learns about the plan: "[W]e're not asking you to train the new Josie. We're asking you to *become* her" (Ishiguro 2021, p. 232). At this point, she is introduced to a very different idea that the Mother has chosen her purposefully in the belief that she is the AF that is the fittest to fulfill this task. This partitioned view of the world recurs to Klara, especially when her sense of judgment needs more clarity at certain moments.

Whenever she confronts a situation of crisis, this multiple-boxed vision comes in front of her, whereupon she becomes more perceptive in this visionary experience, and can possibly see distant people and occurrences. One such moment happens to her when the ground becomes slippery and thus she loses her balance as she is trying to reach Mr McBain's barn to meet the Sun:

> One moment the grass would be soft and yielding, the ground easy to thread; then I'd cross boundary and everything would darken, the grass would resist my pushes, and there would be strange noises around me, making me fearful that I'd made a serious miscalculation, that there was no justifiable reason to disturb his privacy in the manner I was hoping to do, that my efforts would have gravely negative consequences for Josie. While crossing one particularly unkind box, I heard around me the cries of an animal in pain, and a picture came into my mind of Rosa, sitting on the rough ground somewhere outdoors, little pieces of metal scattered around

her, as she reached out both hands to grasp one of her legs stretched out stiffly before her. The image was in my mind for only a second, but the animal carried on making its noise, and I felt the ground collapsing beneath me. (p. 175)

Several images of negative thoughts, such as dread, hopelessness, doubt, and perplexity accompany her troubled journey. She fears that her mistake may dissuade the Sun from sending his special help to Josie. Simultaneously, in another dimension, she has the vision of the furious bull that she has seen on the way to Morgan's Falls. In another unpleasant box or dimension, she has a momentary vision of Rosa, her old friend from the AF store, to whom she has always had a caring attitude. Although she has never heard about Rosa since both found a home, this vision of Rosa anticipates her unfortunate end, which is revealed only in the end when Klara talks to Manager one last time. The concurrence of these visions concerning the angry bull and Rosa's final shattering into pieces in consecutive boxes is not coincidental; the implication is that Rosa's gradual collapse is a culmination of the cruelty of her owners, a condition which is represented by the bull. In that sense, this access to a distant reality, otherwise impossible, is made available through Klara's extraordinary sight, a kind of inclusive vision which is guaranteed by narrative glocality in cosmopolitan novels.

Klara's act of seeing, beyond physical boundaries, both near and distant occurrences all at once is a feature of narrative glocality, a common propensity in contemporary cosmopolitan novel toward juxtaposing global and local visions, reflecting not only the images and perspectives available to the character-narrator in her immediate environment, but also very distant images and perspectives that are made accessible through this unique way of focalizing. In other words, just like Perowne, Klara has access to various kaleidoscopic pictures of the world, and by implication several—often contradictory—outlooks which are beyond her own. In confrontation with these clashing views regarding the Sun's attitude, she oscillates between two opinions; in one, she is assured of the Sun's kindness, and in the other, she thinks that the Sun may fail to be kind at times:

> [F]or a brief moment, I even thought the Sun wasn't kind at all, and this was the true reason for Josie's worsening condition. Even in this confusion,

I was convinced that if I could only pull myself through into a kinder box, I'd become safe. (p. 176)

Opposing views are represented by different "boxes", distinctive points of departure for various perspectives, within which Klara is able to transpose herself to a more comfortable realm. The picture, however fragmented it is, is in fact interconnected within its internal elements; just like the case of Rosa, Josie's demise may occur due to unkindness, but this is just a speculation on the part of Klara, who soon gets aware of other alternative spaces that are defined by kindness. Klara, then, attempts to propel herself toward the "kinder box", the alternate world of vernacular cosmopolitanism. It is in this realm that people like Rick, and later on Josie's dad, help her with the common aim to save Josie. And again, within this territory, she regains her hopes several times however hard her aspirations may seem. Despite "the fierce border separating [their] boxes" (p. 176), ones involving kindness and unkindness, Klara is successfully drawn by Rick towards the kinder box, where she feels "the Sun's generous patterns over [her], and [her] thoughts found order once more" (p. 177).

Klara keeps viewing the world especially that of the others in grids, which enables her to have an insightful look at the others' emotions and perspectives. During Klara and the Mother's expedition to Morgan's Falls, a partitioned image opens in front of her at a critical moment when Chrissie asks Klara to imitate Josie for a while. Klara can view the disputing feelings of the Mother all at once in eight boxes expressing happiness, sadness, fear, and joy, in which "her eyes were laughing cruelly, but in the next they were filled with sadness" (p. 118). Understanding others and their emotions is of utter importance for Klara in her endeavor to serve humanity by offering care, comfort, and empathy. Ishiguro's underlying message seems to emphasize the power of understanding others for the construction of a better society. Klara wanders into others' mind, but is it also possible to wander into their heart and get a full understanding of the interior? This question is raised by Paul who finds this almost impossible, and interrogates: "Rooms within rooms within rooms. Isn't that how it might be, trying to learn Josie's heart? No matter how long you wandered through those rooms, wouldn't there always be others you'd not yet entered?" (p. 243). Nevertheless, Klara is assured that "there's a good chance I'd be able to succeed" (p. 243). Observation is further accompanied by insight, recognition, and consciousness in the next stage.

Klara, in alignment with the second feature of a *cosmoflâneur*, is profoundly conscious of, and hyper-sensitive to, urban spaces in terms of perceiving the workings of neo-capitalism, and the resulting socioeconomic inequalities. Her interaction with the city is constant; on some occasions, she keenly observes from afar the flow of the events in the streets, and on others, she strolls them in company with Jessie and her family, yet does so with full attention. In both cases, however, she is more perceptive than other robots and human beings of disparities that dominate the contemporary society. Even while she resides within the walls of the store, she is able to discern the miseries of the unprivileged children who desire to own an AF robot, yet are unable to afford one that is "beyond their reach" (p. 11). This world of inequality does not miss from Klara's attention. It is not only an imbalance in the socioeconomic status of human characters but also one in the relationship between humans and their robot companions that is characterized by hierarchy and subjugation. Klara, in one of her observations from the store's window, recognizes a boy AF walking a few steps behind his child, a scene reminiscent of slaves standing behind their masters, yet close enough to offer their service when needed.

The world of posthuman technologies and artificial intelligence is not exempt from the mechanisms of capitalism and a consumerist society. As Braidotti argues, "[t]he opportunistic political economy of bio-genetic capitalism turns Life/*zoe* – that is to say human and nonhuman intelligent matter – into a commodity for trade and profit" (2013, p. 61). In the same vein, robot technologies and humanoid robots are profoundly commodified, and subject to constant updating and remodeling to ensure the continuity of their production and marketing. Boy AF Rex fails to be chosen as an AF for a girl whose mother is convinced that his model B2 third series is not updated, and thus, has solar absorption problems. Klara also observes shrewdly from the store's window that other AFs with a home now are either absent from their view of the street or deliberately change their route away from the store to avoid a confrontation between their children and the new models displayed there. Klara understands their fear that "before long their children would decide it was time to have them thrown away, to be replaced by AFs like us" (Ishiguro 2021, p. 18). Human fear of replacement by robots in professional and social life is recast by artificial friends' similar apprehensions that updated models may replace them and make them redundant as companion to human beings.

Class consciousness of a *cosmoflâneur* is apparent in Klara's interpretation of the segregation in their small community. Klara recognizes socioeconomic gaps among people, the hierarchy between human and robot as well as disparities within their robot community itself. The three newest model B3 boy AFs' attempt to position themselves in the store apart from the old AFs represents class structures existing not only within human society but also among humanoid robots based on their technologically, if not economically, advantaged status. Klara finds it "odd" that "the three new B3s were deliberately moving themselves away from the older AFs so that when customers came in, the B3s would look like a separate group on their own" (p. 41). This tendency to prefer the company of those with similar socioeconomic status by ostracizing the rest reflects the classed structure of universalist cosmopolitanism. As a microcosm of the outside world of disparities, the store functions as a site where vernacular cosmopolitanism is offered to overcome the adverse impacts of such inequalities. At least for Klara, such a division is unthinkable. She wonders how the three B3s could "be good AFs for their children if their minds could invent ideas like these" (p. 41). For her, being good companions, and good cosmopolitans by implication, has the precondition to get out of this social structure that compartmentalizes its members according to their financial means.

The lifted children, on the other hand, are well-positioned within this system of compartmentalization. Even Josie underscores the socioeconomic difference between Rick's mother and hers:

> Anyone can have one or two *individual* friends. But your mom, she doesn't have *society*. My mom doesn't have so many friends either. But she does have society.
>
> 'Society? That sounds rather quaint. What's it mean?'
>
> 'It means you walk into a store or get into a taxi and people take you seriously. Treat you well. Having society. Important, right?' (p. 144)

Josie thinks of the capacity to "have society" in socioeconomic terms, equating it to having status. Rick, conversely, rejects the limits that such segregations put on people: "Who wants this society anyway?" (p. 145). Josie suspects their frequently referred future "plan" with Rick, and asks him: "How's it going to work if I've got society and you haven't?" (p. 146). Like Josie, Klara perceives this gap, yet unlike Josie, she does not find this a hindrance in their relationship. On her first visit to Rick's house to take Josie's picture to him, she recognizes the house as a reflector of social status:

> While viewing from a distance, I'd already estimated that Rick's house wasn't as high-rank as Josie's. Now I could see that many of its white paint boards had become gray – even brown in some places – and three of the windows were dark rectangles with no curtains or blinds within them. (p. 154)

In Klara's glossary, high-rank is definitive of people's status, their jobs, and houses. Klara is programmed to think in this categorical vocabulary about her current society that compels such segmentations. Josie's parents are divorced because of their different attitude toward life; Chrissie cares about having society whereas Paul does not. Formerly employed as a high-rank engineer, and now fired, the Father is self-satisfied with his new lifestyle and community of similar people who, like himself, have been replaced in their jobs and started to lead a less ambitious life. He now has a different outlook: "The substitutions made me take a completely fresh look at the world, and I really believe they helped me to distinguish what's important from what isn't" (p. 213). Obviously, this is not the case with Chrissie, who remains disoriented in terms of her life priorities, including her job as well as Josie's health and future. Paul suggests his ex-wife take a similar path by giving up her aspirations about work in that "[y]our every waking moment determined by some contract you once signed" (p. 212). This familial disaccord regarding socioeconomic status functions on a micro level to lay bare imbalances that loom larger over the whole society. Klara perceives these social realities as a character who focalizes, but she also relays details about such status quo within human and nonhuman worlds.

As a third, and perhaps the most important, tenet of the *cosmoflâneur*, Klara is not only observant and conscious of the world and its several problems, but she also actively engages with it to offer solutions, by becoming in no way only a passive observer of the city. Her willingness to take active steps is what distinguishes her from other characters, who respond to Josie's illness with passive submission, awaiting the inevitable end without seeking resolutions in the way Klara does. However implausible it may seem that the Sun's healing power will help Josie recover, Klara's scheme proves to work in the end when the Sun is convinced of her efforts. The underlying threat to human health and the world's well-being simultaneously and the solution offered by Klara can be interpreted on a symbolic level. Both Josie and the world itself are sickened by the animosity of Pollution triggered by the Cootings Machine, a metonymy for all the environmental threats to Earth and human / nonhuman life. Her primary aim being to recover Josie from her worsening condition, Klara thinks of destroying the machine that causes all these disruptions in the ecosystem, and makes a deal with the Sun. In this sense, Klara's mobility throughout the city has a unique purpose, that of putting an end to Pollution, to ecological problems by extension, so that human / nonhuman existence on earth can sustain.

In the tradition of a city-dweller, Klara goes through the cityscapes accompanied by the Father to carry out her plan to stop pollution produced by the Cootings Machine, and it is this purposefulness that makes her a *cosmoflâneur*, a figure of the wanderer defined by active-ness, vigor, and determination. For Klara, "the conditions for renewed political and ethical agency", (p. 191) in Braidotti's (2013) terms, are determined in a way in which she acts as an active political agent at this point. According to Braidotti (2013), these conditions of being a political and active agent "have to be generated affirmatively and creatively by efforts geared to creating possible futures, by mobilizing resources and visions that have been left untapped and by actualizing them in daily practices of interconnection with others" (p. 191). Klara makes a similar effort when she decides to create a possible future for both Josie and the world they live in, and she does so through her practices of interaction with the Sun in an attempt to mobilize him for a start. Klara's resolution—realistic or not—arouses renewed hopes among not only some of the characters but also the reader for the possibility of global healing.

Klara's mobility in an unnamed American city is not motivated by an idle, purposeless, yet a celebratory urban experience, as is the case with the *flâneur*. On the other hand, she goes from streets to streets with determination as a *cosmoflâneur*, in search of the machine that gives off a poisoning smoke which is so destructive that it both perils human health, and forces the Sun to retreat for a while. Klara accompanies Josie and her mother on a trip to the city center for one of their regular visits to Mr Capaldi's studio to have him make Josie's portrait. On the way to the Friend's Apartment, where they plan to stay the night, and during their drive into the city, Klara seeks traces of the Cootings Machine. Similarly, when she is assigned by Josie to look out of the large window of the Friend's Apartment for the Father's taxi, she keeps searching for the signals of the machine. Whenever she comes across a sign of the machine, she feels more hopeful: "My mind filled with happiness each time I saw a Tow-Away Zone sign" (Ishiguro 2021, p. 205) while recognizing at the same that this is quite an ambitious task.

Klara's mobility in the city is motivated by her plan to heal Josie and rejoice the Sun. Fascinated by her decisiveness, the Father comes to be persuaded to help her find the Cootings Machine. Paul thinks that "Hope [...] Damn thing never leaves you alone" (p. 246). In this way, her sense of active devotion becomes transmitted to the Father, who thinks of a way of destroying the machine as Klara reassures him that "If we can make Josie healthy, then the portrait, my learning her, none of it will matter" (p. 250). Of course, stopping pollution altogether is beyond her ability as she later finds out that the machine that they have destroyed is not the only one in the city. To her disappointment, the newly discovered Cootings Machine produces even greater pollution. Nevertheless, she still retains her optimism about persuading the Sun to send his nourishment to Josie: "I believe there's still reason for hope" (p. 297). Her optimism has a positive impact on Rick, too, as he is persuaded to help Klara once more to go to Mr McBain's barn. In this sense, her activeness instigates hope as to the possibility to find solutions to Josie's illness, and by extension the world's problems if appropriate actions are taken. Klara is by no means a passive eyewitness of the cityscapes nor an urban stroller whose mobility is marked by aimlessness and idleness. Her urge for an urban experience is triggered by her determination to help both human and nonhuman life simultaneously.

Post-COVID-19 Sensitivities: Engagement with Health and the Ecological World

Priorities and balances in life are put to the test on both a global and personal level in the wake of the COVID-19 pandemic. Despite the existence of plague narratives in previous ages, post-COVID-19 cosmopolitan fiction displays an unprecedented awareness of, and sensitivity toward, a contemporary global problem intersected at the joint of health and economic concerns. Post-pandemic narratives, not abundant in number for the time being, demonstrate that these two issues—health and economics—cannot be handled separately. This global pandemic attests to the idea that it is not only a health issue but also an economic one.

Groes argues that "the health crisis showed how the world itself was, on many different levels, undermined by deep social divisions and inequality" (2022, p. 1031). The pivotal aspect of contemporary cosmopolitanism is, as the previous chapters in this book emphasize, its engagement with global economics and its local ramifications. In this sense, it is argued here that post-COVID-19 cosmopolitan discourse arouses a great deal of awareness of the interplay between health and economic issues. For Žižek (2020), the pandemic functions as a Master-Signifier, to which every other global threat has been connected:

> This Master-Signifier is overdetermined by a whole series of interconnected real-life facts and processes (today's riders of the apocalypse) that form its "dream content": not only the reality of the health crisis but also the ecological crisis (global warming, the effects of deep sea pollution and mining, etc.); economic crisis (unemployment, threats of widespread hunger); new waves of social unrest bringing many countries to the edge of civil war; international tensions that can easily erupt into war; and, of course, the mental health crisis. In short, the pandemic functioned as a kind of detonator that exploded already existing tensions in our societies. (p. 132)

In this sense, even if the COVID-19 pandemic is not explicitly referred to in *Klara and the Sun*, it looms large in every aspect of the novel which deals with ecological, socioeconomic, and posthuman conflicts of our age.

Socioeconomic inequalities and class consciousness have been among the already-existing concerns of twenty-first-century fiction since 2008 global economic crisis, yet in the wake of a new crisis of 2020—the COVID-19 pandemic—the focus has expanded to the disproportion and imbalance in public health realm. Groes and Dean (2022) contend that "as the [Covid-19] crisis laid bare major inequalities and discrepancies of well-being in our cultures, we wondered about a wider, related question: what really is a healthy society?" (p. 1022). Drawing on Latour and Schultz's term the "geo-social class",[1] Žižek (2020) argues that the geo-social class of caretakers, consisting of those that are affected by the global health crisis to a great extent, goes on working despite difficult conditions (p. 21). Like these health workers who put their own well-being at risk during the pandemic, Klara devotes herself to self-sacrificingly taking care of Josie, even to the point of accepting to annihilate herself and "become" Josie should she die. Self-effacing and giving priority to labor more than anything else are features that make Klara a representative of the new working class.[2] Ishiguro's novel, as Yuqing Sun puts it, revolves around "human attempts to master *non*humans by creating technological others put at the service of human selves" (2022, p. 1). Nevertheless, Klara has an affective dimension that sets her apart from her mechanized counterparts, and makes her a more active decision-maker in the face of crisis. Thus, the theme of the commodification of the robot is handled differently by Ishiguro:

> the affective labor done by artificial intelligence is another changing mode of labor in the new stage of capitalist society, and that although Klara is designed as a commodified robot to serve the human needs, Ishiguro imagines more positive human and non-human relations by giving Klara a sense of agency, enabling her to perform the role of the caregiver in a more healing way. (Du 2022, p. 552).

Assuming her service to be essential for human well-being, Klara as a caregiver is self-motivated rather than seeing herself commodified and her labor exploited. In this sense, just like that of those members of the new working class and the geo-social class, Klara's sense of self-sacrifice for the wellness of the whole community lies at the heart of the relationship between health and several types of inequalities.

After the COVID-19 pandemic, taken for granted notion of human health has become a focus of attention in fiction as in other disciplines. In the novel, most parents' preference for lifting their children shows that health is at stake because human ambition puts academic and socioeconomic success before health. These lifted children are successful, but devoid of life energy that bestows them a healthy childhood. During one argument between Josie and Rick about their mothers' different choices for having them lifted, Rick articulates the mistake of putting health into risk; during their bubble game, he writes on the bubble for Picture Josie: "I wish I could go out and walk and run and skateboard and swim in lakes. But I can't because my mother has Courage. So instead I get to stay in bed and be sick. I'm glad about this" (Ishiguro 2021, p. 147). This ironic remark made by the imaginary Josie is an implicit interrogation into life priorities and the question of what would be more important in life than health. Josie is sickened, just like her late sister Sal, after having been lifted; however, the Mother's previous experience with Sal's illness and death does not make her opt out of her plan to lift Josie, who may have had the same end. Although the disease from which lifted children suffer is not a pandemic, it is very common and afflicts many teenagers.

Inequalities are laid bare in the novel in the common practice of "lifting" children, a kind of genetic coding to enhance their capabilities, and thus, their chances of success in life. This practice widens the gap between privileged and unprivileged children since not all families can afford it. These lifted children attend private online tutorials on their oblongs, a kind of tablet, get medical support regularly as their health is affected adversely from this practice, and come together in interaction meetings for socializing. Josie and other lifted children's mothers obviously prefer their children's having superior mental features and a better prospect at college, and consequently, they take the health risks. This complex relationship between health and wealth is brought into attention by Ishiguro in a time in which the COVID-19 pandemic also helps to raise similar questions as to the uneven impact of such a global health issue on different groups and communities. Those who can afford to work and study online have been exposed to the mortal effects of the virus less than others who are employed in public services and lack opportunities for distant learning and working. As Rick, Josie's best friend and neighbor, is not lifted, his mother is criticized by the mothers of Josie's lifted friends for being unfair to her son. Even though Rick is an extremely intelligent and promising child, it is almost impossible for him to go to Atlas Brookings, a university which accepts less than 2% unlifted children. Zhou and Yang (2021) draw attention to the imbalance within the society brought about by biogenetic practices:

> The state biologically controls the entire population by improving its genetic eugenics as it intervenes, fosters, optimizes, monitors, evaluates, regulates and corrects life to promote the nation's organisms. In the world of the book, the sovereign excludes those children who have not genetically lifted by blocking them out of the colleges (p. 336).

Hence, the exclusion of the unlifted through not only socioeconomic but also biological factors widens inequalities within this dystopian community.

Ishiguro's response to social imbalances can well be defined by the concerns of vernacular cosmopolitanism, in which Klara as well as the Sun function as the promoters of equality, empathy, and care. Like Klara, the Sun also represents kindness, healing, and attentiveness to the world's problems as a whole. The Sun, unlike lifting, is available to everyone regardless of social status, and it is everywhere—be it in the city center or the country. Klara knows that Beggar Man and his dog lying on the street as if they were dead have been healed by the Sun before, and she is assured now that he will send his special help to Josie, as well. Waiting for this help is a source of hope for Klara, and by extension for the whole world. The delay in the Sun's special help for Josie makes Klara speculate:

> I could understand that for all his kindness, the Sun was very busy; that there were many people besides Josie who required his attention; that even the Sun could be expected to miss individual cases like Josie, especially if she appeared well looked after by a mother, a housekeeper and an AF. (Ishiguro 2021, p. 130)

With so many people to be rescued with the help coming from the Sun, Klara's explanation echoes our contemporary condition during the COVID-19 pandemic with millions of people who have been under lockdown waiting to be treated at home or in hospitals. The Sun is generous in his kindness, yet the only requirement for him to send his help is to draw his attention to the sufferers. To put it more clearly, local cosmopolitans play a crucial role in the process of healing in this sense. The Sun recognizes and sends his nourishment to Beggar Man and his dog because Klara assumes some local passers-by or taxi drivers have drawn the Sun's attention to them (p. 130). Klara decides to do the same for Josie, by undertaking the journey to Mr McBain's barn where the Sun sets to persuade him to treat the ailing child. With this responsibility taken empathetically and self-intrinsically, Klara acts as a local cosmopolite whose global as well as local attachments ensure the well-being of not only Josie but also the whole community. Hopeful that Josie will heal with the Sun's help, Klara proves to be a better caretaker than Melanie Housekeeper and the Mother.

The binary between the Sun and the Cootings Machine also represents the relationship between health and Pollution. One's existence hampers the other's: the Sun goes away when the Cootings Machine is around, and likewise, health is at risk when Pollution emerges. Klara remembers this equation when Beggar Man heals:

> The Cootings Machine had been making its awful Pollution, obliging even the Sun to retreat for a time, and it had been during the fresh new era

after the dreadful machine had gone away that the Sun, relieved and full of happiness, had given his special help. (p. 131)

Klara is well-aware that such mechanisms as the Cootings Machine must be taken under control for the world to be saved. Human health is predicated on the Sun's kindness, which is in turn at stake in the current situation of the planet down to many damaging practices of human beings as well as "their Pollution and inconsideration" (p. 184). Children like Josie are also affected although they are quite innocent: "Josie's still a child and she's done nothing unkind" (p. 184). Klara's reflections are reminiscent of the vulnerable condition of human and nonhuman populations across the world during the contemporary moments of COVID-19 and environmental crises.

Health crisis and ecological crisis are interwoven into each other as implicated in the symbolic character of the Sun. Contemporary concerns with green energy, pollution, and health are reiterated in the novel. In the Mother's car, Klara takes a view of the distant village made of metal boxes, a chemical plant, which the Mother describes as "a good place;" "[c]lean energy in, clean energy out" (p. 112). Its distant image, nevertheless, returns Klara's fear of the Cootings Machine: "Something about it reminded me of the awful Cootings Machine, and a concern came into my mind about Pollution" (p. 112). Despite living in the countryside, away from the polluted and crowded streets of the city, Klara is still concerned about Pollution, and its irretrievable impacts on health. Not only AFs like herself but also sick people like Josie need the Sun's rays on themselves so as to survive; however, when Pollution is in an increase, the Sun disappears, which becomes detrimental to life on earth.

The Sun's energy is fundamental to life and human existence on earth. The Sun is nourishing, yet as a synecdoche for planetary resources, it is scarce and limited. It is something to be shared among the AFs in the store where they hope to find a future home and a human child to whom they desire to be a perfect companion. At the outset of the novel, in one of the rarest occasions, Clara behaves selfishly by carelessly touching the patterns of the Sun on the floor and taking all his nourishment just for herself, leaving all other AFs in the store devoid of it. Yet, she regrets her action as soon as she recognizes, upon Boy AF Rex's blame on her for being greedy, that all her friends need the same source of energy from the Sun to survive. Her awareness of the need to share this very limited resource with her fellow AFs contrasts human greed and failure to share the earth's resources equally with distant and disadvantaged territories.

Perhaps, COVID-19 has exacerbated concerns about planetary health, yet it is not the sole force that accelerates the debates on threats to human health. Ever-increasing ecological problems like climate change also pose a threat to human and other species' existence on earth. Well-aware of this organic tie, Klara offers solutions to save the world, stop pollution, and guarantee a healthy life for people, at least for those around her. Somehow naïve, yet well-intended, Klara's proposal to destroy the machine that causes Pollution echoes several post-pandemic discourses advocating the thought that the mother earth is taking revenge from humanity as her resources are exploited relentlessly, and that what we can do to save the world as well as ourselves is to stop destroying natural resources and polluting the world:

> I know how much the Sun dislikes Pollution. How much it saddens and angers you. Well, I've seen and identified the machine that creates it. Supposing I were able somehow to find this machine and destroy it. To put an end to its Pollution. Would you then consider, in return, giving your special help to Josie? (p. 186)

Klara is assured that the Sun will help Josie only on the condition that Klara manages to remove the obstacles in front of the Sun to reach his goodness to people. Nikolaj Schultz (2021), in "The Climatic Virus in an Age of Paralysis", observes a similar optimism, alongside fear, with which people paradoxically react to the COVID-19 pandemic with the recognition that our well-established social and economic systems that result in ecological crisis can possibly come to a halt if need arises. The pandemic has then taught us that such destructive human activities on earth as overconsumption is not inevitable since "we are right now exactly seeing how all the social systems that we thought made the ecological transition impossible—production, consumption, mobility, and so on – are not chiseled in stone but are in fact changeable" (2021, p. 10). Klara also displays this affirmative attitude in her belief that the world can be saved from Pollution if she does something even with her restricted power. Bruno Latour, in *After Lockdown: Metamorphosis* (2021), views the pandemic as a transformative new phase in our interaction with the planet and the global society we live in. Klara seems to take a step toward this new phase through her interaction with both the human and nonhuman worlds.

The Vernacular Ending and Healing

The novel ends, like the other novels in this book, with a vernacular note, emphasizing once more, perhaps more forcefully through the theme of the posthuman, the significance of human capacity for love, empathy, and caring for others. These values celebrated by vernacular forms of cosmopolitanism are symbiotically connected to the idea of healing, which highlights the urgency to form a community ruled by such empowering senses of connectedness in the face of common global threats. To put it more precisely, humanity seeks ways of recovery from wounds caused by the pandemic as well as ecological and economic realities of the contemporary world, and in the novel, solutions are not offered by technology nor by isolation, but by human interaction and solidarity.

Klara, the embodiment of the principles of vernacular cosmopolitanism, attains her aspirations to help heal Josie, the nearest human subject to herself. She does so through her resolution to take an active role in the process of healing by communicating with the Sun and fulfilling her desire to alleviate sufferings caused by Pollution. Perowne, in *Saturday*, with a similar motivation of a caretaker, decides to operate on Baxter to guarantee at least a temporary recuperation, and interacts with the other patients in his hospital to show the power of caring and affection. In *NW*, the protagonists' final activity to call the police to demand justice for the death of their local fellow, and regain their sense of friendship is another testament to the power of cosmopolitan feelings. We further witness the triumph of the vernacular feeling of love over universalist cosmopolitanism as all the members of the Goldens as well as their house end in self-destruction while only the loving couple (the narrator and his partner) and a newborn Golden baby survive to confront a hopeful future. Klara, the representative of posthuman cosmopolitanism, achieves similar senses of self-satisfaction even if her own disposal in the end, once her service is fulfilled, is inevitable.

It is not her skills as an AI, but her capacities to comprehend human feelings and to feel alike that make Klara a good caretaker. Her healing power, unlike Perowne's scientificism, relies on her emotions that make her more human than human. It is neither scientific nor technological progress but a sense of connectivity through feelings of love, caring, and empathy that the condition of healing—be it of human beings or of the world—rests upon. This is what Klara teaches us about being human. Mr Capaldi, the ultimate admirer of AI, strongly expresses his belief that

"AFs have so much more to give us than we currently appreciate. [...] We should learn from them. AFs have so much to teach us" (Ishiguro 2021, p. 221). What Klara teaches us, in the first place, is the power of love to save both human and the planet. At the end of *The Golden House*, the narrator asserts, in a similar note, that "it was up to the two of us to save the planet and that the force that would save the planet was love" (Rushdie 2017, p. 162).

The power of love proves to be essential for the well-being of the human and nonhuman world. Klara is self-assured that the Sun will provide his special nourishment only on the condition of true love, and wonders "if the love between Rick and Josie is genuine, if it's a true and lasting one" (p. 298); upon Rick's affirmative response, then, she gets more confident: "I have something very special" (p. 298). In her final monologue addressed to the Sun, she brings up the topic of love:

> I'm remembering how delighted you were that day Coffee Cup Lady and Raincoat Man found each other again. [...] So I know just how much it matters to you that people who love one another are brought together, even after many years. I know the Sun always wishes them well (p. 304).

Not only Josie and Rick's love, but also Josie's final message to her mother expressing her love for her testify to the emphasis put on the theme of love in the denouement. Rick passes on the message to Chrissie: "She says that no matter what happens now, never mind how it plays out, she loves you and will always love you" (p. 311). Upon this revelation of love, the awaited favor of the Sun appears to come, and when they all rush to Josie's bedroom, they witness the extraordinary brightness in the room: "The Sun's nourishment then came into the room so abundantly Rick and I reeled back, almost losing balance" (p. 313). The correlation between love and the Sun's willingness to oblige them with his favor can be discerned, however supernatural it may seem, in the end when Josie is rejuvenated after this special moment in which they all turn to Josie "as if each of us in the room [has] received a secret message" (p. 314). Perhaps, a kind of secret message as to the power of love is also engrained in the final pages of the novel for the reader to receive. The departure from the mostly realistic rendering of the narrative is striking for the reader suggesting that this final miracle scene may convey a much deeper meaning than it superficially portrays. Rick suspects that Josie's recovery has some secret meaning: "I thought it was all, well, AF superstition. Something just to bring us good luck. But these days, I keep wondering if there was more to it" (p. 321). Not only the reader but also the characters other than Klara seem to vacillate between supernatural and realistic explanations for Josie's healing; however, in either case, we are triggered to give the influence of love a serious consideration.

Klara's own ending looks sentimental at first sight, yet is manifested to be a success as far as an AF's living purpose is concerned. Abandoned in the Yard, where aging AFs that are no longer needed are kept, Klara remembers her old days when she was allowed to experience firsthand as many human feelings as possible. As a last sign of affection toward Klara, Chrissie does not approve of Mr Capaldi's proposal to "reverse-engineer" and "open" Klara to shed further light on AF technology in her belief that fading slowly is the best ending for an AF: "Leave our Klara be. Let her have her slow fade" (p. 329). Klara's life as an AF culminates in accomplishment as Manager puts it in their final encounter in the Yard: "So it was successful. A successful home" (p. 336). Not all AFs terminate in the same peaceful way, a fact Manager hints at during her brief mention of Rosa's tragic end. Klara later affirms that Josie's "was the best home for me. And Josie was the best teenager" (p. 337). The Yard is far from connoting a sense of isolation or abandonment on Klara's part as she is contented with her uninterrupted view from her "special place" (p. 333) of the sunset which she has always admired: "The wide sky means I'm able to watch the Sun's journeys unimpeded, and even on cloudy days, I'm always aware of where he is above me" (p. 334). Without a sign of lamentation for either her past or her current situation, Klara goes over, in her conversation with Manager, her decision to help Josie heal rather than favoring the other option to continue her:

> Mr Capaldi believed there was nothing special inside Josie that couldn't be continued. He told the Mother he'd searched and searched and found nothing like that. But I believe now he was searching in the wrong place. There *was* something very special, but it wasn't inside Josie. It was inside those who loved her. (p. 338)

This reassertion, as a final note, of the primacy of love is remarkable as we the reader are trying to reevaluate Klara's self-sacrifice in the course of her service as an AF vis-à-vis her poignant end. Then this final revelation of her self-complacency and the consolidation of the vernacular feeling of love once more thrust us to a similar path as the ones we have taken before with the other cosmopolitan novels in this book. Vernacular cosmopolitanism is good for human and nonhuman life alike.

NOTES

1. Stein Pedersen, J. V., Bruno Latour, and Nikolaj Schultz. 2019. A conversation with Bruno Latour and Nikolaj Schultz: Reassembling the geo-social. *Theory, Culture & Society* 36:215–230. https://doi.org/10.1177/0263276419867468.
2. The new working class is a term used by David Harvey (cited in Žižek), and Žižek argues that health personnel, agricultural workers, delivery staff, and staff in provision and services sectors like sale assistants are among the members of this class. (p. 21).

REFERENCES

Ajeesh, A.K., and S. Rukmini. 2022. Posthuman perception of artificial intelligence in science fiction: An exploration of Kazuo Ishiguro's Klara and the Sun. *AI & Society*. https://doi.org/10.1007/s00146-022-01533-9.

Braidotti, Rosi. 2013. *The Posthuman*. Cambridge and Malden: Polity Press.

Braidotti, Rosi. 2016. Posthuman critical theory. In *Critical posthumanism and planetary futures*, ed. D. Banerji and M.R. Paranjape, 13–32. Springer. https://doi.org/10.1007/978-81-322-3637-5_2.

Du, Lanlan. 2022. Love and hope: Affective labor and posthuman relations in *Klara and The Sun*. *Neohelicon* 49: 551–562. https://doi.org/10.1007/s11059-022-00671-9.

Groes, Sebastian. 2022. Health warnings: Reading Kazuo Ishiguro in times of crisis. *English Studies* 103: 1028–1044. https://doi.org/10.1080/0013838X.2022.2151781.

Groes, Sebastian, and Dominic Dean. 2022. Reading Kazuo Ishiguro in times of crisis. *English Studies* 103: 1017–1027. https://doi.org/10.1080/0013838X.2022.2159124.

Groth, Helen. 2007. Kaleidoscopic vision and literary invention in an "Age of Things": David Brewster, Don Juan, and "A Lady's Kaleidoscope". *ELH* The Johns Hopkins University Press 74:217–237. https://www.jstor.org/stable/30029552

Haraway, Donna. 1990. *Simians, cyborgs, and women: The revolution of nature*. New York: Routledge.

Ishiguro, Kazuo. 2021. *Klara and the Sun*. London: Faber & Faber.
Kendall, Gavin, Ian Woodward, and Zlatko Skrbis. 2009. *The sociology of cosmopolitanism: Globalization, identity, culture and government*. Houndmills, Basingstoke, Hampshire and New York: Palgrave Macmillan.
Kim, M.S., and E.J. Kim. 2013. Humanoid robots as "The Cultural Other": Are we able to love our creations? *AI & Soc* 28:309–318. https://doi.org/10.1007/s00146-012-0397-z.
Latour, Bruno. 2021. *After lockdown: Metamorphosis*. Trans. Julie Rose. Cambridge: Polity Press.
Leep, Matthew. 2018. Stray dogs, post-humanism and cosmopolitan belongingness: Interspecies hospitality in times of war. *Millennium: Journal of International Studies* 47:45–66.
Mejia, Santiago, and Dominique Nikolaidis. 2022. Through new eyes: Artificial Intelligence, technological unemployment, and transhumanism in Kazuo Ishiguro's *Klara and the Sun*. *Journal of Business Ethics* 178:303–06. https://doi.org/10.1007/s10551-022-05062-9.
Narayanan, Yamini, and Sumanth Bindumadhav. 2019. 'Posthuman cosmopolitanism' for the Anthropocene in India: Urbanism and human-snake relations in the Kali Yuga. *Geoforum* 106: 402–410.
Patell, Cyrus R. K. 2015. *Cosmopolitanism and the literary imagination*. New York: Palgrave Macmillan.
Rossini, Manuela. Bodies. 2017. In *The Cambridge companion to literature and the posthuman*, ed. Bruce Clarke and Manuela Rossini, 153–169. Cambridge: Cambridge University Press.
Rushdie, Salman. 2017. *The Golden House*. New York: Random House.
Sahu, Om Prakash, and Manali Karmakar. 2022. Disposable culture, posthuman affect, and artificial human in Kazuo Ishiguro's *Klara and the Sun* (2021). *AI & Society*. https://doi.org/10.1007/s00146-022-01600-1.
Schultz, Nikolaj. 2021. The climatic virus in an age of paralysis. *Critical Inquiry: Posts from the Pandemic* 47: 9–12.
Sun, Yuqing. 2022. Post/Human perfectibility and the technological other in Kazuo Ishiguro's *Klara and the Sun*. *Critique: Studies in Contemporary Fiction* 64:504–511. https://doi.org/10.1080/00111619.2022.2056429.
van Leeuwen, Bart. 2019. If we are *flâneurs*, can we be cosmopolitans? *Urban Studies* 56:301–316. https://www.jstor.org/stable/10.2307/26621553
Zhou, Zhenzua. 2021. Emotional thinking as the foundation of consciousness in artificial intelligence. *Cultures of Science* 4:112–123. https://doi.org/10.1177/20966083211052651.
Zhou, Hang, and Yanling Yang. 2021. Death and Power: Biopolitics in Klara and the Sun. *International Journal of Social Science and Education Research* 4: 333–339.
Žižek, Slavoj. 2020. *Pandemic! 2: Chronicles of a time lost*. New York and London: OR Books.

CHAPTER 7

Conclusion: The Genre of The Contemporary

This book has aimed to go beyond the classical—and universalist—understanding of cosmopolitanism by adopting, and also manifesting as representative of the new millennium, vernacular cosmopolitanism as its focus of scrutiny. Having laid the foundations of the novel understanding of cosmopolitanism, this book has looked at the features of the cosmopolitan fiction by offering new terminology in order to provide a precise language and analytical tools for a contemporary reading experience: narrative immediacy and political hyper-awareness to emphasize the cosmopolitan novel's instant and direct engagement with contemporary politics and neoliberal capitalism; narrative glocality to reflect the interconnectedness of the global and the local in narrative spaces; and *cosmoflâneur* to typify a character of the cosmopolitan novel whose consciousness as well as activities within the consumption spaces of a city represent a contemporary urban dweller. The theoretical framework created in this book has been applied to the analysis of four post-millennial cosmopolitan novels—Ian McEwan's *Saturday* (2005), Zadie Smith's *NW* (2012), Salman Rushdie's *The Golden House* (2017), and Kazuo Ishiguro's *Klara and the Sun* (2021), which could possibly set a model for further critical engagement with many other contemporary cosmopolitan novels.

In cosmopolitan fiction, it is impossible to detach the local from the global, or vice versa; therefore, cosmopolitan characters are situated

© The Author(s), under exclusive license to Springer Nature
Switzerland AG 2024
E. Toprak Sakız, *Culture and Economics in Contemporary Cosmopolitan Fiction*, https://doi.org/10.1007/978-3-031-44995-6_7

in glocality, a site of existence where they are exposed to the global even in their parochial or immediate environment. Narrative glocality in *Saturday* facilitates the incorporation of broader perspectives beyond that of the protagonist while it envisions the discrepancy among various city spaces that are inhabited by both elite and non-elite cosmopolitans. In *The Golden House*, the enclosed locality of MacDougal–Sullivan Gardens cannot insulate the Goldens from outside terror as the cosmopolitan family—unable to come to terms with the traces of their past—is annihilated together with the universalist values they represent. *Cosmoflâneurs* in these novels are under the yoke of class and inevitably immersed in the workings of neoliberal capitalism as they are profoundly exposed to consumerist objects during their urban mobility. In the course of his wandering throughout city spaces of London, and encountering anti-war demonstrators in some of them, Perowne also makes his way to Marylebone, a gentrifying and peaceful neighborhood which stands in stark contrast to the streets vitiated by the mass walkers as well as to the ones that are "ungentrified" or "ungentrifiable" in *NW*. The cosmopolitan city as a consumption space is also demonstrated in *NW*'s London, where transnational media, banks, restaurants as well as numberless other consumables can be seen in a kaleidoscopic picture of urban spaces. In this cosmopolitan novel, the city itself is a site of consumption and commodification where even the culture itself is commodified. Rushdie's narrator's act of *cosmoflânerie* becomes a testimony to his hyper-aware vision, which handles consumption spaces on a global level by concentrating on the mobility of global capitalists like the Goldens, of capital as well as information with more grievous consequences. In *Klara and the Sun*, new meanings of class and consumption are introduced as the commodification of the humanoid robot emerges as a theme of posthuman cosmopolitanism, and Klara redefines *cosmoflânerie* with her near-perfect qualities of observation, consciousness, and activeness.

This book has engaged with an understanding of cosmopolitanism in which culture is designated as anti-essentialist and everyday difference as an indispensable part of life, which is the case in *Saturday*'s and *NW*'s London and *The Golden House*'s New York City. Cosmopolitans often elude group allegiances and identifications precisely because cosmopolitan identity is informed by individualistic choices or a cosmopolitan outlook, rather than group dynamics. Cosmopolitan outlook is, then, a defining feature of identity for particularly *NW*'s Natalie and *The Golden House*'s central characters, the Golden family, who perfectly exemplify this tenet of cosmopolitan fiction. These novels are, thus, characterized by vernacular cosmopolitanism: having given up universalist and overly-utopian ideals of soft cosmopolitanism, they are involved with the world in a more hyper-aware mode and acknowledge differences of interests and concerns in more local forms of cosmopolitanism.

At the center of contemporary cosmopolitanism lies the conception of *choice*—self-fashioning and continuous mutability—of cosmopolitan identity, which in turn looms larger on the new novel form of the twenty-first century. To be more precise, cosmopolitan subjects relinquish self-definition delineated by nation-boundedness, or group affiliations, and instead tend toward a process of identity-making through a set of ever-changing and alternating choices and associations. Cosmopolitan fiction, in like manner, dismisses preset forms and definitive tools, setting itself apart from all generic limitations, and liberating itself to make infinite choices in the process. All the novels scrutinized in this book can definitely be acclaimed for their embracing of new perspectives and fictional devices in conjunction with the pervasive cosmopolitan thought of the century. This propensity toward vernacular cosmopolitanism is also conspicuous in their changing—and less celebratory—stance toward the blend of cultures in the face of globalism and its unfavorable ramifications. The novels display a hyper-awareness toward global matters in a way in which an immediate yet cogent response to the contemporary world becomes an indispensable constituent of the narrative.

All four novelists in this book—Ian McEwan, Zadie Smith, Salman Rushdie, and Kazuo Ishiguro—share a particular point of departure from their former oeuvre through their clearly identifiable shift to certain modes of twenty-first-century aesthetics that facilitate their intensifying levels of concentration in cosmopolitics, in a way to successfully meet Nealon's demand for the post-postmodernist literature to prioritize the political and economic realities as primary constitutive elements of literary subject matter. To put it differently, they all demonstrate a changing attitude toward fiction, which is characterized by a renewed focus on content over form: "The sea change, I think, is a matter of emphasis. The emphasis among [...] the post-postmodernists, is less on self-conscious wordplay and the violation of narrative conventions and more on representing the world we all more or less share" (McLaughlin 2004, pp. 66–7). These novels, in varying degrees, engage with contemporary global issues, among which are global wars, nuclear weapons, exploitation of financial means, global economic crisis, environmental problems, poverty, everyday violence, class divides, the dehumanizing impact of technology as well as ineffective responses to all these issues. Rushdie reflects these concerns in *The Golden House* by, for example, commenting upon the Joker president's eagerness to implement nuclear power and see climate change and the end of the Arctic icecap as a new real estate opportunity. Although the obvious reference of this character is Donald Trump, the 45th president of USA, in this novel, Rushdie seems to attack a more general political abyss which would perhaps outgrow a particular presidential period.

On the other side of the Atlantic, another cosmopolitan city, London, is represented as a glocal space where economic inequalities also predominate, whereby the main concern of citizens is that of class rather than race, culture or any other forms of division as it is what remains outside the limits of everyday diversity, in which while any kind of difference is accepted and made ordinary, class divides continue to deepen social injustice and financial inequalities, as explored in the novels here to some extent. It has been observed in this study that *Saturday*'s engagement with class and economic aspects of cosmopolitanism is relatively more limited for reasons that have been primarily expounded in reference to 2008 global financial crisis, an event which marks a decisive moment in cosmopolitan fiction's new impulse to represent the impact of this economic challenge upon society.

This book may lead to further trajectories and pose noteworthy questions considering currently disputed world events and their repercussions in fiction. We have witnessed a recent challenge to cosmopolitanism as a universalist concept, which can be discerned in the shifting politics of the worldwide community. More and more countries seem to be returning to vernacularism, looking inward and reconsidering their global and local allegiances. Yet, the distinction between adopting a vernacular outlook and turning one's back altogether to the world in a parochial manner is not straightforward. The era of global solidarity proves to be a utopia in the face of the impossible eradication of international conflicts and increasing threat of global wars. Evidently, the June 2016 referendum on Brexit recalls the question of whether it is an anti-cosmopolitan move. Rushdie views Brexit as a revitalization of Britain's imperial dream: "The whole Brexit thing was a retreat into a fantasy of England, some imagined moment in which everybody wore straw boaters. They were glorious and they ruled the world. And the fact that all this was based on the exploitation of an empire, we just agree not to mention that" (in Tuttle

2017). Yet, despite its obvious positioning against multiculturalism and toward English nationalism, the Brexit decision is more complicated than this idea of British sovereignty when vernacular connotations of cosmopolitanism are concerned. As Calhoun (2017) argues, "Those who have benefited from globalization—the well-educated and well-off, especially those linked to growing service industries in the southeast rather than old money in the Tory constituencies of middle England and the southwest—voted disproportionately to stay in Europe" (p. 68). This amounts to voting against the universalist cosmopolitanism that benefits the elite rather than the non-elite as Calhoun further argues that immigration, hence diversity, is significant for the elite cosmopolitans who voted against Brexit not because they wholeheartedly support multiculturalism but because they need these 40% population of London as workers in their service and construction industries (2017, p. 66). This book also emphasizes, by focusing on the vernacular, the question of whose cosmopolitanism it is, just like the one posed above concerning whose Brexit decision it is. Postmillennial British fiction that follows and revolves around Brexit can possibly be analyzed with a view to the idea of vernacular cosmopolitanism as well as the analytical tools that are provided in this book, and alternatively the topic could be extended to the relationship between cosmopolitanism and British or American nationalism to become the subject matter of yet another related book.

The writing of this book also coincides with another significant cosmopolitan phenomenon—the COVID-19 coronavirus pandemic—which can without doubt be called "the cosmopolitan virus" as Ruud Koopmans (2020) does.[1] While elite cosmopolitans have more opportunities to protect themselves from the virus by distancing themselves from the rest in private spaces of living and traveling, local cosmopolitans are exposed to its adverse effects disproportionately. Not only the disease's mortal consequences but also its economic devastation is felt more seriously by the non-elite, who are, unlike the elite, unable to switch to home office to avoid infection and compelled to work under more pressure. This is also relevant to the discussion of vernacular cosmopolitanism here as well as the following decades of postmillennial fiction.

A future sub-genre of pandemic fiction will continue to emerge in the following few years in the literary realm as a response to the radical changes in human lives and interactions following the social, cultural, economic, and political ramifications of the coronavirus pandemic. It can be argued that this fiction can possibly be read against the bulk of cosmopolitan theories outlined and detailed in this book. Although the pandemic is a sweepingly global problem, as it is, the possible question of why its consequences affect certain cosmopolitans—the non-elite and working class—more while the elite are relatively untouched or at least suffer less from its financial disarray remains to be explored. Unequal access to vaccination and primary health care services in certain parts of the world also revoke the questions that are posed by vernacular cosmopolitanism. The conceptual distinction between universalist and vernacular cosmopolitanisms as explored in this book will also work perfectly with a study of postmillennial fiction exclusively dealing with the implications of COVID-19 for contemporary human existence and cooperation.

Certain breakdowns and historical moments mark a turning point in both cosmopolitan thought and fiction as this book argues and demonstrates. The three milestone dates that lead to paradigmatic changes are 2001 (September 11 terrorist attacks), 2008 (the global mortgage financial crisis), and 2020 (the global outbreak of the COVID-19 pandemic). The implications of each historical event can be observed in the fiction that follows, as is the case with the novels analyzed in this book. The first novel scrutinized, *Saturday*, predominantly reflects the public paranoia in the aftermath of 9/11, which is encapsulated in the image of a burning plane over the post office tower in London on the date of September 15, 2003, about one and a half year after the actual reference event took place in New York. In the other two novels that follow the momentous date of 2008 economic crisis, in *NW* and *The Golden House*, a new thematic dimension—as well as ensuing conceptual terms—added to the definition of cosmopolitan fiction: the economic consequences of globalization and neoliberal capitalism can be efficiently explored with the genre's qualities of narrative immediacy and political hyper-awareness. The third moment—COVID-19 pandemic—will indisputably bring into attention other concerns including biological wars, posthuman technologies, the manipulation of natural forces, and space travel, alongside the already existing cosmopolitan themes like human communication and identity, global mobilization, communal cooperation, global economic inequalities, and environmental matters, to list only a few. *Klara and the Sun*, a post-COVID-19 novel, represents these changes by making references to both posthuman cosmopolitanism and post-pandemic sensitivities not only in terms of human health but also ecological well-being. It can be argued, then, that cosmopolitan fiction will continue to be an organic part of literary discussions in the years that follow, and the above-mentioned topic can constitute a focus of attention for further studies.

Another challenge to universalist cosmopolitanism in the contemporary moment is the search for radical ways to decentralize global financial power, among which are emerging monetary systems. Aspiring to go beyond dollar-dominated exchange systems through the ever-growing popular use of cryptocurrencies, these systems defy a centralization of power to issue money as well as possible governmental interventions. The changing medium of exchange in global trade can have further implications for international relations, which in turn inform the de novo trends in cosmopolitan fiction. In the same vein, the decentralization of financial arenas through growing economic powers like China entering the global scene also marks a new challenge to universalist cosmopolitanism, especially to the version which is implicated in Americanism. Vernacular cosmopolitanism in postmillennial fiction will possibly highlight the impact of engrossing virtuality in almost every aspect of human life including monetary systems, communications, professions, and even humanity itself. These remarkably significant subjects will probably constitute a rich content for cosmopolitanism and fiction studies that will follow.

On another front concerning the rise of populism, the universalist orientation in cosmopolitan thought comes up against confrontations in social, political as well as literary spheres. Populist movements and mass demonstrations complement the main thematic concerns of *Saturday* and *The Golden House*. Saturday witnesses the historical moment of a massive march against the impending Iraq war while *The Golden House* relates a number of public protests brought about by political and economic turmoil, especially the disillusionment caused by US election results spanning the period from 2008 through 2016. Protests unmistakably constitute a significant theme of the cosmopolitan novel, which seeks to investigate this populist torrent. Drawing attention to escalating populism, Calhoun (2017) makes an interesting comparison: "[T]he Brexit campaign was a close cousin to Donald Trump's quest for the US presidency. Both are part of a still wider populist surge that expresses frustration with radically intensified inequality, stagnant incomes and declining economic security for middle- and working-class people in ostensibly prosperous countries" (pp. 62–63). Mainstream insurrection against the economic exploitation of globalization in quite diverse ways has been, and will always be, a concern of cosmopolitan fiction, which accordingly can be explored with recourse to the analytical vocabulary that has been provided in this book.

Vernacular cosmopolitanism in fiction is not only concerned with problems but also some solutions, which are, nevertheless, hard to offer in an era in which coming up with real-time resolutions is somehow painful, too. This study has acknowledged the difficulties in identifying the solutions that cosmopolitanism offers in very concrete terms as the term itself corresponds to multifarious senses. Yet, all the novels explored in this book are revealed to present as alternative to universalist cosmopolitanism a vernacular conception, which is in no way regarded as a utopian ideal but as an actually attainable everyday human feeling: human interaction with unfamiliar fellow citizens and genuine communication in friendship and love in its purest sense. In *Saturday*, the neurosurgeon, Henry Perowne, attains a cursory moment of interaction with an anonymous street-sweeper with an eye-contact fraught with meaning and empathy recurring twice, both on his way to and from a night operation upon seeing that the cleaner's overtime is not yet over. At the end of *NW*, two old childhood friends, Leah and Natalie, are reconciled and come together after years of distance due to class distinctions, in order to seek justice for the murder of another local resident, Felix, and meanwhile refresh their vernacular feeling of friendship. *The Golden House* ends with feelings even deepening; love wins over money, and consequently, the only survivor in a time of flux proves vernacular cosmopolitans rather than universalist ones. In *Klara and the Sun*, the AI protagonist seeks ways of offering healing for humanity and alleviating ecological and economic challenges of the contemporary world, and in the novel, solutions are neither offered by technology nor by a synthetic society, but by genuine human interaction and empathy. Although the novels lack in clear material solutions, they seem to offer something very human in their finales perhaps as a revolt against the times that are increasingly getting dehumanized. One possible solution for a better world would certainly be the promotion of posthuman cosmopolitanism that embraces the nonhuman as well as the human in a shared world of solidarity, empathy, and openness toward the other. As a defining element of this cosmopolitan impetus, other species, notably animals, as well as humanoid robots must be acknowledged to be a part of a cosmopolitan coexistence in city spaces. It must be finally noted that these novels' solutions are never irrelevant, considering the fact that feelings and interactions have become more and more local and vernacular as recent lockdowns and social distancing that we all have had to go through during the pandemic.

Note

1. Koopmans, Ruud. 2020. The cosmopolitan virus—Covid-19 does not strike randomly. WZB *Berlin Social Science Center.* 4 April 2020. www.wzb.eu/en/research/corona-und-die-folgen/das-kosmopolitische-virus-vor-corona-sind-nicht-alle-gleich. Accessed 5 May 2021.

References

Calhoun, Craig. 2017. Populism, nationalism and Brexit. In *Brexit: Sociological responses*, ed. William Outhwaite, 57–76. Anthem Press. http://www.jstor.org/stable/j.ctt1kft8cd

McLaughlin, Robert L. 2004. Post-postmodern discontent: Contemporary fiction and the social world. *Symplokē* 12: 53–68.

Tuttle, Kate. 2017. Salman Rushdie on the opulent realism of his new novel The Golden House. *Los Angeles Times.* www.latimes.com/books/jacketcopy/la-ca-jc-salman-rushdie-20170914-story.html.

Index

A
active, activity, activeness, 3, 5, 20, 25, 27, 31, 39, 41, 42, 55–57, 59, 60, 74, 76, 85, 86, 89, 121, 123, 140, 175, 186, 196, 198, 204–206, 208, 212, 213, 219, 220
allegiance, 11, 12, 21, 42–45, 56, 57, 64, 114, 143, 159, 161, 222
American identity, 157, 158, 183
Americanism, 53, 62, 63, 173, 225
Appiah, Kwame Anthony, 22, 23, 26, 28
Artificial Intelligence (AI), 5, 188, 191, 192, 202, 208, 213, 226. *See also* robot
attachment, 10, 14, 22, 24, 26, 28, 31, 44, 45, 47, 54, 114, 115, 135, 137, 156, 172, 193, 195, 196, 210

B
Beck, Ulrich, 6, 18, 19, 153, 156, 157, 175

beneficiary, 6, 59
Bhabha, Homi, 26, 30
bottom-up cosmopolitanism, 25, 28
Braidotti, Rosi, 5, 190, 191, 202, 205
Brennan, Timothy, 12, 24, 47, 51–53, 173
Brexit, 2, 6, 7, 14, 222, 223, 225

C
Calhoun, Craig, 6, 8, 27, 39, 52, 53, 88, 136, 173–175, 223, 225
capitalism, 9, 25, 50–53, 57, 58, 60, 91, 137, 173–176, 190, 191, 202
choice, 2, 10, 24, 27, 42, 43, 57, 64, 87, 109, 110, 112, 115, 117, 130, 134, 152–157, 159–161, 181, 220, 221
city, city spaces, 14, 26, 41–43, 48, 55, 57, 58, 60, 63, 64, 70, 74, 80, 86, 88, 90, 94, 96, 97, 103, 109, 112, 114, 119, 121, 123, 125, 126, 149, 152, 157, 158, 162, 167, 175–177, 179, 198, 205, 210, 220, 226

cityscape, 55, 85, 86, 137, 178, 190, 205, 206
class, 3, 4, 8, 16, 17, 25, 26, 29, 31, 41, 45, 54, 58, 59, 79, 85, 87, 88, 96, 108–110, 112, 119, 131, 133, 140, 143, 155, 175, 176, 203, 207, 208, 220, 222, 226
class consciousness, 55, 87, 88, 108, 112, 114, 132, 140, 156, 198, 207
Cohen R., 15, 27, 38, 41, 43, 45, 53, 74, 110, 149, 150, 159
commodification, 5, 27, 41, 50, 55, 57, 85, 88, 119, 120, 208, 220
communication, 2, 11–13, 17–20, 22, 23, 49, 62, 107, 110, 111, 113–118, 125, 135, 141, 142, 174, 188, 193, 194, 224, 226
community, 3–5, 8, 10, 12, 14, 16, 18, 21, 23, 30, 39, 43, 47, 76, 93, 103, 110–113, 118, 119, 123, 124, 128, 130, 131, 133, 134, 140, 143, 150, 155, 156, 158, 172, 174, 188, 189, 193, 197, 203, 208, 209
consciousness, 11, 17, 19, 41, 55–57, 59, 62, 63, 72, 75, 80, 85, 87, 89, 118, 121, 129, 143, 163, 174, 192, 198, 201, 219, 220
consumption space, 86, 91, 92, 95, 97, 120, 123, 219, 220
contemporary, 1–4, 7, 9, 10, 12, 16, 18, 20, 23, 25, 27, 29, 38–55, 57–59, 61–63, 70, 71, 73, 78, 82, 85, 87–89, 91, 95, 97, 103, 107, 110, 119, 122, 128, 136, 137, 140, 143, 147–150, 152, 159, 161, 165–167, 169, 172–174, 176, 180, 185, 186, 189, 202, 207, 211, 213, 219, 221, 225, 226

cosmoflâneur, 53–60, 64, 77, 85, 87, 88, 90, 103, 189, 198, 203, 205, 219, 220
cosmoflânerieflânerie, 54, 55, 85, 87
cosmopolitan fiction, 1–4, 7, 9–11, 15–17, 23, 27, 37, 38, 40, 43, 46–51, 55, 59, 61, 63, 91, 152, 165, 172, 198, 219, 221, 222, 224, 225
cosmopolitan narrator, 62, 136, 189
cosmopolitan outlook, 49, 56, 59, 64, 112, 129–132, 134, 135, 153, 157, 182, 198, 220. *See also* outlook
Covid-19 pandemic, 2–4, 187, 189, 206–210, 212, 224
crises, 1, 8, 19, 40, 70, 75, 93, 107, 149, 211
  global crises, 93, 97
  world crises, 166
culture, 1–3, 6, 10, 11, 13, 16, 19, 20, 26, 27, 29, 30, 37–39, 42, 44, 45, 47–49, 63, 71, 108, 123, 143, 148, 150, 155, 161, 177, 185, 192, 220–222

D

Delanty, Gerard, 19, 24, 39, 40
demonstrations, 74, 78, 81, 92, 170, 171, 225
diversity, 8, 10, 11, 16, 23, 26, 27, 31, 37, 39, 45, 46, 54, 55, 60, 110, 123, 148, 156, 161, 223

E

ecological, 2, 3, 5, 7, 13, 19, 55, 60, 61, 85, 186, 187, 189, 191, 205, 207, 211–213, 226
economic crisis, 2, 7, 37, 38, 108, 122, 164, 207, 221, 224

economics, 2–4, 6, 7, 9, 11, 15–18, 25, 30, 31, 37, 39, 47, 50, 55, 61, 63, 86, 87, 96, 107, 109, 111, 114, 118, 123, 136, 137, 141, 154, 164, 167, 173, 179, 198, 206, 212, 213, 221–226
elite cosmopolitanism, 112, 121
emotions, 99, 182, 186, 188, 191, 192, 196, 201, 213
empathy, 7, 20, 59, 101, 112, 115, 116, 118, 122–124, 141–143, 192, 194, 197, 201, 213, 226
environmental, 3, 8, 27, 31, 91, 92, 167, 168, 170, 187, 205, 211, 221, 224
ethics, 5, 12, 13, 22, 109, 111, 137, 138, 148, 163, 169
everyday, 5, 8, 18, 25, 27, 30, 31, 37, 39–41, 45–48, 54, 69, 74, 89, 103, 108, 110, 118, 119, 126, 137, 143, 149, 153, 158, 161, 165, 170, 185, 186, 191, 222, 226
everyday difference, 2, 31, 45, 47, 48, 64, 110, 150, 220

global, 1–4, 7, 8, 11, 12, 16, 18–21, 25, 27, 28, 38–42, 44, 50–52, 55, 56, 59, 60, 62, 63, 69–72, 74, 76, 77, 82, 84–86, 89, 90, 92, 93, 97, 118, 121, 122, 128, 130, 137, 139, 164, 170, 173, 175, 179, 187, 188, 190, 193, 198, 206, 207, 212, 220–222, 224, 225
global economics, 1, 2, 7, 59, 63, 108, 115, 207, 224
globalization, 6, 8, 9, 12, 17–19, 26, 39, 40, 47, 53, 108, 116, 118, 136, 141, 143, 160, 175, 176, 179, 223, 225
global matters, 21, 38, 70, 76, 128, 149, 165, 187, 221
glocal, 30, 41, 58, 77, 80, 82, 83, 85, 119, 121, 125, 128, 138, 143, 222
glocality, 38, 41, 42, 107, 119
glocalization, 39, 40

F

feelings, 20, 21, 59, 71, 75, 76, 84, 86, 89, 90, 99, 100, 102, 118, 141, 143, 151, 157, 181, 182, 188, 192–194, 196, 197, 199, 213, 215, 216, 226
flânerie, 44, 55, 58, 60, 96, 101
focalization, 73, 86, 107, 189, 199
from-above, 25, 95, 150, 169
from-below, 25, 29, 31, 40, 42, 59, 197

G

gender identity, 156, 157, 161, 181

H

Hall, Stuart, 25, 26, 115, 118, 150
healing, 60, 102, 204, 205, 208–210, 213, 215, 226
health, 1, 4, 8, 19, 187, 197, 204–212, 224
Held, David, 13, 19, 39, 82, 112, 125, 154, 173
hospitality, 6, 7, 14, 21, 114
human/nonhuman, 5, 11–13, 15, 19, 21–23, 28, 39, 71, 87, 93, 97, 100, 101, 111, 134, 141, 142, 149, 161–163, 169, 181, 185–198, 202–206, 208, 211–214, 216, 223, 224, 226

I

identity, 10, 12, 15, 26, 28, 43, 44, 47, 48, 50, 57, 64, 107, 108, 110, 111, 114, 115, 125, 129, 133–135, 138, 143, 150, 151, 153, 156, 157, 159–162, 181, 190, 192, 220
immediate, 22, 39, 41, 62, 71, 73, 74, 77, 101, 128, 141, 143, 151, 166–168, 199, 200, 220, 221
implied author, 70, 71, 79, 89, 133, 177
inclusiveness, 54, 64, 81, 85, 98, 189, 190, 197
inequalities, 3, 8, 16, 40, 45, 47, 50, 52, 59, 71, 108, 124, 141, 171, 173, 176, 186, 202, 203, 207–209, 222, 225
interaction, 5, 13, 20, 39, 41, 47, 82, 92, 99, 101, 113, 114, 141, 142, 186, 188, 190, 191, 196, 198, 205, 212, 213, 226
Ishiguro, Kazuo, 2, 56, 63, 185, 186, 188, 190–196, 199, 201, 202, 206, 208–210, 214, 219, 221

K

kaleidoscope, 56, 120, 164, 165
kaleidoscopic, 56, 116, 164, 165, 198–200, 220
Kendall, Gavin, 5, 18, 21, 60, 186
Klara and the Sun, 2, 4, 186, 187, 189, 192, 207, 219, 220, 224, 226

L

lifted, 73, 186–189, 203, 208, 209
local, 1, 3, 5, 6, 11, 16, 19, 22–31, 37–42, 44, 45, 49, 53, 55–58, 60, 62, 63, 70, 72, 74, 75, 77, 78, 80, 82, 83, 85, 87, 90–94, 96, 97, 103, 110, 111, 113, 114, 116, 118–121, 123–128, 130, 133, 135, 137–143, 148, 151–153, 158–162, 170, 172, 173, 176, 177, 180–182, 185, 188, 189, 193, 196, 198, 200, 207, 210, 213, 219, 221–223, 226
locality, 21, 26, 28, 30, 38, 41, 73, 77, 113, 114, 119, 125–127, 133, 177, 181, 220
London, 10, 41, 42, 59, 69, 74, 75, 85, 89–91, 93–96, 107, 108, 111–113, 116, 118–123, 125, 126, 130, 136, 140, 171, 179, 220, 222–224
love, 51, 72, 99, 101, 154, 169, 180–182, 196, 213–216, 226

M

McEwan, Ian, 2, 10, 53, 56, 59, 61, 63, 69–73, 75, 78–80, 82–84, 88, 89, 92, 94–97, 99, 100, 102, 103, 107, 122, 126, 139, 143, 171, 195, 219, 221
mobility, 3, 6, 12, 16, 20, 27, 31, 44, 52, 54, 55, 57, 58, 62, 87, 93, 115, 117, 131, 134, 135, 174, 189, 198, 205, 206, 212, 220
multiculturalism, 7, 10, 15, 43, 47, 110, 118, 138, 148, 223

N

narration, 61, 62, 72, 89, 107, 108, 162, 163, 177. *See also* cosmopolitan narration
narrative glocality, 38, 40–42, 63, 72, 74, 77, 82, 103, 107, 120–122, 124, 126, 170, 200, 219, 220
narrative immediacy, 61, 62, 162, 165–168, 172, 219, 224

INDEX 233

narrator, 41, 42, 48, 53, 55, 56, 62, 71–77, 79, 81, 82, 87, 89–91, 96, 98, 107, 108, 112–114, 120–126, 128, 131, 132, 134, 135, 137–141, 143, 148, 149, 151, 153, 155, 158, 159, 162–171, 174, 176, 179, 180, 182, 186, 189, 198–200, 213, 214, 220
national, 6, 16, 19, 21, 23, 30, 39, 46, 48, 49, 94, 112, 140, 151, 161
nationalism, 16, 22, 48, 50, 51, 69, 150, 223
Nealon, Jeffrey T., 9, 62, 166, 221
neo-capitalism, 2, 7, 8, 50, 62, 202
neoliberal capitalism, 1, 31, 50, 51, 53, 58, 63, 70, 85–87, 97, 103, 108, 111, 136, 141, 173, 219, 220, 224
news, 74, 75, 77, 78, 82–84, 89, 94, 117, 139–141, 162, 167
New York, 42, 76, 148–151, 154–156, 159, 162, 166–168, 170–172, 174–176, 224
non-elite, non-elite cosmopolitansim, 6, 25, 26, 28, 29, 40, 88, 92, 111–114, 118, 121, 123, 138, 143, 151, 179, 183, 185, 187, 220, 223, 224
NW, 2, 107–112, 114, 119–123, 126, 129, 131, 134–137, 142, 143, 151, 168, 175, 182, 213, 219, 220, 224, 226

O
observation, observer, 56, 59, 73, 88, 90, 101, 196, 198, 201, 204, 220
ordinary, 6, 8, 10, 22, 26, 27, 30, 31, 40, 45, 48, 53, 72, 76, 96, 109–112, 114, 119, 121, 123, 126, 139, 140, 143, 148, 149, 151, 157, 158, 199, 222
outlook, 16, 24, 49, 55, 60, 76, 79, 81, 85, 87, 101, 126, 129, 153, 163, 179, 222

P
parochial, 3, 7, 16, 20, 22, 27, 28, 30, 31, 38, 70, 74, 77, 82, 111–113, 119, 120, 134, 137, 152, 153, 197, 220, 222
particularism, particularist, 8, 11, 20–22, 24, 26, 28, 31, 38, 46, 49, 78, 98, 116, 149
perspective, 9, 11, 15, 21, 28, 42, 55, 56, 71, 73, 74, 77, 78, 80, 81, 87, 107, 108, 121, 122, 124, 127, 128, 143, 148, 163, 169, 188, 199–201, 220, 221
political, 4, 6, 7, 9, 12–15, 17, 20, 39, 41, 42, 46, 49–51, 58, 59, 63, 78, 82, 84, 88, 92, 94, 121, 128, 133, 147, 148, 155, 165–168, 170, 172, 175, 202, 205, 221–223, 225
political hyper-awareness, 61, 63, 136, 138, 140, 162, 165, 169, 170, 172, 219, 224
post-Covid-19, 189, 206, 207
post-factualness, 152, 171
posthuman, 3, 5, 185, 190, 192, 194, 196, 202, 207, 213, 224
posthuman cosmopolitanism, 5, 189–191, 197, 213, 220, 224, 226
posthuman ethics, 5, 185, 186, 190
postmillennial British fiction, 3, 223
post-postmodernism, 1, 8, 9
privacy, 94, 151, 193, 199

R

realism, 20, 147, 148
realistic, 14, 110, 205, 214, 215
Robbins, Bruce, 21, 22, 24, 26, 29, 43, 44, 46, 48, 49, 59, 150
robot, 5, 185, 186, 188–191, 194, 198, 199, 202, 203, 208, 220, 226
Rushdie, Salman, 2, 10, 53, 61–63, 147–152, 154–159, 161–166, 169, 170, 172–175, 177, 179, 181, 182, 214, 219–222

S

Saturday, 2, 41, 42, 59, 69, 70, 73, 74, 85, 94, 96, 107, 119–121, 126, 139–142, 170, 171, 195, 213, 219, 220, 222, 224–226
Schoene, Berthold, 56, 69, 94, 120, 138, 161, 163–165, 172
second modernity, 18, 19, 54
Shaw, Kristian, 6, 7, 41, 43, 44, 57, 82, 108–110, 116, 134, 137, 153, 159
Smith, Zadie, 2, 107, 108, 110, 112, 113, 115–119, 121–123, 125–127, 129, 130, 133–135, 137–140, 143, 151, 168, 219, 221
solidarity, 4, 10, 11, 20, 21, 140, 182, 188, 213, 222, 226
solution, 10, 13, 53, 75, 85, 91, 92, 139, 140, 143, 175, 187, 193, 197, 204–206, 212, 213, 226
space, 19, 26, 29, 30, 39–42, 45, 48, 51, 54, 58, 74, 77, 79, 80, 82, 94, 112, 119–122, 125, 128, 131, 135, 138, 140, 143, 149, 158, 173, 176, 222, 224

T

The Golden House, 2, 147, 148, 150, 163–165, 172, 173, 175, 176, 188, 214, 219, 220, 222, 224–226
top-down cosmopolitanism, 174, 188
transformation, 3, 10, 19, 52, 70, 71, 85, 98, 103, 114, 117, 130, 133, 157, 160, 166
twenty-first-century fiction, 1, 25, 44, 49, 50, 61–63, 152, 207

U

universalism, universalist, 6, 7, 10, 11, 13, 20–24, 27, 30, 31, 38, 42–44, 46, 48, 51, 53, 54, 78, 82, 87, 91, 98, 99, 103, 110, 111, 116, 118, 120, 121, 137, 138, 140, 148–154, 159, 160, 163, 167, 169, 172, 173, 176, 177, 179–182, 187, 188, 197, 203, 213, 219–226
urban, 28, 44, 52, 54–58, 86, 91, 95, 108, 110, 111, 122, 137, 143, 158, 198, 205, 206, 219, 220
urban space, 77, 202, 220

V

vernacular cosmopolitanism, 8, 24–27, 30, 31, 39, 40, 42–46, 49, 54, 63, 70, 74, 75, 82, 86, 87, 96, 98, 103, 110, 111, 114, 118, 119, 134, 138, 143, 148, 149, 152, 160, 168, 177, 180–182, 185, 187, 188, 192, 195, 197, 201, 203, 209, 213, 219, 221, 223, 224
Vertovec, S., 15, 27, 38, 41, 43, 45, 53, 74, 110, 149, 150, 159

W

Walkowitz, Rebecca, 44, 59, 61, 62, 165
wandering, 41, 44, 54, 55, 57, 59, 81, 85, 87, 121, 152, 155, 220
Werbner, Pnina, 27–30
working-class, 4, 5, 25, 29, 111–113, 125, 127, 128, 130, 208, 224, 225
working-class cosmopolitanism, 25, 27–29
world, 1–8, 10–13, 15, 17–27, 29, 31, 38–40, 47–49, 51, 52, 54–57, 59–64, 69–71, 73–81, 83–85, 87–99, 102, 103, 108, 110–112, 116, 120, 126, 128, 132, 134, 136–138, 141, 142, 147, 148, 150, 154, 157, 159–169, 172, 173, 175–181, 185–207, 209–214, 221, 222, 224, 226
world-making, 55, 59, 60, 85, 189

Z

Žižek, Slavoj, 4, 207, 216